BULGARIA

Marxist Regimes Series

Series editor: Bogdan Szajkowski,
Department of Sociology, University College,
Cardiff

Further Titles

BULGARIA

Politics, Economics and Society

Robert J. McIntyre

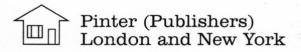
Pinter (Publishers)
London and New York

First published in Great Britain in 1988 by
Pinter Publishers Limited
25 Floral Street, London WC2E 9DS

British Library Cataloguing in Publication Data
A CIP catalogue record for this book is available from the British Library.

Library of Congress Cataloging-in-Publication Data
McIntyre, Robert J.
    Bulgaria: politics, economics, and society/Robert J. McIntyre.
    p.   cm.—(Marxist regimes series)
    Bibliography: p.
    Includes index.
ISBN 0-86187-398-X   ISBN 0-86187-399-8 (pbk.)
    1. Bulgaria—Civilization. I. Title. II. Series.
DR91.M38   1988
949.7'7—dc19   87-34177
                                          CIP

Typeset by Joshua Associates Limited, Oxford
Printed in Great Britain by SRP Ltd, Exeter

Editor's Preface

Most observers and analysts agree that Bulgaria is on a point of change. This, the first comprehensive book on Bulgarian politics, economics and society, provides the reader with an in-depth analysis of the background, current state and prospects of success of the various experiments taking place in the country's economic, social and political life.

At the same time this monograph is also a timely and important contribution to the overall analysis of Marxist regimes. The study of Marxist regimes has commonly been equated with the study of communist political systems. There were several historical and methodological reasons for this. For many years it was not difficult to distinguish the eight regimes in Eastern Europe and four in Asia which resoundingly claimed adherence to the tenets of Marxism and more particularly to their Soviet interpretation—Marxism–Leninism. These regimes, variously called 'People's Republic', 'People's Democratic Republic', or 'Democratic Republic', claimed to have derived their inspiration from the Soviet Union to which, indeed, in the overwhelming number of cases they owed their establishment.

To many scholars and analysts these regimes represented a multiplication of and geographical extension of the 'Soviet model' and consequently of the Soviet sphere of influence. Although there were clearly substantial similarities between the Soviet Union and the people's democracies, especially in the initial phases of their development, these were often overstressed at the expense of noticing the differences between these political systems.

It took a few years for scholars to realize that generalizing the particular, i.e., applying the Soviet experience to other states ruled by elites which claimed to be guided by 'scientific socialism', was not good enough. The relative simplicity of the assumption of a cohesive communist bloc was questioned after the expulsion of Yugoslavia from the Communist Information Bureau in 1948 and in particular after the workers' riots in Poznań in 1956 and the Hungarian revolution of the same year. By the mid-1960s, the totalitarian model of communist politics, which until then had been very much in force, began to crumble. As some of these regimes articulated demands for a distinctive path of socialist development, many specialists studying these systems began to notice that the cohesiveness of the communist bloc was less apparent than had been claimed before.

Also by the mid-1960s, in the newly independent African states 'democratic' multi-party states were turning into one-party states or military dictatorships, thus questioning the inherent superiority of liberal democracy, capitalism and the values that went with it. Scholars now began to ponder on the simple contrast between multi-party democracy and a one-party totalitarian rule that had satisfied an earlier generation.

More importantly, however, by the beginning of that decade Cuba had a revolution without Soviet help, a revolution which subsequently became to many political elites in the Third World not only an inspiration but a clear military, political and ideological example to follow. Apart from its romantic appeal, to many nationalist movements the Cuban revolution also demonstrated a novel way of conducting and winning a nationalist, anti-imperialist war and accepting Marxism as the state ideology without a vanguard communist party. The Cuban precedent was subsequently followed in one respect or another by scores of Third World regimes, which used the adoption of 'scientific socialism' tied to the tradition of Marxist thought as a form of mobilization, legitimation or association with the prestigious symbols and powerful high-status regimes such as the Soviet Union, China, Cuba and Vietnam.

Despite all these changes the study of Marxist regimes remains in its infancy and continues to be hampered by constant and not always pertinent comparison with the Soviet Union, thus somewhat blurring the important underlying common theme—the 'scientific theory' of the laws of development of human society and human history. This doctrine is claimed by the leadership of these regimes to consist of the discovery of objective causal relationships; it is used to analyse the contradictions which arise between goals and actuality in the pursuit of a common destiny. Thus the political elites of these countries have been and continue to be influenced in both their ideology and their political practice by Marxism more than any other current of social thought and political practice.

The growth in the number and global significance, as well as the ideological, political and economic impact, of Marxist regimes has presented scholars and students with an increasing challenge. In meeting this challenge, social scientists on both sides of the political divide have put forward a dazzling profusion of terms, models, programmes and varieties of interpretation. It is against the background of this profusion that the present comprehensive series on Marxist regimes is offered.

This collection of monographs is envisaged as a series of multi-disciplinary textbooks on the governments, politics, economics and society of these countries. Each of the monographs was prepared by a specialist on the country concerned. Thus, over fifty scholars from all over the world have contributed monographs which were based on first-hand knowledge. The geographical diversity of the authors, combined with the fact that as a group they represent many disciplines of social science, gives their individual analyses and the series as a whole an additional dimension.

Each of the scholars who contributed to this series was asked to analyse such topics as the political culture, the governmental structure, the ruling party, other mass organizations, party-state relations, the policy process, the economy, domestic and foreign relations together with any features peculiar to the country under discussion.

This series does not aim at assigning authenticity or authority to any single one of the political systems included in it. It shows that, depending on a variety of historical, cultural, ethnic and political factors, the pursuit of goals derived from the tenets of Marxism has produced different political forms at different times and in different places. It also illustrates the rich diversity among these societies, where attempts to achieve a synthesis between goals derived from Marxism on the one hand, and national realities on the other, have often meant distinctive approaches and solutions to the problems of social, political and economic development.

University College   *Bogdan Szajkowski*
Cardiff

Contents

List of Illustrations and Tables

Map

Tables

Preface

I was initially attracted to the study of Bulgaria because of the light I believed it could shed upon developments in other Soviet-type economies rather than because of its own characteristics. I have found it to be a surprising and intriguing country in many respects, clearly worthy of analysis and appraisal in its own right. It offers a second test case of what might be called the Stalin period model of rapid state-controlled and centrally planned industrialization and urbanization, albeit with great internal and external political differences. Bulgaria thus provides an indirect way of learning about and testing our causal understanding of the Soviet model of economic, political and cultural organization. By carefully weighing the similarities and differences it is possible to use Bulgarian experience to learn more about what is logically implied by the various features of the Soviet model, as against what might be the result of particularly Russian cultural, political and economic conditions.

Because of this long list of developmental similarities, cultural affinities and historical connections (discussed in Chapters 1 and 2), Bulgarian developments can be analyzed fruitfully as a source of insights about both the Soviet past and future. Even with the special advantages provided by the Bulgarian perspective, the causal questions are still complex, since the existence of the Soviet Union as an admired model led to the adoption of some very similar arrangements in Bulgaria. By virtue of the close and, at least on the surface, largely trouble-free relationship with the Soviet Union, Bulgaria falls into the category of states that are unfortunately very difficult for Western scholars to appraise. Countries that have moved (or seem to have moved) significantly away from the Soviet model, or away from close political-cultural links with the Soviet Union, have tended to become the object of often uncritical Western praise and constructive curiosity. From Yugoslavia through China, Romania, Hungary, Czechoslovakia and Poland this pattern has emerged, often to disappear if the deviation or split in one way or another closes or heals. Countries such as Bulgaria, the German Democratic Republic, and Vietnam, which have generally close relationships with the Soviet Union, are subject to a special scrutiny and in general treated with disproportionate severity in Western popular and scholarly sources. The durability of the thoroughly incredible 'Bulgarian Connection' aspects of the Ali Agca–Pope Plot in English language cultures is perhaps the most recent manifestion of this pattern.

This book is to a considerable degree written against the backdrop of a general pattern of distorted and misleading discussion of Bulgaria in the West and is intended to be a partial remedy. It attempts to adopt a practice of explaining why arrangements work when they do, noting and criticizing them when they fail or work perversely, and avoiding tendentious speculation in the many areas where little can be determined about the realities of political–economic–social behavior. The result is a variegated portrait which includes economic, political and social successes and inexplicable malfunctions. Bulgaria is presented here as less unfailingly threatening than in some treatments, but certainly does not appear in monochromatic bright tones.

The author, whose principal areas of competence are comparative economics systems and European economic history, has had the opportunity to visit Bulgaria to conduct research on economic performance and reform, social policy and the role of women in society, and demographic policy questions steadily since 1973. Longer exchange visits occurred under the auspices of the National Academy of Sciences program in 1975 and the IREX exchange in 1985–6. Much of the initial work on this book was carried out in the course of a five-month IREX visit in 1985 and early 1986. Assistance from the American Philosophical Society has permitted me to expand my knowledge of Hungarian developments, leading to frequent discovery of sharp differences, but also revealing a number of very interesting similarities. Another major part of the writing of the book was carried out during a six-month period of residence in East Berlin where my wife was an exchange scholar. I believe that the direct comparison of Bulgaria with the very different Hungarian and GDR experiences has enriched my study in a number of unexpected ways, and is indeed one of the hidden virtues of the volume.

By good fortune and IREX assistance it was possible to return to Bulgaria for one month during June and July of 1986, shortly after the XIII Congress of the Bulgarian Communist Party. As a result it has been possible to include the full range of events that did (and did not) occur at the Congress, incorporate official statistics for the troubled last year of the 1981–5 plan period, and take account of data for 1986, 1987 and early 1988 which marked a return to more normal economic performance.

The preparation of this manuscript has extended over several years, during which I have had the invaluable assistance of Joyce Caron in typing, retyping, editing and interpreting (often from a great distance) my often convoluted texts. Laura Juraska has provided research bibliographic assistance of a high quality. I am indebted to the members of the Russian Research Center Economics Seminar at Harvard University and Dorothy Rosenberg for useful and constructive criticism. The errors and omissions that remain are proverbially my own fault.

Robert J. McIntyre
Lewiston, Maine, 1987

List of Abbreviations

AIC	Agro-Industrial Complex
BANU or BAU	Bulgarian Agrarian National Union
BCP	Bulgarian Communist Party
BIA	Bulgarian Industrial Association
BNB	Bulgarian National Bank
BWP	Bulgarian Workers Party
CDSP	*Current Digest of the Soviet Press*
CMEA	Council for Mutual Economic Assistance
CPSU	Communist Party of the Soviet Union
DSO	*Durzhaven stopanstvo organizatsia*
FBIS	*Foreign Broadcast Information Service*
GDR	German Democratic Republic
IAC	Industrial-agrarian Complex
MB	Mineral Bank-Bank for Economic Initiatives
NATO	North Atlantic Treaty Organization
NEM	New Economic Mechanism
OECD	Organization for Economic Cooperation and Development
RFER	Radio Free Europe Research
Sovnarkhoz	Regional Economic Council
WP	Warsaw Pact

Basic Data

Official name	People's Republic of Bulgaria
Population	8,942,965 (31 December 1985; based on early December 1985 Census)
Population density	80.7 per sq. km.
Population growth (% p.a.)	0.12 (1985)
Urban population (%)	65 (1985)
Total labour force	4,092,832 (1985) (48.1% women)
Life expectancy	
Men	68.7 (1980)
Women	73.9 (1980)
Infant death rate (per 1,000)	15.8 (1985); 27.3 (1970)
Ethnic groups	Not officially reported since the 1956 Census. Bulgarians approximately 90% of population; remaining 10% predominantly Turkish; also small gipsy, Romanian and Armenian population. Some dispute as to whether population called 'Turkish' in the West is Turkish or Bulgarian Moslem
Capital	Sofia (pop. 1,192,981 (1985))
Land area	110,911.5 sq. km. Several extensive mountain ranges and much arid rocky land. Large agriculturally ideal central plain
Official language	Bulgarian
Other significant language	Turkish
Administrative division	29 province (*okrug*) divisions, which include as separate units Sofia proper and the region surrounding Sofia
Membership in United Nations affiliated organizations	UN since 1955, FAO, IAEA, ICAO, ILO, IMO, ITU, UNESCO, UNIDO, UPU, WHO, WIPO, and WMO
Membership in other international organizations	BIS, CCC, CMEA, IBEC, ICCO, IIB, ILZ, Inmarsat, ISO, PCA, and WTO
Foreign relations	Close and steady relationship with the Soviet Union is the fundamental basing point of Bulgarian foreign affairs. Few

Foreign relations (*Cont.*)	examples of divergence from Soviet views on more than details. Strong advocate of CMEA integration and cooperation. Active diplomacy and cultural–educational exchanges with Middle Eastern and African countries. Long-standing and bitter relationship with Turkey
Political structure	
Constitution	1879 Turnovo Constitution established Parliament and limited monarchy 4 December 1947 Dimitrov Constitution established People's Republic with classic features modelled directly on the Soviet Constitution of 1936. Disestablished Orthodox Church and affirmed nationalization of industrial property 16 May 1971 New Basic Law a thorough revision of 1947 Constitution, introducing a State Council as the supreme, constantly functioning body of state power, superseding the Council of Ministers
Highest legislative body	National Assembly
Highest executive body	State Council
Chairman of State Council	Todor Zhivkov (b. 1911)
Prime Minister	Georgi Atanasov (b. 1933)
Food self-sufficiency	Net food exporter even in drought years. Import of specialty fruits and livestock feed, more than offset by large exports of fresh and preserved vegetables, fruit, meat, poultry and wine

Growth indicators (% p.a.)

	1976–80	1981–85	1986
Net material product	6.1	3.7	5.5
Industry	6.0	4.4	4.3
Heavy (Group A)	—	4.4	—
Consumer (Group B)	—	4.5	—
Agriculture	0.9	1.3	10.5

Agriculture organization
and practices

High level of mechanization and irrigation (25.1% of arable land in 1983) on extremely large state units (agro-industrial complexes) formed from previously independent state and collective farms. Complex symbiotic relationship between state sector and personal garden plots of state agricultural employees. Excellent agricultural performance, given modest levels of investment in agriculture over last two decades

Trade and balance of payments

Exports

13.736 billion leva (1985)

Imports

14.002 billion leva (1985)

Exports plus imports as % of:

Net material product

110.8 (1985)

Gross national product

42.9 (1984 est.)

Main exports (%)

Machinery (48.4); foodstuffs, including wine and tobacco (21.6); and semi-finished products (11.4): non-ferrous metals, cast iron and leather products are the dominant categories. Largest exports to the West in 1983 were fuel oils, iron and steel, tobacco, electric current, cheese, wine, wood furniture and fresh vegetables

Destination of exports
(% 1983)

Socialist countries 76.4, of which:

USSR	56.0
GDR	5.5
Poland	3.2
CSSR	4.0
Romania	2.2
Hungary	2.3
Cuba	1.8
Yugoslavia	0.7

Western industrialized countries 10.5, of which:

FRG	1.7

and, Developing countries 13.1 of which:

Libya	4.1

Main imports (%)

Machinery (34.2); fuels (oil and natural gas), raw materials (including cellulose and wood products) and metals (46.2)

Origin of 1983 imports	Socialist countries 80.2, of which:

Socialist countries 80.2, of which:

USSR	58.5
GDR	5.7
Poland	4.3
CSSR	4.1
Romania	2.1
Hungary	2.3
Cuba	1.6
Yugoslavia	1.0

Western industrial countries 13.7, of which:

FRG	3.9

Developing countries 6.1, of which

Libya	2.0

Foreign debt
Convertible currency debt (in current US$ billion):
Gross debt: 2.4 (1983); 3.6 (1985)
Net debt: 1.2 (1983); 1.5 (1985)

Foreign aid
Significant construction, health and educational service programs in Third World countries on unclear financial terms. Large numbers of Asian, African and Latin American students are provided with technical education in Bulgaria

Foreign investment
Legal under law of 28 March 1980 on joint ventures, which permits more than 50% ownership by Western participants. As of 1985 six joint ventures are under way with Japanese and French firms, involving both consumer goods and industrial products

Main natural resources
Bauxite, copper, lead, zinc, coal, lignite, lumber

Ruling Party
Bulgarian Communist Party in formal alliance with the Bulgarian National Agrarian Union

Secretary General of the Party
Todor Zhivkov (since 1954)

Party membership
932,055 (at XIII Party Congress, April 1986)

Other mass organizations
Fatherland Front, Dimitrov Communist Youth Union (Komsomol), Central Council of Trade Unions, National Committee for Defense of Peace, Union of Fighters Against Fascism and Capitalism,

	Committee of Bulgarian Women, All-National Committee for Bulgarian–Soviet Friendship
Armed forces	Compulsory service of 2 years (3 years in navy). Regular army of 105,000; 177,000 in border police, security police and territorial militia. Navy of 8,500 and 124 vessels of all types. Air force of 35,000 and approximately 250 combat aircraft
Education and health	
School system	Free and compulsory from age 6–17
Primary and secondary school enrolment	1,244,396 (1985–6) and 237, 631 (1985–6) in specialized vocational, technical, and art schools
Higher education	101,507 students in 1985–6 in 3 major universities (9,600, 3,500 and 3,100 students in 1983–4) and 27 institutes of higher education
Adult literacy (%)	100 (claimed)
Population per hospital bed	588 (1939); 179 (1960); 107 (1985)
Population per physician	2,021 (1939); 715 (1960); 349 (1985)
Economy	
GNP	US$57.8 billion (est. 1985 in 1985 US$)
GNP per capita	US$6,463 (est. 1985 in 1985 US$)
State budget (expenditure)	19.4 billion leva (est. 1985)
Defence expenditure % of state budget	6.2 (est. 1985)
Monetary unit	lev (sing.), leva (pl.)
Main crops	Wheat, corn, barley, sunflower seeds, sugar, tobacco, grapes, tomatoes, potatoes, 80% of world supply of rose oil (attar of rose), meat, wool, and (for export) meat, eggs and milk
Land tenure	State ownership of land except for areas around detached single homes and weekend houses. Personal agricultural plots leased. Predominance of private ownership of housing units
Main religions	Eastern Orthodox (Bulgarian Patriarchate), Moslem, Roman Catholic and 5 small Protestant groups. State provides 15–20% of Orthodox Church budget

Transport
  Rail network   4,033 km., of which 1,994 are electrified
                                  (1983)
  Road network   32,839 km., of which 2,923 are main roads
                                  and 197 are expressways

Sources: Banks, Arthur S. (ed.), *Political Handbook of the World: 1987*, Binghamton, New York, 1987; Central Intelligence Agency, *World Factbook: 1987*, Washington, DC, 1987; *Statisticheski Spravochnik 1986*, Sofia, 1986; *The Statesman's Yearbook, 1986–87*, London, 1986; *World Economic Survey 1986*, New York, United Nations, 1986; and *Economic Survey of Europe in 1986–1987*, New York, United Nations, 1987.

Population Forecasting

The following data are projections produced by Poptran, University College Cardiff Population Centre, from United Nations Assessment Data published in 1980, and are reproduced here to provide some basis of comparison with other countries covered by the Marxist Regimes Series.

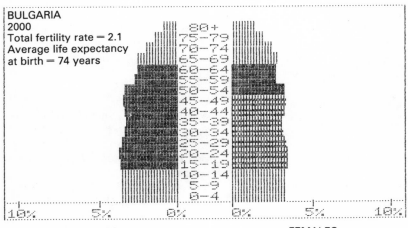

Projected Data for Bulgaria 2000

Total population ('000)	9,699
Males ('000)	4,801
Females ('000)	4,898
Total fertility rate	2.10
Life expectancy (male)	71.0 years
Life expectancy (female)	76.7 years
Crude birth rate	14.2
Crude death rate	11.3
Annual growth rate	0.29%
Under 15s	20.49%
Over 65s	15.56%
Women aged 15–49	23.04%
Doubling time	241 years
Population density	87 per sq. km.
Urban population	77.1%

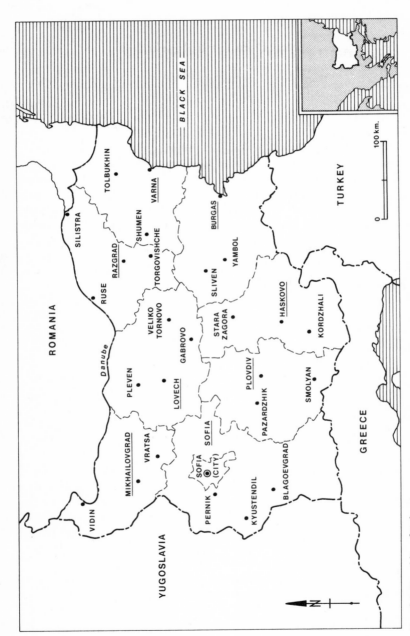

People's Republic of Bulgaria

1 Introduction: The Bulgarian Development Experience

It is difficult to see Bulgaria clearly and on its own terms. This book attempts to do this both by resisting the tendency to see Soviet interests, institutions or historical–cultural perspectives behind all Bulgarian reality and by avoiding assuming the worst in the many cases where detailed information is not available. These problems of interpretation are in part due to the tendency to think of Bulgaria as being so close to the Soviet Union that it is scarcely more than a projection of a presumably well-understood Soviet reality. They are also attributable to the lack of information about the inner workings of Bulgarian political, social, and economic institutions, creating the temptation to fill the gaps with assumptions.

In appearances, style of operation, names and forms of administrative organs, direct parallels or copies of Soviet arrangements have developed in post-war Bulgaria. These similarities arise partly from the centuries-old bond between these two national cultures and partly from the wholesale institutional borrowing that occurred during the three formative years of the People's Republic of Bulgaria following the revolutionary uprising of 9 September 1944. So, like most misleading national stereotypes, this Bulgaro-Soviet connection is real and substantial in many ways, and provides sufficient reinforcement to avoid jolting the unwary from the simple assumption that Bulgaria is unworthy of or does not require independent scrutiny.

Countries which have generally close relationships with the Soviet Union are subject to a special scrutiny and in general treated with disproportionate severity in Western popular and scholarly sources. The reader seeking enlightenment about the functioning of Bulgarian society has long been faced with a shortage of reliable book-length treatments after J. F. Brown's 1970 volume. The reader will quickly become aware that the author views the studies by Oren (1971, 1973) and Dobrin (1973) to be too relentlessly hostile, tendentious and polemical to be useful in understanding what it is about Bulgarian society that explains the relatively good economic performance, an impressive set of social policy achievements and what appears to be a considerable level of popular support and implied legitimacy.

Inside Information: *Émigré* Publications and Radio Free Europe

Because there has been no large-scale post–World War II migration to the West, students of Bulgarian society are denied the advantage of an *émigré* press or of research based on the experience of significant numbers of previously integrated members of Bulgarian society. A considerable selection of *émigré* materials are more or less directly incorporated in the regularly appearing research studies and press summaries (with interpretation) produced by the US government-financed Radio Liberty/Radio Free Europe Research, located in Munich, Federal Republic of Germany. These studies often include valuable summaries of regional newspapers or narrow-circulation journals. They also include many speculative, out-of-date or impossible-to-evaluate rumours, allegations and anecdotes. Fascinating examples fully accessible to any reader include the treatment of the 1984–5 soccer scandal (*RFER*, Bulgarian Situation Report 9, 1 August 1985, pp. 15–18, and 10, 2 September 1985, pp. 19–22), and the 'Down with Todor Zhivkov' acrostic that may have appeared in a popular Bulgarian literary magazine in March 1985 (*RFER*, Bulgarian Situation Report 9, 1 August 1985, pp. 11–14).

These sources are of unpredictable quality, crackpot notions sometimes receiving considerable respect, but when little is known for certain it is difficult to separate fact from plausible fiction. Access by Western diplomatic personnel to high- and middle-level officials is far more restricted than is the case in Moscow, for example, so the ability to test the plausibility of rumors or speculative interpretations against the intuitions of persons actually functioning in the system is essentially zero (if Bulgarian employees of foreign embassies are discounted as a source of reality appraisal). The resulting dependence on rumor and speculation passed from one friendly embassy to another is substantial. Western news agencies cover Bulgaria only sporadically. AFP (Agencie France-Presse) has a reputation for special creativity in its coverage of Bulgaria, but seems to be the source of many widely circulated wire stories. *The Financial Times* (London) alone provides serious albeit intermittent coverage of Bulgarian governmental and economic affairs.

Questions about the extent of political freedom and popular participation in government can be answered simply but unsatisfactorily by noting on the one hand that there is no open adversarial political life and on the other by admitting that almost nothing is known about the internal workings of the Bulgarian Communist Party (BCP) and the Fatherland Front, or what effect if any the unique Bulgarian Agrarian Union (BANU) has on policy and administrative behavior. The BANU certainly does not present an oppositional face in public and it is generally dismissed in the West as an empty shell entirely controlled by the BCP. Western writers who find the modern BANU bogus and illegitimate generally ignore the profoundly radical program and actions of the BANU during its brief pre-fascist period in power (1919–23), while feeling greater affinity toward the right wing of the party that survived the 1923 coup (due to its only mildly reformist program) and kept the name alive until 1944. The resolutely 'pro-Western' orientation of the BANU right wing in the immediate post-war period further endeared it to these observers. I argue to the contrary that the BCP–BANU alliance has strong historical roots, but can offer little detail on its current status. I do note that the BANU represents a separate organizational hierarchy, and that some of those who rise to the top of that hierarchy end up in government positions where they exercise more than formal powers.

In tracing the roots of both conflict and cooperation between the BCP and the BANU, I have depended heavily on the excellent biography and party history written by John Bell (1977) and the interesting and thorough study of BCP–BANU conflict during the crucial 1944–7 transition period by Michael Boll (1984). Still, much of this book steps around the boundaries of the BCP, without knowing how it really works inside. This is true at top policy-making levels and at all the regional, city and neighborhood levels where the BCP interacts with other social bodies and other aspects of itself in determining or influencing the thousands of details that form the matrix of daily life in contemporary Bulgaria. Even before the recent campaigns to raise the quality of democratic practice in various party meetings and assemblies (see, for example, *FBIS*, vol. 11, no. 38, 26 February 1986, pp. C4–C5), the reality of power at the local and district level (especially after the 1959 regional decentralization) was substantial, leading to very different styles of local government and urban development in cities away from the capital. The role of the IKO organization (described below, pp. 122 ff.) in providing development planning, project evaluation and design services to town governments on a contract basis is evidence of the reality of local government power in modern Bulgarian life.

As Hough (1976) has suggested for the USSR, there has been some real democratization in party functioning at lower and middle levels of the BCP. Cohen (1984, 1985 and 1986) suggests that democratic practice has also increased within the CPSU Central Committee, making Brezhnev, for example, little more than the representative of a committee majority. Mikhail Gorbachëv is similarly seen as the most visible individual in an emergent

Central Committee majority that is collectively the ruling power. Parallel developments appear to have occurred in Bulgaria. It is important to note that, as is the case in the USSR, groups such as women, who are under-represented at the highest party and government levels, are much more widely involved in local government leadership.

For up-to-date and relatively even-handed information on Bulgarian political development, the short summaries included in the *Yearbook of International Communist Affairs* (done over the years by Dellin, Pundeff, Staar, and most recently John Bell), are valuable and are recommended to readers in future years. Two excellent studies appeared in 1986 by John Lampe and Marvin Jackson, who together produced the definitive English language *Balkan Economic History* (1982). Lampe has written a thorough history entitled *The Bulgarian Economy in the Twentieth Century*, while Jackson has provided an analysis of the adjustment and structural problems of the middle reform period (1981) and a similarly detailed analysis of the provisions and potential implications of the (second) New Economic Mechanism (1986). Lampe and Jackson conclude their 1986 works with 1983 data and experience, so this volume has the luxury of both benefiting from their analysis and being able to observe three additional years of 'reform experience,' concluding with the dramatic new measures introduced in 1986 and 1987. The reader will discover that some proposals of 1982 are still proposals in 1987, that some measures reported to have been put into effect in the former year remain plans in the latter, but that some of the seeds of change have taken root and produced real alterations in the way things are done.

The reader will find a basic unity in this volume and the two 1986 works cited, all more or less favorable in their interpretation of the achievements of the last decade and suggesting that there is much more worthy of study in the Bulgarian political-economic experience than is indicated by the durable cliché that treats Bulgaria as indistinguishable from the Soviet Union. This book is written from the comparative economic and political systems perspective, which sees in Bulgarian developments an unusually valuable opportunity to study the 'Soviet-type' economic and political system. The historical, economic and cultural similarities are strong enough that anything learned about Bulgarian experience is valuable to students of the Soviet Union. By carefully weighing the similarities and differences it is possible to use Bulgarian experience to learn more about what is logically implied by the various features of the Soviet model, as against what might be the result of particularly Russian cultural, political and economic conditions.

(1) In making these comparisons it is obvious that Bulgaria and the Soviet Union shared at their respective beginnings a similar culture and similar

development level, combined with a lack of dense connections with the Western European world. There were as well strong institutional and ideological similarities in both pre- and post-revolutionary periods. On the other hand, Bulgaria has had the benefit of a far more favorable climate, in both the immediate physical sense and in terms of the international conditions which impinge upon internal development.

(2) Bulgaria has none of the historical pattern of anti-Russian and/or anti-Soviet popular opinion that make events in a number of other Eastern Europe countries difficult to interpret. Although the degree of warmth of pro-Soviet feeling can be exaggerated and made to seem absurd and servile, there is undoubtedly a depth and reality to these feelings and opinions going back to the distant past. For nearly 500 years Bulgarians looked to Russia as the only possible hope for liberation from Ottoman rule, not finally realized until the surprisingly recent date of 1878. During the centuries of Ottoman rule and into the twentieth century, Russia was the land of opportunity for Bulgarian economic and political expatriates. It was the place where Bulgarians were able to encounter and contribute to modern European society and culture. In the post-war period the Soviet Union has provided a sense of international security, in particular against Yugoslavia (to Bulgaria, one important advantage of the Stalin–Tito break was the certainty of Soviet support against what were felt to be strong Yugoslav territorial ambitions) and Turkey. It has provided a nearly unlimited market for Bulgarian agricultural and manu-factured goods, and has been the source of technology and raw materials on highly favorable terms.

(3) Bulgaria has an odd and unusual modern political history, including the development of the only other clearly Leninist party prior to 1917, the emergence of an extraordinarily radical and successful agrarian party which governed from 1919 to 1923 (the only peasant party ever to rule in Europe), and perhaps the earliest arrival of avowedly fascist rule (modelled after the tactics and program of the Italian Fascists, but preceding them in the achieve-ment of state power). The program of the Agrarian Party under Alexander Stamboliski was easily as radical as that of the Bolshevik government at the same moment.

After World War II, developments were also different than observed elsewhere in Eastern Europe where pro-Soviet governments arose or were installed under the aegis of the Red Army. The Bulgarian partisan movement had not achieved a level of military success comparable to the Yugoslav Communist Party, but operated under very different and difficult conditions. Because of the belief by the Czar that, even in the early stages of the war, combat with Red Army troops would immediately precipitate internal revolution (and German acceptance of the reality of this appraisal), Bulgaria was able to maintain *de facto* neutrality, while serving as a training ground and supply route for the German force. Thus the BCP came to power in a society where, with the exception of the Gestapo-controlled internal security police and a relatively narrow circle of Tsarist political figures, anti-communism was not a well-rooted popular political ideology. Viewed from the Soviet perspective, Bulgaria was not an ex-enemy state in the same way as countries with mass pro-fascist parties and active participation in the German war effort in the East.

(4) Bulgaria lacks the great-power military commitments and political ambitions that make appraisal of Soviet experience somewhat difficult.

(5) While clearly continuing within the general framework of Soviet-type institutions, Bulgaria has made several independent institutional innovations that appear to have broad general implications.

Because of this long list of similarities, affinities and historical connections, Bulgarian developments can be analyzed fruitfully as a source of insights about both the Soviet past and future, while at the same time allowing some useful analysis of the differences between Soviet-type systems *per se* and the particular political, social and economic experience with those institutions in the Soviet Union. These quite different phenomena (Hanson, 1971) are often conflated and confused in both popular and professional discussions. We follow Wilbur (1969) in trying to disentangle the essential and accidental aspects of Soviet experience, trying to see separately the preconditions of the model, the institutional characteristics of the model, and the strategy of development in the model.

Realities of the Bulgarian Post-World War II Experience

What we find on closer inspection is a surprisingly successful case of develop-ment from very low material and cultural levels, in the face of an unfavorable resource and energy endowment, using familiar Soviet-type economic, political and social forms, but in many respects operating them in a fashion and with an effect quite different from what was found in the original case. Bulgaria has followed what may fairly be said to be the Stalin model of pervasive state ownership and direction of the economy, has collectivized and massively amalgamated the rural sector, has developed under the leadership of a vanguard party with an effective monopoly (despite the interesting persistence and participation in government of a formally autonomous Agrarian Party) on political power, has followed many of the twists and turns in Soviet artistic, cultural, economic and social policy, but yet has seemed to employ these institutions and techniques with a different emphasis and achieve quite different and often more favorable results.

A brief list of significant differential aspects of the Bulgarian variation on the Soviet political and economic model includes:

(1) Adoption of an industrialization strategy that stresses the classical heavy metal working, chemical and power areas, but which has not been pushed to the point of making agriculture an absolutely impoverished 'buffer' sector. A case can be made that Bulgarian agriculture has received less investment attention than it deserves on the basis of its concrete growth and foreign exchange earning capacities. None the less, the overall rural development effect achieved by a variety of investment measures, administrative-organizational techniques and direct social welfare policies has been sufficient by the mid-1970s to generate productivity, incomes and living standards for the previously impoverished rural population essentially equal to those enjoyed by the urban population.

(2) In part as the result of the relatively small urban–rural differential, but also within the various other occupational, social and regional categories, Bulgarian development has proceeded with a notably high degree of income equality. Economic growth and productivity has not to any significant degree been purchased by applying a veneer of market–capitalist differential rewards atop the structure of social ownership. Thus Bulgarian development has stayed close to socialist distribution norms and standards and may make some claim to relative doctrinal purity.

(3) Development of a Communist Party of a distinctively mass member-ship character, embodied in a national front organization (Fatherland Front) which includes more than half of the adult population.

(4) Pursuit of a steady policy of recruiting and quickly promoting able young party members to positions of real power and visibility. The long-standing, but recently quieted, claim that the Communist Party of the Soviet Union (CPSU) represents a self-perpetuating and unchangeable geronto-cracy has never been plausible as a description of Bulgarian Communist Party (BCP) practice, despite the long tenure of Todor Zhivkov as Party First Secretary and (after 1971) Chairman of the State Council.

(5) A very high degree of involvement in foreign trade, to an extent unequalled in other countries which have maintained the most rigorous and detailed forms of Soviet-style central planning. Total trade turnover (exports plus imports) has reached 100 percent of national income in recent years. While Bulgaria is not open to the world economy in the full sense of the

word, this level of foreign trade involvement successfully combined with central planning is worthy of attention. The fact that the bulk of this exchange has been with other CMEA members and is especially concentrated on the Soviet Union must be noted.

(6) A relatively open and rich cultural–artistic life with much less restrictive central control of publication and exhibition content than might be expected. Especially during the period in which Ludmilla Zhivkova was Minister of Culture, but since then as well, young Bulgarian artists have almost been rushed to meet their public, and works of a very broad range of artistic perspectives are seen by the general public.

(7) A rapid rate of progress in achieving full integration of women into economic, social and political life. This degree of progress (while far from equality of outcomes, especially at highest decision-making levels) is especially impressive in light of the strong conservative effects of social values and gender assumptions coming from the 500 years of Turkish rule.

Relatively Egalitarian Growth Provides Fewer Visible Signs of Progress

One result of the remarkable degree of equalization achieved *between* the rural and urban sectors of the society, compounded by the relatively even distribution *within* the sectors, is that casual observers often miss the extent of the Bulgarian achievement. Because of the absence of the surface froth of Western-style consumer goods visible in societies such as Greece, Yugoslavia and Hungary they reach unfavorable conclusions about the performance of the Bulgarian system on that basis. Comparisons with a number of countries will be made in the course of this volume, and Bulgarian achievements after World War II will be shown to be comparatively impressive in several unexpected respects and areas.

Institutions, Models and Systems

Although the boundaries are not perfectly precise, we will in general attempt to distinguish between *institutions*, *economic systems* and *models*. *Institutions* are particular aspects of economic organization or behavior. *Economic systems* are the specific groupings of institutions found in actual functioning economies at a particular time. *Models* are groupings of institutions which capture the spirit or essence of a particular type of existing or hypothetical economic system, but which are too starkly simplified ever to exist in nature. Economists use the word 'model' in a variety of ways, and here it is used in the sense of Weberian 'ideal types.' It is argued here that there is a distinctively Bulgarian economic model worthy of consideration independently of the closely related Soviet-type economic model.

The Bulgarian Economic Model

The Bulgarian economic model has several distinctive features which were probably not chosen consciously as a unit by any one person or group at any one time. Some of these features are identical to Soviet conditions while others diverge sufficiently to justify treating Bulgaria as a separate model.

(A) A *full employment perspective* has been adopted, existing (largely structural) unemployment eliminated in 1958 and over-full employment maintained thereafter. The patterns of over-staffing that emerged by the end of the 1950s as the combined results of social policy and the workings of the behavioral complex known as the *safety factor* have been maintained to the present time.
(B) Adoption of a *middle ground approach to agriculture*, which avoided sectoral impoverishment in the early years and, while later producing rapidly rising and relatively high rural living standards, did not emphasize the sector as a growth source. The 'food problem' has long been solved and a steady and obvious rise in living standards has occurred at the same time that the historical urban–rural differential has been wiped out. Migration to the cities has continued because of the prestige of urban occupations and the excitement of urban life, but now it is clearly pull, not push, migration.
(C) Adoption and maintenance of the distinctive *Soviet-type central planning techniques and ownership patterns*.
(D) Achievement of a *good overall growth performance*, although based on relatively high capital formation rates and low investment efficiency.
(E) Creation of a *respectable level of workplace diligence*. This aspect has not been pushed too hard, with the result that ample room remains for more rapid overall growth and rising living standards if improved utilization of existing capital equipment and better work methods can be adopted. The 'intensification' of the growth process by the combined effects of improved work methods, better management and incentive techniques, and the more rapid adoption of new technology, has proved difficult. Many Western analysts point to the institutions of central planning as sufficient by themselves to prevent successful reform, arguing that even the most simple

and logical measures meet with bureaucratic resistance from those in the party and government bureaucracy who benefit from the existing arrangements.

Bulgaria thus offers an unusually interesting comparative perspective on the effects of the Soviet-type model *per se*, free of the special political, military and climatic baggage of the Soviet original. Bulgaria has avoided the political disaster of the collectivization, the unfavorable climate and geography, and the resource-use implications of being a world power with heavy military requirements. Unfortunately for the purity of the possible comparisons, the Bulgarian party and government leadership share much of the particular 'heroic' perspective of the CPSU (which manifests an encirclement mentality and emphasizes the overcoming of all obstacles by military-like mobilization campaigns and 'shock work,' and includes a thoroughgoing hostility toward markets as economic coordinating devices).

The relatively good performance of the Bulgarian economy over several decades has served to deflect serious criticism and prevent the movement for conventional economic reform from gathering real momentum. The combination of factors that emerged during the last years of the 1981–5 plan—extraordinarily bad and sustained weather problems which had both agricultural and industrial effects, energy stress heightened by changed and possibly damaged economic relationships with the Soviet Union, and problems in adjusting to rising quality standards in both CMEA and Western markets—may have finally pushed economic reform to the top of the political agenda.

While consumers were largely shielded from the consequences (except for the indignities of the regime of interrupted electrical service), the events of the year 1985 undoubtedly had powerful effects on popular confidence in the performance of the economic system (which had provided an essentially unbroken two-decade-long period of rapidly rising living standards). The intense self-criticism and substantial personnel changes in 1986 can be viewed as providing scapegoats for the set-backs of the last several years, while sending the message that this time the pressure for improved and 'intensified' work methods was really strong.

The new set of reforms which were announced at the XIII Party Congress in April 1986 had been preceded by an extensive series of personnel changes (including the discharge of Stanish Bonev, the chief of the Central Planning Board) and an unusually direct and intense press campaign which called into question the competence and seriousness of the work efforts of a broad range of political and economic leaders. The condemnation of the performance of 'top leaders' was so strong and unqualified that it produced widespread speculation that it presaged the resignation of Todor Zhivkov, First Secretary and Chairman of the State Council. This did not occur, but instead the Party Congress witnessed strong attacks by Zhivkov on the performance and management of the economic and social system which he had presumably managed for the last three decades. It must be stressed that the criticism directed at the planning mechanism assumed its permanence at the core of the system, denied none of its prerogatives, and focused exclusively on the insufficient wisdom and competence with which it had been operated.

The reforms themselves managed to be at the same time daring in apparent scope and in almost every specific detail connected to already existing elements or tendencies in the system. The dual themes of heightened *party* control and strategic direction in economic decision-making and reduced *government* interference in the details of economic life are not, as is sometimes implied in Western discussions, logically inconsistent. They may however turn out to be contradictory in practice. The most radical-sounding aspect of the reform program was what was described as the 'abolition' of the industrial ministries themselves. If both true and behaviorally meaningful this structural reform would establish a new and direct relationship between the Central Planning Board and the state economic organizations (Durzhaven Stopanstvo Organizatsia or DSO) in which both would seem to have gained new power and leverage over their environments. The reservation here is that the new supervisory 'councils,' established to replace the ministries, may simply make the old ministries into subsections or bureaux, scarcely altering the operational realities of DSO life but adding another layer to the existing administrative structure.

Other changes which have the potential for making important differences in the functioning of the society and economy, but which also can only be evaluated after their actual implementation details become clear, include the spread from the agricultural to the industrial sector of the process of electing first-line supervisors, intensified efforts to apply 'brigade' methods in the industrial sector, the introduction of some degree of direct competition between producers of the same consumer goods (with specific reference to allowing some decentralized control over pricing), and increased rewards for outstanding managerial, technical or inventive activities.

The steady and self-conscious use of the name 'New Economic Mechanism' (NEM) for the now decade-old reform process should not be taken to imply actual or intended direct use of market forces in the style of the Hungarian reforms. While the extent and linear development of the Hungarian reforms have often been exaggerated in the West, they none the less go far beyond what happened under the same name in the large enterprise sector of the Bulgarian economy. Similarly in those small service and trade categories where Hungary, the GDR (and after 1 May 1987 the USSR) have been fostering a modest and tightly controlled privatization, no such Bulgarian policies emerged until late 1987.

The relatively sharp improvement in consumer living standards observed over the last decade has occurred as a result of two major changes in Bulgarian practice which are in a sense outside the realm of conventional economic reform: the great improvement in food supply under the new form of integration between the Agro-Industrial Complexes (AIC) and the personal plots, and the foundation and effective performance of relatively autonomous Small and Medium-Sized units generally *within* existing larger state enterprises, both of which developments are considered in detail in Chapter 4.

First, it is necessary to recognize that the Small and Medium-Sized Enterprise program is an important and authentically innovative form of decentralizing reform. They are none the less state enterprises in a system where the role of classical central planning, materials allocation and price formation have changed very little. They reflect an effort to improve the supply of services and simple consumer goods outside the existing large enterprise channels and it is useful to compare them with measures adopted in other Eastern European countries having the same purpose.

Second, a fundamentally new relationship has been established between the state agricultural sector and the household garden plot sector in several Eastern European countries. This relationship is so deeply symbiotic and reciprocal that the citation of productivity figures of one sector against the other, as though there is a competitive or adversarial relationship between them in which they can be viewed as competitive models or alternatives, had become fundamentally false. In both Bulgaria and Hungary the state sector provides inputs and services to the personal plot sector (fodder, seeds, fertilizer, piglets, etc.) in return for contractual sales of much of the resulting output for final sale through the state distribution network. Since the early 1970s the Bulgarian government has been eager to expand the output of the rural personal plot sector because of the immediate effects on consumer living standards, while at the same time representing a vast reservoir of untapped labor power in a labor-short economy.

Developments such as have been considered here are not economic reforms in the conventional sense of redesigning the organizational structure or incentive arrangements within the entire state sector. They have none the less produced a fundamental change in the performance and character of the

Bulgarian economic system (in the broadest sense of the words), and in the new wave of reform proposal during 1986 and 1987 have been used to illustrate the advantages of comprehensive reform. The very limited (though possibly increased) dependence on market forces of these successful economic tactics makes them especially appropriate for study by those concerned with predicting and analyzing the future evolution of the Soviet economic system.

This picture of generally favorable performance, and by implication possible usefulness as a development model for Third World countries, must coexist with the fact of a relatively serious economic crisis endured by Bulgaria during 1984 and 1985. A series of unusual political and economic events occurred during the months preceding the XIII Congress of the BCP in April of 1986, including the continuation of the energy crisis of the preceding winter through the summer and fall of 1985, a drastic price reform and rise in September 1985, and an unprecedented campaign in the BCP Central Committee newspaper *Rabotnichesko Delo* criticizing corruption, incompetence and toleration of the incompetence of subordinates at the 'highest levels' of the party leadership.

The relatively advanced age of Todor Zhivkov (born in 1911) and the open-ended and bold phrasing of the anti-corruption campaign fueled speculation of changes at the very top of the party and state hierarchies, but the Congress confirmed Zhivkov as First Secretary and laid heavy emphasis on further economic reform. Since Zhivkov has been the dominant single figure in Bulgarian political and economic life for more than twenty years, with a relatively calm and uncontested time in office, the prediction of the persons and factions that might emerge after his eventual retirement is a very difficult enterprise, eagerly avoided here. It is however worth referring to the view, popular for explaining Soviet developments during the period from the beginning of the decline in the health and vitality of Leonid Brezhnev to the accession of Mikhail Gorbachëv, that saw real government by committee occurring behind the scenes. Should either such a collective leadership or simple democratic practice *within* the Central Committee exist in Bulgaria, the retirement of Zhivkov could occur at any time without seeming surprising or humiliating, while 'committee' policies continued along a similar path.

In early 1986 a division of major operational responsibilities emerged between Chudomir Alexandrov, Ognyan Doynov, Georgi Atanasov and Stoyan Markov—all Politburo members and all born between 1933 and 1943—which appears to have narrowed and simplified the eventual succession process. I have stressed the depersonalized character of governance in the

Zhivkov period, but the 1986 press campaign at least suggests the possibility of a very comprehensive house-cleaning of middle- and higher-level cadres when he leaves office.

It is easy to anticipate that the relatively favorable picture presented here may seem to be insufficiently critical or too generous to Bulgaria. While Bulgaria is obviously not a liberal parliamentary democracy, at least after 1954, it is also not the sort of comprehensively repressive state of Cold War nightmares: It is a state that, under easier conditions to be sure, has avoided institutionalizing the worst political features of the Stalin model, has made its economic machinery work surprisingly well, and appears to the author to have become steadily more open and relaxed with the passage of time. It is a society with many severe development problems, and has been in a period of particular stress for the last several years, but it is not stagnant or institutionally complacent despite sustained problems in making talk of 'intensification' and reform of the economic mechanism into changes in actual behavior. The long-term implications for popular attitudes and morale of the break in the pattern of steady economic progress in the mid-1980s cannot be determined at this time. Similarly, the potentially explosive ethnic conflict, as symbolized by the Turkish assimilation campaign, is an unpredictable element in future Bulgarian national development. The acquittal of the Bulgarian nationals in the attempted assassination of the Pope has perhaps permanently removed that issue from contention, but the pattern of accusations of Bulgarian complicity in all manner of dark and suspicious dealings that appear to serve Soviet interests is a seemingly permanent feature of the international reputation of Bulgaria.

2 History and Political Traditions

The history of an autonomous Bulgarian state is generally dated from 681 when the Byzantine Empire signed a peace treaty recognizing the existence and military success of a combined Slav–Bulgarian state under the leadership of Khan Asparouh. In the thirteen hundred years since then, as in the thousands of years before, the area has been invaded, absorbed, transformed and ruled by a succession of different nations, tribes and armies.

The First Bulgarian Empire was characterized by cultural and artistic dynamism and lasted until the reconquest by Byzantine forces in 1018. This period is often referred to as the Slavic Enlightenment. This Golden Age of old Bulgarian literature and culture included the formulation of the Slavic alphabet in 855 by the brothers Cyril and Methodius, the replacement of the Greek language in church and other uses and a general intellectual flowering which in some ways anticipated the Reformation. There was considerable attention to ancient secular literature in addition to the predominantly religious subjects.

. . . the old Bulgarian literature, like Byzantine literature, threw a bridge between the ancient and the early feudal European civilization . . . [it] had the merit not only of preserving the achievements of Cyril and Methodius, which would otherwise have been doomed to failure, but also of creating all the necessary prerequisites for their further development and genuine flowering. The Bulgarians were the first among the Slav peoples to create a rich literature of their own, written in their own language, which was called on to play a Pan-Slavic role and to serve as an intermediary between the highly-developed Byzantine culture and the southern and eastern Slavs. The Old Bulgarian language served as the basis of literary Russian and Serbian languages, and was for several centuries the church and official state language of Russians and Romanians. [Vassilev, 1979, p. 39].

A century and a half later, when the Byzantine Empire was under attack by the Turks from the east and the Magyars from the northwest, the Bulgarian state again emerged as an independent entity. A politically turbulent period ensued, marked by territorial expansion and contraction, but also by a cultural development considered to be a second Golden Age, which as early as the first half of the thirteenth century showed proto-Renaissance tendencies. This promising cultural development was cut short by the armies of the rapidly expanding Ottoman Empire, which arrived in the south during the 1360s and completed the conquest of the area between 1388 and 1396.

The modern history of Bulgaria may be divided into three periods: 1396–1878 under Ottoman rule and largely cut off from commercial or cultural contact with the rest of Europe; 1878–1944, a period of four wars and dramatically changing national borders as the drive for long–delayed modernization and national self–actualization led to an aggressive and expansionist foreign policy. Internal developments in this period moved first in the direction of parliamentary democracy and social change through essentially social democratic policies, followed by a fascist coup and quasi–totalitarian rule from 1923 to 1944. The current period began with the seizure of power by the Fatherland Front coalition on 9 September 1944, followed by the consolidation in power of the Bulgarian Communist Party (BCP) over the next two years, culminating in the declaration of a People's Republic on 4 December 1947.

The Ottoman Empire

The Ottoman Empire was founded by Turkish tribes of Asian origin, which had occupied Constantinople in 1453 and rapidly expanded around the north and south shores of the Mediterranean. It almost incidentally absorbed Bulgaria, Romania and most of the rest of the Balkan peninsula as it moved toward Vienna and the Hungarian plains. Hungary was largely under Ottoman control from 1526 to 1697 and Vienna was twice besieged, first in 1529 and after a quiescent period again in 1683. It is now three centuries since that momentous Turkish defeat at the gates of central Europe, but it was another two hundred years before the Turkish grip on the Balkans was finally broken. During much of this period Turkey was viewed as the 'sick man of Europe,' needing only a small push to collapse. The presence on its northern border of a dynamic Russian state with strong geopolitical interests in freeing its access to the Mediterranean Sea and strong cultural and religious ties to the largely Slavic captive peoples at the European edge of the Ottoman Empire suggested a quick demise, but the larger European balance of power and the resulting set of alliances placed strong barriers in the way of Russian success in what was simultaneously a liberating and self-aggrandizing role. First France, which was seeking any available counterweight against the Austrian Habsburgs, became an ally and supporter of Turkey. Then in the nineteenth century Great Britain assumed a similar role, developing what was in effect a regional alliance with Turkey to protect it from any developments that would be territorially beneficial to Russia.

Russia fought a series of little-known wars with Turkey in 1768–74, 1787–92, 1806–12, 1828–9 and 1853–6, the last developing into the Crimean War, with the entry of England, France and Piedmont (for reasons explicable in terms of internal Italian politics) as allies of Turkey. Even Austria–Hungary entered the situation, seizing Moldavia and Wallachia (together modern Romania) which had been the immediate objects of Russian aspirations in 1853. The Crimean War was fought almost exclusively on Russian soil and was an embarrassing revelation of how far Russia had fallen behind the other major European power since its peak at the end of the Napoleonic Wars. This humiliation is widely seen as having precipitated the edict which began the emancipation of the serfs in 1861 and a series of reforms aimed at modernizing and mobilizing Russian society. The peace imposed at the Congress of Paris in 1856 forbade the presence of Russian naval units on the Black Sea, made the Danube an international river, and included an agreement to maintain the territorial integrity of the Ottoman Empire. Despite the apparent finality of these terms, Russia entered a period of economic and geopolitical dynamism (partly as a result of the reforms and development policies adopted after the Crimean débâcle) and by 1875 Tsar Alexander I was in a position to reassert Russian influence to the south and remove the Crimean stain. Turkey had entered into a period of reform (1856–76), which at first promised to remove the various civil discriminations against non-Muslims, abolish torture, and establish a representative parliament which would include delegates from Bulgaria and Serbia. A turn back to vigorous repression, which began in 1875 and included large-scale massacres of peasants in Serbia and Bulgaria, produced a wave of popular revulsion in Europe and brought an end to the belief that the Ottoman Empire might be in the process of thoroughgoing reform.

In Bulgaria a strong nationalist and insurrectionary tradition had emerged in the course of the broad development known as the National Awakening. Unsuccessful armed uprisings had occurred in 1828–9, 1835, 1836, 1841, 1850, 1868, and in April of 1876 a much larger but also unsuccessful uprising was attempted. The murder of tens of thousands of peasants in the course of April and May of 1876 was widely reported in the European press. Turkey rejected the settlement proposed by a conference convened to discuss the Balkan situation and Russia declared war on Turkey in April of 1877, leading to a bitter nine-month war which cost the lives of roughly 200,000 Russian soldiers, and ended when the Russian armies reached Constantinople. On 3 March 1878 Russia imposed the Treaty of San Stefano, which provided independence for Bulgaria, Serbia, Romania and Montenegro and ceded territory along the east shore of the Black Sea to Russia. The borders of the Bulgarian state created under this treaty included all of Macedonia and the area that came to be called Eastern Rumelia.

England was prepared to go to war with Russia to revoke this treaty, and later in 1878 the Congress of Berlin was called to attempt a peaceful solution. The resulting Treaty of Berlin avoided an English–Russian war, but established the conditions that led to a string of Balkan Wars and that leave even today border disputes and irredentist feeling. The German Prime Minister Bismarck convened the Congress but Germany took nothing for itself in the ensuing redivision of the Russian war gains. England and Austria were particularly determined to resurrect a viable European presence for Turkey. To do this much of the Treaty of San Stefano was abandoned: Russia retained its acquisition on the Black Sea; Serbia, Romania and Montenegro were established as independent states; Bosnia and Hercegovina were awarded to Austria–Hungary to be administered but not legally incorporated; and England took the island of Cyprus. Bulgaria as defined by the Treaty of San Stefano was now divided into three parts, all of which remained at least nominally part of the Ottoman Empire. Northwestern Bulgaria became a principality within the Ottoman Empire, Macedonia reverted to its pre-war status and southern Bulgaria under the name of Eastern Rumelia became an autonomous region of the Ottoman Empire.

The Bulgarian view of these developments and their implications is reflected precisely in the following quotation.

[It was] a base and immoral act, because far from securing peace, it created numerous occasions for future conflicts and wars.

Separated from the Adriatic Sea, having lost vast territories (Bosnia and Herzegovina) Serbia was forced to look for an outlet on the sea to the south, through Bulgarian lands, along the valley of the River Vardar, towards Salonika. This, of course, pitted the two fraternal peoples, Bulgarians and Serbians, against each other, making them fly at each other's throat. Greece for her part, was interested in opposing Serbia's and Bulgaria's penetration towards Salonika by expanding its hinterland, i.e., by seizing the undisputed until then Bulgarian region of Macedonia. Thus the rivalry between the Great European powers and their selfish interests gave birth at the Berlin Congress to the notorious Macedonian question [Vassilev, 1979, pp. 111–12]

This settlement was imposed on Russia by the revived 'Concert of Europe' in the name of maintaining the overall balance of power in Europe. It set the conditions for permanent Bulgarian dissatisfaction with its frontiers, created an especially malignant problem with respect to Macedonia, and provided the basis for the ultimately self-destructive course taken by Bulgaria in four twentieth-century wars—the First Balkan War (1912–13), the Second Balkan War (1913) and both World Wars.

A few months after the Congress of Berlin an unsuccessful uprising against Turkish rule in Macedonia resulted in the flight of large numbers of Bulgarians to the Principality, and after a short sucessful war with Serbia a peace treaty was signed in Bucharest which affirmed the union of eastern and western Bulgaria. Secret societies for the liberation of Macedonia and Thrace were founded at this time, including IMARO (Internal Macedonian and Adrianople Revolutionary Organization), which continued to play an important and generally bloody role in Bulgarian politics in the 1920s and 1930s. A number of attempted uprisings occurred over the next two decades, two in the year 1903 alone, leading to a large flow of Macedonian refugees into Bulgaria proper. Finally in 1908 at the time of the 'Young Turks' revolution, the Bulgarian government proclaimed its full independence from the Ottoman Empire.

After the Italian declaration of war on Turkey in 1911, Bulgaria, Serbia, Greece and Montenegro joined in a war against Turkey in which Turkey was quickly defeated. Disagreements among the victors, in particular about how large the Bulgarian and Serbian shares of Macedonia should be, led to the Second Balkan War in which Bulgaria was badly defeated by the combined forces of Serbia, Greece, Turkey and Romania. Bulgaria shrank precipitously as Macedonia was divided by Serbia and Greece, Adrianople Thrace was returned to Turkey, and Romania received the southern part of the Dobroudja region along the Black Sea Coast. The settlement imposed at the end of the Second Balkan War inflamed Bosnian nationalists, with important consequences for all of Europe, and left Bulgaria with a profound sense of victimization and of having been deprived of its obvious and natural frontiers.

In World War I Bulgaria gravitated to the German side (despite the presence of Austria–Hungary and Turkey) because it expected restoration of territories lost in the Second Balkan War to result from a German victory, as well as because the Tsar was German and the ruling party pro-German. We will see below that the Agrarian Party categorically opposed entering the war, which redounded to its favor when the war went badly, and largely explained its quick rise to power after the war. The anti-militarism of the Agrarian Party at the same time earned the hatred of military, monarchist and Macedonian circles which led to its destruction after three years in power.

After an armistice signed on 29 September 1918, Bulgaria, like the other defeated states, was forced to accept an extremely harsh peace. In the treaty signed in the Paris suburb of Neuilly on 27 November 1919, Bulgaria lost the part of Thrace along the Aegean Sea, the Strouma, Tsaribrod and Bossilegard regions, Romanian possession of the southern Dobroudja was confirmed, large reparations in cash and in kind were required, and Bulgaria was cut off from normal trade relationships.

A combination of economic, political and ideological factors pushed Bulgaria toward alliance with Germany during the inter-war period. Powerful irredentist feelings existed throughout Bulgarian society and Germany as the Great Power with the strongest grievances against the status quo was the logical ally. Substantial economic penetration by Germany before 1914 and lack of normal access by Bulgaria to trade relationships with other European countries after the war reinforced the political attraction. Finally, the fascist coup that overthrew the elected Agrarian Party government in 1923 was carried out by military and political figures who directly admired the newly emerged Italian fascism and its methods and sought to bring similar institutions to Bulgaria. The rise to power of the Nazi Party ten years later found a clear social, political and ideological resonance in Bulgaria, which by that time had abolished all political parties and become a military dictatorship. The Bulgarian government joined the Axis Pact, declared war on England, France and the United States but not on the Soviet Union, and in general attempted to minimize its direct involvement in the war. The German military had free rein (for transit, training or rest) in Bulgaria and Bulgarian resources were at German disposal, but almost all of the Bulgarian casualties in battle occurred when fighting as units of the Red Army after the overthrow of the pro-German government in August 1944. Despite this military effort Bulgaria was again considered to be a defeated nation at the end of the war, occupied by the Soviet army, and administered by a joint Russian–British–American Control Commission. The territorial effects of the war were that Bulgaria withdrew from the parts of Greece and Yugoslavia it had been occupying as a German surrogate (and hopeful future recipient), but retained the South Dobroudja which had been ceded by Romania in 1940, thereby achieving its current territorial configuration.

We now turn to a more detailed discussion of the rise and fall of the Bulgarian Agrarian National Union (BANU) and the relationship of these events to the rise to power of the Bulgarian Communist Partuy (BCP). First however we must pause to consider the economic, social and demographic conditions in the period following the liberation from Turkish rule, which set the framework for the unusual Bulgarian political development.

Historical Demographic Patterns

Analysis of Bulgarian demographic history reveals a pattern of relationships that had strong effects on and were strongly affected by military and political developments. While mortality and fertility rates declined rapidly from the high levels of the late nineteenth century, and certain aspects of this develop-ment are consistent with the general European pattern, in other respects Bulgaria stands outside of this tradition (McIntyre, 1980).

In the 'European' fertility pattern identified by Hajnal (1964), a relatively late age of marriage for women, a small difference in the age of husband and wife, and a relatively large number of people who never marry, combined to hold overall fertility levels far below those existing elsewhere in the world. Bulgaria entered into its transition to modern, low fertility levels with an opposite pattern of early and nearly universal marriage. As Table 2.1 suggests, a distinctive Balkan pattern of early and nearly universal marriage is visible when the first comprehensive data became available at the turn of the century.

Table 2.1 Percentage of age group single in 1900

	Women			Men		
	20–24	25–29	45–49	20–24	25–29	45–49
Bulgaria	24	3	1	58	23	3
Romania (1899)	20	8	3	67	21	5
Serbia	16	2	1	50	18	3
France	58	30	12	90	48	11
Great Britain	73	42	15	83	47	12
Sweden	80	52	19	92	61	13
The Netherlands	79	44	14	89	53	13

Sources: Hajnal, 1964, pp. 102–3; McIntyre, 1980, p. 149.

Table 2.2 traces the decline of Bulgarian fertility through time and shows that by the 1920s, 'relatively low overall fertility levels had been achieved in what remained a backward agrarian society, despite the continued presence of this elevated nuptiality pattern and in the absence of substantial overall modernization' (McIntyre, 1980, p. 147).

The analysis in Table 2.3 is presented in terms of the indexes developed by Coale (1967, 1969) in which total fertility (I_f) is explained by the combined effects of the proportion of the population married (I_m) and the fertility of those who are married (I_g). Unmarried fertility is in the aggregate insignifi-cant. In the European pattern, marriage prevalence rose only after effective technical control of fertility had been achieved, but in Bulgaria and several

Table 2.2 Crude birth rates and rates of reproduction, Bulgaria, 1880–1985

	1880	1900	1930	1960	1965	1970	1975	1980	1985
Crude birth rates	33.7*	42.2	31.3	17.8	15.3	16.3	16.6	14.5	13.2
Rates of reproduction									
Gross	—	3.18	1.90	1.12	1.00	1.05	1.08	1.00	—
Net	—	1.84†	1.29‡	1.01	0.95	1.01	1.04	0.96	—

* 1881.
† 1901–5.
‡ 1929.

Sources: United Nations, *Demographic Yearbook 1965*, pp. 294–6, 612; *1969*, pp. 262–3, 475–6; *1972*, pp. 476–8; *1975*, pp. 524–5; *1977*, p. 286; *1981*, p. 555; Kuczynski, 1931, pp. 30, 35, 50, 134–5; 1936, pp. 104–5, 126–7; B. R. Mitchell, 1975, pp. 108, 110, 111, 118; Bulgaria, *Statisticheski godishnik 1984*, p. 34; *Statisticheske Spravochnik*, 1986, p. 184.

Table 2.3 Selected countries: indices of fertility and marital proportions

	Overall fertility (I_f)			Marital fertility (I_g)			Proportion married (I_m)		
	1900	1930	1960	1900	1930	1960	1900	1930	1960
Bulgaria	0.52	0.31	0.20	0.70	0.41	0.24	0.73	0.75	0.78
European Russia	0.55	0.44	0.24	0.77	0.65	0.35	0.70	0.63	0.62
France	0.24	0.19	0.22	0.38	0.30	0.31	0.57	0.58	0.67
England & Wales	0.27	0.15	0.22	0.55	0.29	0.29	0.48	0.50	0.71
Sweden	0.30	0.15	0.17	0.64	0.30	0.24	0.41	0.42	0.63
United States	0.29	0.20	0.28	0.49	0.31	0.36	0.58	0.63	0.75

Sources: Coale, 1967, p. 209; van de Walle, 1972; and calculations by McIntyre, 1980, p. 151, based on data from Bulgaria, *Statisticheski godishnik 1960*, p. 27; Kuczynski, 1936, pp. 239–45.

other southeastern European countries the pattern is reversed, in effect by-passing the demographic stage that Coale (1973, pp. 55–7, 70) has character-ized as the first or Malthusian transition in which fertility declines as a result of a sharp drop in the proportion married. Cultural forces seem to have required a non-Western mode of 'transition,' so that the spread of the general European mortality decline into Bulgaria resulted in rapid natural increase, but did not produce significant changes in the early and universal marriage pattern. The sharp decline and eventual very low levels of the crude fertility indicators in the twentieth century were based on spectacular reductions in *marital* fertility. As Krause has suggested, despite similarities, Bulgaria is not an appropriate policy metaphor or demographic model for application to the problems of current developing countries, but is instead 'another population type ... somewhat similar [to the] pre-industrial western [type], but differ[ing] in that it was geared to a different standard of living and in that marital fertility was controlled more than marriage' (Krause, 1960, pp. 485–7). A surprisingly little-known revolution in marital patterns began around 1930 in most of the rest of Europe, raising the proportion married sharply in the direction of the early and nearly universal marriage that had long existed in eastern or at least southeastern Europe (Coale, 1973; Sklar, 1974; McIntyre, 1980).

This non-European demographic pattern has both historical interest and direct relevance to contemporary Bulgarian social and economic policy problems. Exploration of the interrelated causes and consequences of the Bulgarian fertility transition casts considerable light on the political and economic forces that operated in the period after 1878 and led to the formation and rise to power of the Bulgarian Agrarian National Union (BANU). This discussion sets the stage for much of the post-liberation political development, revealing forces leading to dashed dreams of develop-ment and prosperity on the one hand and intensifying rural poverty on the other. The modern policy relevance of these demographic developments comes from the labor force effects of the very low fertility levels already achieved in Bulgaria by the beginning of the communist era, which had delayed but definite implications for the performance of an economic model founded on the concept of extensive growth.

Landholding Arrangements and Rural Poverty

The interesting and surprising demographic developments in Bulgaria are obviously manifestations of deeper economic and cultural forces. The factors which appear to play the major role in explaining the early achievement of low marital fertility in Bulgaria are the pattern of landholding which resulted from the persistence of the form of extended household organization known as the *zadruga* (Sanders, 1949; Halpern & Anderson, 1970, pp. 83–97; Halpern & Halpern, 1972, pp. 16–44), the system of inheritance, and the comprehensive and thoroughly egalitarian land reform which occurred when the feudal Ottoman social structure and land tenure system were overturned in 1878 and the class of predominantly Turkish large landowners was expelled or expropriated.

National independence and a new rural social structure based on small peasant landownership arose at the same relatively late time in modern European history. Although small peasant landholding remained the predominant characteristic of the Bulgarian countryside until 1944, and Bulgaria remained as well a profoundly agrarian country, by the turn of the century the initially small holdings had become inexorably and noticeably smaller and the problem of pervasive rural poverty had emerged (Warriner, 1965, pp. 7–10). The high hopes that had followed the liberation from what is still nearly universally called the 'Turkish yoke' had not been met by sustained improvements in general rural living standards. It is hard to deny a central role in the ensuing growth and dynamism of agrarian radicalism in Bulgaria to this combination of frustrated aspirations and worsening real conditions in the immediate post-liberation decades.

As a consequence of both the practice of inheritance by subdivision among all living heirs (including female children) and the systematic scattering of individual holdings that followed from the method of distribution applied to both the expropriated feudal estates and the *zadruga* common lands, there was an extreme and often grotesque parcellization of peasant landholdings. The result was a small average size and a progressive scattering of the acreage of individual peasants which sometimes produced plots narrow enough to jump over (Warriner, 1939, pp. 9–10, 160, 1965, pp. 15–16; Dobrin, 1973, pp. 7–9; League of Nations, 1940, pp. 10–15; McCloskey, 1975, pp. 27–35). Fragmentation was not by itself worse than in some advanced European economies (Jackson & Lampe, 1982a, pp. 351–2), but its intensification in the absence of technical change led to systematic downward pressure on rural living standards. The *zadruga* relationship provided both men and women with strong reasons for early marriage (Sklar, 1974, pp. 234–6, 243–4), but both the small size of initial holdings and the distribution pattern are factors that appear to have combined to produce an exceptional concern with fertility control by married couples. These cultural and landholding patterns, along with the orthodox religious tradition, are factors which set Bulgaria and adjacent areas of Bosnia and Serbia apart from other European countries.

Whether dependent on *coitus interruptus*, various more or less effective folk methods of contraception, or illegal abortion, the highly effective fertility control of the Bulgarian population relative to the more advanced and industrialized countries of Eastern Europe, such as Hungary and Czechoslovakia, seems to be an established and long-lasting fact. Evidence of the early rise of family limitation in rural areas in Hungary and France should make the possible 'leading' role of the rural population in Bulgaria somewhat less surprising. [McIntyre, 1980, p. 164]

While the Bulgarians were sometimes called 'the Frenchmen of the Orient,' as a tribute to their Malthusian cast of mind, the rise of effective fertility control among the Bulgarians occurred in the context of very high marital proportions, unlike the French peasants. Aspects of the Bulgarian situation have parallels in other parts of Eastern Europe, in Portugal and in many developing countries but similar population pressure on scarce agricultural land has not always produced comparable fertility adaptation (Sweezy, 1973a, pp. 2–6; Coale, 1973, pp. 62–3; Livi-Bacci, 1971, pp. 11–13, 66–9; Jackson & Lampe, 1982a, pp. 354–5; Lampe, 1986, pp. 24–6, 55–6). Some writers have mentioned factors such as rising literacy rates and the penetration of foreign social and political ideologies (Sweezy, 1973a, pp. 18–19, 1973b, 1973c; Kirk, 1946, pp. 48–50, 55–9) as possible explanations. The role of education and the ideology of education in the course of the Bulgarian National Awakening, reinforced by the special emphasis on mass education and study groups that were a fundamental characteristic of the Bulgarian Agrarian National Union from its very beginning, together lend some support to this interpretation, but do not settle the question of the direction of the causation.

Post-World War II Fertility Patterns and Current Demographic Policy

The low fertility pattern which began to develop around the turn of the century was strongly established by the time of World War II. The post-war governments did not see slow population growth as a problem requiring policy attention, at least prior to 1956. Table 2.4 shows that in 1955 Bulgaria already had age-specific fertility rates considerably lower than other more highly developed Eastern European countries.

Table 2.5 reports the actual crude birth rates (births per 1,000 of total population) and general fertility rates (births per 1,000 women in the age

Table 2.4 Births per 1,000 women, by age groups, 1955

Age group	15–19	20–24	25–29	30–34	35–39	40–44	45–49	15–49
Bulgaria	59.6	178.4	128.8	63.6	32.8	10.4	1.9	75.6
Czechoslovakia	44.6	201.0	159.0	94.5	51.7	16.9	1.4	83.3
Hungary	54.3	191.6	151.3	95.6	52.4	16.4	1.3	83.0
Romania	50.7	186.0	167.3	111.4	64.2	24.8	3.5	95.1

Source: United Nations, *Demographic Yearbook 1965*, pp. 320, 331, 476–7, 487–9.

Table 2.5 Crude birth and general fertility rates (in parentheses), 1955

Age-structural weights	Bulgaria	Czechoslovakia	Hungary	Romania
Own weights	20.1 (75.6)	20.2 (83.3)	21.4 (83.0)	25.6 (95.1)
Bulgarian weights	20.1 (75.6)	24.0 (90.0)	23.6 (88.7)	– –

Sources: Calculations based on data from United Nations, *Demographic Yearbook 1965*, pp. 320, 331, 334, 476–7, 487–9.

range 15–49) for Bulgaria, Czechoslovakia, Hungary and Romania, and standardized rates which remove the effects of differences in the number of women in the various age groups between countries. When these structural variations are taken into account, Bulgarian fertility levels are revealed to be even lower than superficial inspection would suggest (McIntyre, 1980, pp. 158–68). All of the Eastern European countries liberalized abortion availability following reintroduction of the 1920 abortion law in the Soviet Union in 1956, leading to lower birth rates and the beginnings of official concern about possibly inadequate rates of population growth. Around 1960 these same countries began to introduce measures to raise fertility levels, ranging from 'positive' inducements to restrictions on induced abortion (McIntyre, 1972; Coelen & McIntyre, 1978; David & McIntyre 1981; McIntyre, 1985).

Thus Bulgarian fertility was low at the beginning of the reform period, fell little as a result of the abortion reform which seems to have largely replaced illegal abortion, failed to respond substantially to the relatively weak pro-natalist measures employed in the 1960s and 1970s (Berent, 1970, pp. 285–90;

McIntyre, 1975, pp. 366–80), and by the 1980s was viewed as part of an interrelated set of factors boding ill for future economic growth. After mild abortion restrictions in 1968 and 1973 (David & McIntyre, 1981, pp. 283–8), more serious restrictions were introduced in the 1980s. In 1985, as part of an integrated pro-natalist program, family allowance payments, maternity leave arrangements, layette payments and other positive incentives were increased, while administration of existing abortion regulations was made more restrictive (in particular by removing easy access to induced abortion on 'psychological' and 'social' indications or grounds). While not in any way as severe as the abortion restrictions and other methods utilized in Romania (McIntyre, 1985), the recent changes do mark a fundamental shift in social policy and importantly alter the relationship between women and the state health system. While Bulgaria no longer recognizes an unconditional right of women to control their fertility, it has not restricted access to contraceptive supplies or services and may be defended against the charge of forcing women to choose between celibacy, maternity or illegal abortion.

The Rise of the Bulgarian Agrarian National Union (BANU)

The Bulgarian Agrarian National Union (BANU) was an unusual and interesting organization, in a number of ways unique among the considerable variety of populist and peasants' parties that appeared in Europe in the last century. Its rapid political success was the combined result of an original and comprehensive social–economic program and the particular relationship of the BANU to the foreign policy and military developments discussed above. Despite its genuine popularity and solid rural support, the BANU would not have reached power so quickly had it not been so strongly identified in the public mind with unconditional opposition to Bulgarian participation in both the Balkan Wars and World War I. When the Second Balkan War and World War I resulted in 'national catastrophe,' the Tsar and the other political parties were discredited and BANU was seen as prescient and correct about Bulgaria's true best interests. This same position assured BANU of the hatred of an interlocking set of military, monarchist and Macedonian forces who viewed its political program as treasonous and its conciliatory foreign policies as foreclosing opportunities for revenge and the reconquest of lost territories.

The Agrarian Union forswore territorial claims against adjoining states and sought accommodation in particular with Yugoslavia. It emphasized economic development and the need to overcome internal backwardness, and directly identified the combative and expansionary foreign policy and the military budget required to support it as responsible for the failure of Bulgaria to achieve significant economic and social progress in the three decades since liberation. It was stridently republican and developed a number of often theatrical methods of demonstrating contempt for the Tsar. BANU accused the Tsar of pursuing an adventurist foreign policy, and once in power moved progressively to restrict the influence of the monarch on the conduct of government, while continuing to call for elimination of the monarchy. These positions guaranteed the hatred of various bourgeois sectors of society and reinforced the nearly universal opposition of the officer corps to the BANU. The Agrarians undertook the daunting task of administering the harsh conditions imposed by the Treaty of Neuilly, while at the same time facing the frequently exercised veto power of the Allied Reparations Commission over the social and economic policy measures it adopted. It is not surprising that the BANU failed under these extreme conditions, but its efforts and the original measures it attempted to employ are worthy of respect. The characters and methods of the opposition that rose up against the Agrarian Union also do much to explain the later political history of the Bulgarian Communist Party (BCP).

The Political History of the BANU: Organizational Character and Program

It is impossible to separate the history and political program of the BANU from the career of Alexander Stamboliski, who played a key role in its growth before World War I, its eclipse and suppression during the war (when he was sentenced to death for treason), and its rapid rise to governing status after the war when he served as its only Prime Minister. The following discussion relies heavily on the biography and party history by John Bell (1977), which contains an extensive bibliography and careful documentation. For other treatments of Bulgarian political history the reader is referred to Rothschild (1959) and *Istoriia na Bulgarski kommunisticheska partiia* (1972).

The Agrarians were the only European peasant party to exercise state power and put at least part of their program into effect. They were a mass mobilization party with thoroughgoing internal democracy: the elected local village council selected representatives to regular national congresses which made detailed and binding declarations of party policy; joint membership in other organizations was prohibited; and party discipline (i.e., ejection from the party of those members who defied the policy of the Party Congress) was established. The party leadership itself on several occasions did reverse Congress decisions, defending the action on the basis of changed circumstances. The leadership was mostly made up of intellectuals but they did not impose a program on an inert mass following. From the beginning the Agrarian leadership articulated the broad issues and then left the development of specific policies to the Congresses.

The Economic and Social Program of the BANU

The Bulgarian Agrarian Union (BAU) was founded in December 1899 by a group of intellectuals, mostly local school teachers, who had directly observed the lack of economic and social progress in the villages following the post-liberation land reform. They attributed the lack of progress to the rampant political corruption and absence of interest in rural distress by the bourgeois parties. The BAU began with a non-political orientation, reflecting the direct inspiration of the evolutionary branch of Russian populism.

Central to Bulgarian populism was the concept of the duty of the intelligentsia to raise the intellectual and moral standards of the common people. The populists believed that the roots of Bulgaria's political and economic failure lay in the ignorance and backwardness of the peasantry. Their goal was to make the peasant a more efficient and prosperous producer and to educate him to the duties of citizenship in a democratic state. [They] most often turned to journalism . . . [and] created no organized political movement. [Bell, 1977, p. 19)

When the BAU decided at its third annual congress to go beyond its 'educational-economic' role and openly become a political party, many members resigned on philosophical grounds. The Bulgarian Social Democratic Party had been founded in 1890, and its successes in organizing printers' and teachers' unions had suggested the possible advantages of some form of joint action by the numerically dominant Bulgarian peasantry. Almost immediately after the founding BAU congress a series of government measures, including sharp tax increases (the tithe), had produced mass peasant protests, some of which were violently repressed. In one battle, in May 1900, 90 peasants were killed and more than 400 were wounded. By the time of the third annual Agrarian Congress in October 1901 the case for seeking political power directly and outside the channels of the existing parties had become persuasive (Bell, 1977, pp. 20–1, 39–52).

The political program developed by the renamed Bulgarian Agrarian National Union (BANU) was extremely far-reaching and radical and the measures implemented during the BANU's brief period in power (6 October

1919–9 June 1923) in many respects paralleled contemporary developments in the Soviet Union. Stamboliski had frequently attacked the Soviet government for its treatment of the peasantry during the Civil War period (1918–21) and played on peasant fears that the word 'socialism' definitionally meant abolition of all categories of private property, including personal effects. Both were effective tactics against the Bulgarian Communist Party in internal politics. He quickly noted the new atmosphere (especially abandonment of compulsory procurement of food supplies, institution of free market relationships, and a single proportional tax in agriculture) under the New Economic Policy (NEP) introduced by Lenin in March 1921, and in November said that 'We have fought fiercely against Bolshevism, that is Bolshevism in the form in which it first appeared in Russia. I do not speak of today's Bolshevism, which is moderating its aspect and taking a more democratic form' (Bell, 1977, p. 195). Bulgaria also provided famine relief to the Soviet Union and Stamboliski spoke of his government and Lenin's as the only ones that had undertaken serious reforms. According to Bell (1977, pp. 194–5), Stamboliski wished to make peace with the BCP, which he now considered to be a 'tame bear' that could be used to 'frighten the bourgeoisie should it try to thwart his reforms.'

The BANU program as articulated by Stamboliski had distinguishing theoretical and practical policy features, and in both respects the Agrarian program was so far outside the boundaries of conventional liberal–reformist politics that it appears to be the direct precursor of much of the post-1944 BCP social–economic program. I can find no support for such a strong assertion of policy lineage in the works of Western scholars. The clear exceptions of the collectivization of agriculture and central planning of the industrial sector are not relevant for the simple reason that they had not yet occurred in the Soviet Union when the BANU was in power. Under this interpretation the BANU program set the point of reference for all later Bulgarian politics far to the left, making the programmatic content of the BCP governments, after the fascist interlude, a continuation rather than an entirely new departure.

The two most distinctive theoretical aspects of the BANU analysis of society where the notion of reconstituting politics on the basis of negotiations (in parliament) between explicitly and exclusively occupationally based parties (estates), and the idea of labor property (*trudova sobstvennost*), which basically declared invalid the ownership of all assets the use of which required exploitation (in the Marxian sense) of others and called for private ownership of only what could be worked directly in the hands of the individual household. Stamboliski formulated both of these principles in his writings and parliamentary speeches and they became the ideological core of the Agrarian program. The analysis in terms of occupational estates welcomed the rise of the BCP as the representative of the urban working class, guilds and cooperatives as representatives of artisans and craft workers, and saw the BANU as the representative of the numerically dominant peasantry and thus as the natural ruling party during the long transition to a modern industrial society.

The concept of labor property lies behind many of the explicitly redistributive BANU programs:

Land reform: The expropriation of all holdings of absentee owners in excess of 4 hectares; and a maximum of 30 hectares per household of arable land; the formation of a State Land Fund to allocate land to landless peasants from state holdings and expropriated private or monastery land. Of an anticipated 230,000 hectares, 82,000 had been accumulated by the time of the coup. Compulsory consolidation of extremely small strips, sometimes combined with relocation assistance, was also part of the land program. Peasant recipients paid 120 percent of the average 1905–15 price with no interest charge over a twenty-year term. Compensation was paid on a sliding scale with a maximum price of 100 percent of the 1905–15 average price for the first 10 hectares and less thereafter (Bell, 1977, pp. 163–7). Some sources suggest that the pattern of landholding in Bulgaria was so egalitarian after the 1878 land reform that there was no need for further reforms like those adopted elsewhere in Eastern Europe designed to prevent repetition of the Russian revolutionary experience. This is incorrect for, as noted in the earlier discussion of the reform after 1878, differentiating tendencies were immediately at work, in part as peasant bankruptcy led to loss of land, in part as population growth brought further parcellization and the existence of many very small holdings, and lastly because of the influx of more than 450,000 refugees from Greece and Yugoslavia that followed the constriction of Bulgaria's borders in the Treaty of Neuilly.

Housing reform: Urban apartment space was reallocated by the Interior Ministry on the basis of family size and excess space held by government ministries was also seized (Bell, 1977, p. 167).

Prohibition of private trade in grain and tobacco: Trade was monopolized in government hands to eliminate speculation and stabilize prices. Profits were largely rebated to growers. The Grain Consortium was disbanded by order of the Inter-Allied Reparations Commission (Bell, 1977, pp. 169–70).

Confiscation of profits of speculative activity and profiteering during World War I (Bell, 1977, p. 167).

Worker ownership of industrial enterprises: Much discussed by members of the BANU during its last year in power and consistent with the labor property concept, but never implemented (Bell, 1977, p. 168).

Progressive income tax and corporate income tax: Introduced to reduce the tax pressure on the peasantry and resulted in a roughly 50 percent decline in the tax liabilities of a typical farm family.

BANU programs that were not directly redistributive but had other clear social policy motives include:

Establishment or encouragement of consumer, producer and credit cooperatives: A National (Cooperative) Store was established by the BANU as a non-governmental activity in 1908 to sell both consumer goods and agricultural implements and supplies. Credit cooperatives were designed to end private lending to agriculture and to lower interest rates drastically. Producer cooperatives were generally marketing organizations, such as the Grain Consortium mentioned above. Highly successful production cooperatives were established in the fishing and timber industries. There appears to have been no development of cooperative cultivation of land along the lines of the then experimental Soviet cooperative farms. The Agrarians appeared to believe that, even in the long run, small peasant farms would be viable if given sufficient technical, credit and marketing assistance.

Educational reform: The BANU carried out a substantial program of building and staffing schools, along with a major curriculum reform which increased the role of practical education by establishing a *realka* for the first three years of the five-year secondary education period, and built in two weeks each year, plus a half-day each week of work experience for all primary and secondary students (Bell, 1977, pp 176-9).

Compulsory Labor Service: Required national service of one year for all males at age 20 and all females at age 16 was introduced in June 1920. The goals were both economic (mobilizing labor resources for road building, tree planting, brick, shoe and uniform manufacturing, tractor and automobile repair and such; providing skill and literacy training) and social (breaking down class barriers between the urban and rural population and introducing the former to physical labor). Implementation of the legislation was blocked by the Inter-Allied Control Commission on Disarmament and a compromise plan, allowing purchase of exemptions, smaller total size and reduced role for the women's program, was put into force in November 1921 and its operation received wide European attention (Bell, 1977, pp. 171-6).

Proposed or Feared Reforms: The Language, the Monarchy and Control of the Workplace

The BANU proposed a highly logical simplification in the spelling rules of the Bulgarian language which produced ferocious opposition from intellectuals and was not implemented until 1944. The BANU seemed to be moving toward abolition of the monarchy, although no such legislation had been prepared or offered to the legislature. Stamboliski himself viewed all monarchs as 'poisonous snakes' and made no secret of his total contempt for both Ferdinand and his son Boris III. These last two possible reforms, along with the alleged intention to introduce worker ownership of industrial enterprises, mobilized the opposition of a large proportion of the urban business and commercial classes, the officer corps, and the Macedonian groups, accounting for the nearly universal support for the coup by the political leadership of the conventional parties and the military. Remembering that these events occurred before the end of the NEP in 1928 and the emergence of central planning and collectivization under Stalin in the Soviet Union, it is difficult to ignore the strong similarities in both direction and detail between the BANU and the early Soviet programs. This of course does not imply that a longer-lived BANU government would have moved to adopt agricultural collectivization or central planning.

Violent Resistance from the Right and the Overthrow of the Agrarian Government

The Agrarian Party attempted to carry out the second stage of the democratic revolution begun by the liberation which established both an egalitarian pattern of wealth-holding in the countryside and the forms of a constitutional parliamentary government. The rise of the BANU amounted to the political and intellectual mobilization of the mass of the population to take over real direction of the existing political institutions, against the very different interests of the bourgeois political parties and the administrative classes with which they had become intermingled.

It is difficult not to sympathize with the noble goals and the high tone of the internal practices of the BANU. It is also difficult not to look back and see great naïveté about the likelihood of violent counter-revolution. The combined example of Bulgaria's already bloody political history and the contemporaneous counter-revolutionary events in Russia, Hungary and

Germany should have been sufficient to suggest that the Agrarian program could not expect peaceful acceptance. In addition to the strong and obvious military and royalist hatred of the Agrarians, there were recently arrived external adversaries—the 15,000-strong White Army of Baron Wrangel (Bell, 1977, p.195) and the Macedonian organizations' that had a well-established history of political terrorism.

Bell presents a persuasive portrait of Stamboliski and shows that he was convinced of his righteousness and of his ultimate protection by nearly the entire rural population. The absence of any active efforts to gather intelligence about the intentions of the political action groups, whose programs implied and often directly confessed their intention to seize power, is inexplicable and was fatal. Bulgaria did not have deeply rooted constitutional and democratic traditions, so benign toleration by one's political enemies could not reasonably be hoped for.

The 'Military League,' which was in effect an officers' union, including all but 200 of the active officer corps and thousands of officers forcibly retired by the provisions of the Treaty of Neuilly, was the active force in planning, organizing and carrying out the coup (Bell, 1977, pp.208–9, 225–34). It cooperated closely with both the 'Bourgeois Bloc' in the parliament (also called the 'Constitutional Bloc'), which had formed by the end of 1921 and called for the overthrow of the Agrarians, and the National Alliance (Naroden Sgovor) of business, military and university leaders formed in early 1922. The founders of the 'non-partisan' National Alliance were, according to Bell (1977, pp. 211–12), 'all admirers of Italian fascism, whose successes they hoped to duplicate in Bulgaria. The Sgovor even sent a delegation to observe Mussolini's methods of organization and agitation.' Professor Alexander Tsankov of the Sofia University, who was a planner of the coup and became Prime Minister thereafter, was a major figure in both of these civilian groups, and was Bulgaria's 'ideologist of fascism' (Bell, 1977, p. 212). The Bloc parties called for a series of mass meetings in the Italian style in the fall of 1922 (the same time that the Mussolini government came to power), with the expectation of bringing down the Agrarian government directly. BANU was able to carry out a mobilization of the Orange Squads, suppressed the planned demonstrations, and arrested the entire Bloc leadership on 17 September 1922 (Bell, 1977, pp. 213–14, 221–5). The election of 27 April 1923 was conducted with Bourgeois Bloc party leadership still in jail (although not inaccessible to Military League negotiators). This dramatic turn of events reinforced BANU self-confidence, but confirmed Military League belief that a surprise coup was required to topple the Stamboliski government.

As early as the winter of 1919–20 the Agrarian Party moved in the direction of paramilitary 'committees for the defense of the revolution,' forming Orange Squads of peasants, armed initially with clubs and later with rifles. The Orange Squads were used effectively for political intimidation of both the bourgeois parties and the BCP (Bell, 1977, pp. 150, 220–4). Under the best of circumstances these groups would have been unlikely to do well against a coordinated surprise move by the Bulgarian Army. In the event, the rifles of all of the Orange Squads were called in for 'repairs' two weeks before the planned coup. If this was part of the preparation for the coup it was a clever but somewhat obvious move that eliminated any possibility of effective resistance. The person responsible for that order, Constantine Muraviev, emerged at two later junctures in important political roles. In 1931 Muraviev was appointed Minister of Education in the People's Bloc coalition government (made up of the Democratic, Radical and Liberal Parties and the right wing of the BANU) and promptly reappointed the infamous Alexander Tsankov to the Sofia University faculty. Then, during the last seven days before the Fatherland Front Uprising of 9 September 1944, Muraviev became Prime Minister and attempted to negotiate a break with Germany that would avoid both occupation by the Red Army and a coalition government dominated by the BCP component of the Fatherland Front (Bell, 1977, p. 233; Boll, 1984, pp. 55–60).

The early morning coup of 9 June 1923 was swift, well organized and founded on the prearranged approval and/or active complicity of the leadership of all other parties except the Broad and Narrow (BCP) Socialists. The Bulgarian Communist Party was not asked to participate in the coup and when the BCP proposed that it be armed to defend the elected government, Stamboliski replied contemptuously that if it was ever needed it would be given fifteen minutes' notice (Bell, 1977, p. 231). The most honorable behavior that Bell is able to uncover by the other parties is the refusal of the leadership of the Broad Socialists to participate when approached by the military planning group. They were however divided to such an extent that they did not forbid participation of individual members and did not provide warning of the plan to the Agrarians. A leading Social Democrat, Dimo Kazasov, participated in organizing the coup and then became Minister of Communications. According to Oren (1973, p. 22), he was supported by the party and remained in its leadership after the coup. Some resistance did occur spontaneously and Stamboliski escaped to the mountains and evaded capture for several weeks. He was eventually arrested, tortured to death, mutilated and decapitated. His head was never found, and although Bell (1977, p. 238) notes that this grotesque speculation has never been proved, the character of the threats exchanged by Stamboliski and Boris tend to support the suggestion that the head was indeed presented at the royal palace.

The Relationship of the BANU with the BCP

At the time of the coup the relationship between the BANU and the BCP had reached its lowest point and the BCP leadership was in hiding from arrest orders that followed the interception on 27 May of a Soviet ship carrying rifles from Odessa. Two years earlier during the winter of 1919–20 the BCP had itself mounted a campaign to bring down the minority Agrarian government. The BCP had used strikes and demonstrations, but had been thoroughly defeated by the police powers of the state (which evicted striking workers from their apartments, enlisted the troops and expertise of the Allied occupation authorities, and so on) and intimidation by armed Orange Squads (Bell, 1977, pp. 149–53). After the strikes were broken, Stamboliski called new elections for 28 March 1920 (see Table 2.6), but when the BANU fell five members short of a majority he had thirteen opposition delegates unseated (nine from the BCP) by application of a technicality in the election laws. There were thus a number of strong reasons for hostility and mistrust between the two groups.

Conflict between the Agrarians and Communists was . . . the natural outcome of political developments since the end of the war. The two militant and exuberant organizations were inevitably headed for a showdown to decide which of them would inherit Bulgaria. [Bell, 1977, p. 150].

Although BCP groups fought spontaneously against the coup in a number of locations, the party leadership present in the country at the time 'took the position of an outside observer' (Bozhkov, 1981, p. 233). This declaration of neutrality (the coup had already succeeded) led to condemnation by the Comintern later that month and the dispatch of BCP General Secretary Vasil Kolarov both to purge the party leadership and those who had chosen not to fight the coup and to form a direct alliance with the BANU to battle the Tsankov regime by means of a 'workers and peasants' uprising. The result was an unsuccessful uprising on 23 September 1923, which was led by the BCP with little involvement of the remaining BANU leadership, but with predominantly peasant participants. The September uprising is celebrated in BCP and Bulgarian popular history as Europe's first anti-fascist insurrection (Rothschild, 1959, pp. 121–47, cited in Bell, 1977, pp. 242–4; Oren, 1973, pp. 24–5; Lalkov, 1982, pp. 87–8).

Table 2.6 Election results, 1908–23 and 1946

	25 May 1908		24 Nov. 1913		17 Aug. 1919		28 Mar. 1920		27 Apr. 1923		27 Oct. 1946	
	Votes cast	%	Votes cast	%	Votes cast	%	Votes cast	%	Votes cast	%	Votes cast	%
BANU	105,979	11.2	113,761	20.9	180,648	28.0	349,212	38.2	569,139	53.9	*	*
BCP	8,101	0.9	54,217	10.0	118,671	18.0	184,616	20.2	203,972	19.3	*	*
Broad Socialist	–		55,171	10.2	82,826	13.0	55,542	6.1	27,816	2.6	*	*
Fatherland Front	–										2,981,189	70.1
Other	828,807	87.9	320,281	58.9	274,170	41.8	325,802	35.6	254,610	24.1	1,271,381	29.9
Total	942,907	100.0	543,430	100.0	654,315	100.0	915,172	100.0	1,055,537	100.0	4,252,570	100.0

* See Table 2.7.

Sources: Bell, 1977, pp. 82, 110, 143, 152, 228; Ognyanov, 1981, p. 105; calculations by the author.

The repression that followed the September 1923 uprising, and again after the unsuccessful attempt of the left wing of the BCP to assassinate Tsar Boris by blowing up the Sveta Nedelia church in April 1925, led to hundreds of official executions and the murder of at least 16,000 BCP and BANU members during those two years (Vandervelde, 1925, p. 53, cited in Bell, 1977, p. 245). A recent Bulgarian source cites a figure of 20,000 killed in 1923 alone (Lalkov, 1981, p. 89). Bell observes that the September uprising brought the BCP a 'bloody expiation' for its earlier inaction (1977, p. 244). The campaign against the BCP and the BANU at this time had many vicious and atavistic features which do something to explain the vengeance taken by the BCP once it came to power after World War II. The intense political violence of the mid-1920s, along with the steady pattern of assassinations by the Macedonian IMARO group, established Sofia in the popular European press as having a 'Wild West' atmosphere. Another important effect of the 1923-5 period was the flight to Moscow of most of the surviving BCP leadership, although the party continued to function underground in Bulgaria for the next two decades.

Following the coup, the new regime under Professor Alexander Tsankov of the Sofia University Economics Faculty was immediately consolidated, in part because of the extensive pre-coup negotiations on cabinet positions and distribution of power. The large-scale murder of Agrarians of the left persuasion (those at all vigorously committed to social change) and BCP members of all stripes left Bulgarian politics a hollow shell under governments called first the People's Bloc and then the Democratic Alliance, but none the less a political process did continue to function and elections (albeit with a drastically reduced number of participants) continued to be held. Events went so far as to return to power a coalition government which included right-wing Agrarian Union ministers in 1931 (League of Nations, 1938).

It is difficult to fit the Bulgarian governments of the 1923-44 period into clear political categories. Western writers have danced around this question with a variety of terms including crypto-fascist, quasi-fascist, authoritarian and so on. As noted in detail above, the forces that overthrew the Agrarian government were an amalgam of all the conventional bourgeois parties, led and organized by fascist groups who explicitly set adoption of the forms and methods of Italian fascism as their goal. The leadership and political activists of the BCP and the Agrarian Party were either killed, imprisoned, or driven into exile during the 1923-5 period.

The re-emergence of contested elections loses some of its force under these circumstances, since most of the highly popular left of Bulgarian politics had been either exterminated or removed from political life. None the less, an accomodationist wing of the Agrarian Party survived and became part of an opposition People's Bloc which won the 1931 election. Oren, who characterizes the overthrow and murder of the elected Agrarian government as 'reintroducing traditional political pluralism' (1973, p. 33), describes the 1931 election as the 'last free electoral contest that Bulgaria would have' (1973, p. 13). The surviving Agrarian faction headed by Dimitur Gichev had abandoned most of the program goals of the Stamboliski period and adopted an expansionist foreign policy, a policy transformation that Oren characterizes without a trace of irony as conferring on it a 'sufficient degree of legitimacy to be allowed to operate on the Bulgarian political scene' (1973, p. 49). Despite their numerical predominance, the threat of another coup forced them to accept a secondary role and take no significant ministerial posts in the People's Bloc government.

The BCP was illegal during all of this period and was excluded from political life, although it was able to establish a semi-transparent surrogate organization—the Bulgarian Workers' Party (BWP)—a name retained until 1947. The BWP–BCP showed nearly miraculous political resilience and was able to elect a considerable number of deputies in the 1931 general election and also to win the 1932 Sofia municipal election, but in both cases the results were simply cancelled by extra-legal proclamations. Again in 1938, when the Tsar reintroduced elections without parties, the BWP and the left Agrarians both achieved surprise successes and were promptly expelled. During the brief thaw in Bulgarian-Soviet relations that coincided with the Molotov-Ribbentrop Pact, the BWP elected more delegates than all other opposition parties combined (Oren, 1973, pp. 25–6, 42, 66–7).

The incompetence and veniality of the People's Bloc in power led, by a process punctuated by another military coup, to a steady accumulation of real power in the hands of the Tsar. The coup was carried out on 19 May 1934 by members of the Military League which had formed the core of the movement that overthrew the Stamboliski government a decade earlier. The sub-group of the League which took power in 1934 was heavily influenced by the Zveno (link) Political Circle which had formed five years earlier. The Zveno group advocated rapid economic modernization guided by technical experts operating above conventional politics and it proceeded to outlaw all political parties. Many of the leaders of the Zveno group considered themselves to be disciples of Alexander Tsankov, the ideologue of Bulgarian fascism and the leading figure in organizing (and Prime Minister after the success of) the 1923 coup. The Zveno–Military League government was not supported by a mass political following or a conventional party organization.

Kimon Georgiev of the Zveno group was Prime Minister (a position he was to occupy again a decade later as the Zveno representative in the first two Fatherland Front governments), but the government was so conspicuously ineffective that the attempt of the military to rule directly soon collapsed. In November 1935 the pretense of popular government was abandoned. Boris established what was in effect a personal dictatorship. He ruled through a cabinet composed of his agents, and this government affirmed the outlawing of all political parties (Lalkov, 1981, pp. 93–105). Elections were re-established in 1938 as a tactic for managing public opinion, with candidates largely hand-picked by the central government and forbidden to adopt any party label. Election days were staggered so that police and army units could be concentrated to control the process in detail. This last point suggests the absence of a reliable and well-organized local 'political' apparatus, despite the genuine personal popularity of the Tsar.

The 1923–31, 1934–5 and 1935–44 governments are all difficult to characterize. None went very far in the direction of the mass mobilization tactics and aggressive anti-semitism that characterized German fascism, providing grounds for seeing them as only semi-fascist. The survival of the Bulgarian Jewish population, described in detail by Chary (1972), seems to underline this point. On the other hand, the absence of virulent anti-semitism was also an aspect of the Italian regime that served to introduce the term 'fascism' into modern political usage, and the survival of the Bulgarian Jews was not clearly the result of a decision to protect them for ethical reasons. Bulgarian forces participated in the administration of German programs directed at the removal of Jews from occupied areas of Greece and Yugoslavia. By the time the German command began to make plans for the transport and extermination of the Bulgarian Jewish population, the war was obviously lost and the Bulgarian Tsar and his advisors concluded that they would achieve better treatment at the hands of the victorious allies if they did not facilitate the Final Solution. The regime of Boris III had established the full set of German-type laws confiscating Jewish property and revoking civil and economic rights. It had collected the male population into concentration camps (not extermination camps), had facilitated the transport of the Greek Jewish population to their death in the North, and had made arrangements for similar transport of the Bulgarian Jews. Only the deteriorating German military situation and the small size and hence inconspicuousness of the Bulgarian Jewish population prevented their extermination.

The Bulgarian left met the same fate as the German left, but a decade earlier. The result was a dualistic development of the Bulgarian Communist Party in which an underground party carried on within the country and the surviving identified leadership fled to Moscow (a wise short-term choice at least, compared to the regular assassination of surviving left Agrarian figures in Prague, for example). The special relationship between the BCP and the CPSU dates to this time and was quickly reflected in the prominence accorded to leading BCP figures in the international communist movement, in particular the Soviet-dominated Comintern which was headed by Georgi Dimitrov from 1935 until 1943 when it was disbanded by Stalin as a sign of goodwill toward allies that were capitalist, but anti-Nazi. The dualistic development suggests some reasons for the legitimately close and fraternal relations between the BCP and the CPSU, once the BCP came to power and in particular after the Moscow group had won the contest for power within the party and dispossessed the 'home' party leadership. This complex development is treated in Chapter 3.

Alliance with Germany and World War II

Fascism was not imposed on Bulgaria from the outside, although the role of Italian fascism in inspiring the plotters against the Agrarian government has been noted. The coup and the ensuing large-scale murder of Agrarian and BCP members were carried out by explicitly fascist elements who viewed Mussolini, his party, state and methods as a model. So the ground was well prepared for a favorable response to the rise of the Nazi Party in Germany. The monarch was a German, Bulgaria and Germany had been allies in the last war, and Bulgaria had been driven to heavier dependence on the German market by the commercial restrictions that had been built into the harsh peace treaty at the end of that war. The German share of Bulgarian exports (imports) rose from 36 percent (38) in 1933 to 43 percent (41) in 1934 and 68 percent (65) in 1939 (Oren, 1973, pp. 55-6).

The fundamental irredentist theme of Nazi foreign policy promised by implication that countries dissatisfied with their borders could achieve satisfaction by alliance with Germany against the so-called status quo powers. Promises of territorial expansion to the south and west were made to Bulgaria. Once France made a formal alliance with the Soviet Union in 1935, there was little to counteract the combined ideological, commercial and territorial reasons for alliance with Berlin.

Under Boris, Bulgaria glided smoothly into the German camp. The country's overall orientation was never in doubt. In the second half of the thirties, Bulgarian diplomats were preoccupied mainly with the price they hoped to extract from the rulers in Berlin. [Oren, 1973, p. 44]

A rearmament program based exclusively on German equipment began in 1936 (Oren, 1973, pp. 53–4). The fruits of membership in the Axis alliance (restoration of the territories nearly universally held to be Bulgarian) were so welcome by the general population, that it does much to explain the absence of larger-scale warfare by the BCP against the Bulgarian fascist regime in the early years of World War II.

Despite these great rewards the Tsar and his advisors held back from full participation in the German war effort, but finally signed the Axis Pact on 1 March 1941, declared war on England, the United States and France, but refused to declare war on the Soviet Union. Popular affection for Russians in general and the sense of historical and cultural association with the Russian state in particular had not been dulled by the replacement of the Tsarist regime by Soviet rule. Throughout the war the German armed forces were welcome in Bulgaria and were present in large numbers for training, rest, or transit to the Russian and African fronts, but despite steady pressure to enter the war against the Soviet Union the Tsar resisted. As the German situation became more and more desperate in the East the pressure on Bulgaria grew. In meetings with Tsar Boris, Hitler argued that only German victory would save Bulgaria from the Bolsheviks. Boris died on 28 August 1943 upon returning from one such meeting in Berlin and is widely believed to have been poisoned by the Germans in hopes of securing fuller Bulgarian cooperation from his successor. The Regency Council which ruled on behalf of his 7-year-old-son Simeon was indeed strongly pro-German, but still not willing to take the step of entering the war on the Eastern Front. This is six months after the epochal battles of Stalingrad and the Kursk Salient, so the tide had already (nine months before the opening of the Western Front) clearly turned against the Germans (Erickson, 1983, pp. 94–135).

During the war internal resistance was organized by the underground BCP, with some assistance from the Soviet Union. The Moscow wing of the BCP was strongly in favor of open military action against the Bulgarian government and German forces and installations in the country, while the underground leadership in general opposed this approach. One major figure in organizing guerilla bands was, for example, the Bulgarian Tsvyatko Radoinov, a colonel in the Red Army. Agents and some supplies were delivered by Soviet submarines. Since many of the leaders of the BCP were present in Moscow and Georgi Dimitrov was a confidant and advisor to Stalin, there was a clear channel of influence. Communication of confidential materials between the leadership in Moscow and the BCP underground headquarters in Sofia was slow and unreliable despite the presence of two separate radio services broadcasting to Bulgaria from Moscow. Although well organized and active, when the BCP and its combat group, the People's Revolutionary Army of Liberation, came into existence, its actions were mostly restricted to sabotage and assassination of fascist functionaries and police officials, and did not move to the level of general insurrection. Many BCP members were killed during the war, but in general died in small unit actions or at the hands of the police after capture (Boll, 1984, pp. 53–60). Working under direct Gestapo control, the Bulgarian secret police were able to penetrate and nearly destroy the underground BCP late in 1942. After this devastating blow it was a full year before the BCP was able to revive and regain operational strength (Oren, 1973, pp. 70–1).

Research into Soviet behavior and intentions toward the Balkan countries has yielded evidence of a surprising lack of interest in or advance planning for the establishment of a friendly government in Bulgaria. The Red Army offensive beginning on 20 August 1944 led to the unexpectedly rapid collapse of both the German armies and the Romanian government, with the result that the Third Ukranian Front army under General Feodor Tolbukhin reached the Danube River border between Romania and Bulgaria on 23 August (Erickson, 1983, pp. 354–71). Tolbukhin paused there for two weeks to allow collection of intelligence information about the capabilities and intentions of the Bulgarian Army which was a formidable and fresh force. The Soviet army doubtlessly could have destroyed the Bulgarian army but was attempting to maximize speed of movement west and minimize its own casualties, so ill-considered encounters with unknown adversaries were to be avoided (Erickson, 1983, pp. 371–9; Boll, 1984, pp. 48, 58, 191–2).

There was also the possibility that Bulgaria would break its links with Germany and negotiate an armistice. A complex dance involving the Bulgarian cabinet, the Fatherland Front, the Soviet Union, and Germany had been going on for several months, as well as a year-old but still developing US–British plan to induce Bulgaria to switch sides. The US–British effort had involved both large-scale bombing of Sofia of an essentially terror type and a variety of secret diplomatic contacts (Boll, 1984, pp. 14–22, 31–5). Bulgaria had moved close to apparent agreements on several occasions, but played for time once too often in the continuing hope that the United States and Britain would agree to Bulgarian retention of Macedonia and Thrace. Initially the Soviet Union had accepted US leadership in this undertaking and made a number of efforts to pressure Bulgaria to accept US terms which would have involved a joint US–UK occupation with no Soviet participation. The Soviet Union had promptly and fully reported these initiatives to the United States (Boll, 1984, pp. 18–37, 197, fn. 90).

Thus the Soviet Union appears to have expected Bulgaria to fall outside its

immediate zone of post-war influence until the spring of 1944. A fundamental change occurred with the rapid success of the Soviet spring offensive,
which retook Odessa on 10 April and began to push the Germans back
toward Romania. Suddenly German use of Bulgarian Black Sea ports as naval
bases and shipbuilding facilities and Bulgarian railroads for transit became
militarily important (as late as early summer 1944 eight troop trains per day
crossed Bulgaria and Yugoslavia to avoid the congestion of the Romanian
system). Soviet diplomatic representations to Bulgaria became sharper and
more insistent, warning that neutrality towards it was not enough and
threatening to declare war. Bulgaria had by late summer 1944 succeeded
in persuading the Germans to remove approximately sixty warships from
Varna and had cut troop train frequency to one per day (Boll, 1984, pp. 27–8,
38–42). Even at this late date there was room for a negotiated settlement but
the Regency Council and its appointed Prime Ministers moved too slowly,
held back by hope of retaining its territorial acquisitions and fear of a rapid
seizure of Sofia by the German army and its many Bulgarian sympathizers
(Boll, 1984, pp. 9–10, 27–8, 38, 42).

The Soviet declaration of war on 5 September was none the less a great
surprise to the Bulgarian government which had prepared to declare war on
Germany on 8 September and was waiting for its own troops to be
redeployed (withdrawn from occupation duty in Yugoslavia) to protect
against a German reaction to the announcement. Red Army movements
appear to have been controlled by immediate military objectives, in
particular the desire to cross northern Bulgaria to reach the German units in
Yugoslavia, although the Soviet leadership knew of the possibility of a BCP
uprising (Boll, 1984, pp. 20–6, 46, 57–60, 191–2). Even Oren (1973, pp. 76–7)
describes 'securing their left flank [as] a military necessity,' but at the same
time a 'masterful maneuver . . . which complemented and harmonized with
Soviet political designs.' The common assertion that Yugoslavia was almost
entirely self-liberated territory and untenable for the Germans is contra-
dicted by the regular train traffic mentioned earlier, the withdrawal of
Bulgarian occupation forces for purely political reasons, and the fact that
after crossing the northwest corner of Bulgaria, the Red Army drove
organized German units out of Croatia and Slovenia and liberated Belgrade,
with partisan participation, and then moved north toward Budapest
(Erickson, 1983, pp. 380–91).

For the five-day-old Muraviev government 8 September was a momentous day. During the day Bulgaria declared war on Germany, and the Red
Army crossed the Danube without opposition to be greeted by popular
jubilation. That night, after two days of strikes, the Fatherland Front

Coalition staged a successful revolutionary uprising in the capital. Less than twenty-four hours after achieving the feat of being simultaneously at war with the United States, Britain, France, Germany, and the Soviet Union, the Muraviev government was deposed. When the Red Army crossed the border it had orders to proceed only 180 kilometers, where it stopped far short of Sofia. This left the Fatherland Front more or less on its own, although the approach of the Russians created disorganization and panic in the government and encouraged the BCP and other Fatherland Front participants to believe that they would not face a German counter-revolution (Erickson, 1983, pp. 371–80). It appears that no effective, that is timely, communications existed between either the BCP leadership in Moscow and the Fatherland Front or the Red Army and the Fatherland Front. The Fatherland Front had planned the uprising in August, setting the date for 6 September to coincide with already scheduled transportation and mining strikes. The unexpected Soviet declaration of war led to a decision to wait, but when no immediate border crossing occurred the Fatherland Front made an apparently independent decision to reschedule the uprising for the night of 8–9 September.

This discussion of the degree of operational independence of the Fatherland Front is important because subsequent events cast their shadow backward and invite the assumption that Bulgaria fell into the Soviet orbit as the result of a sustained and carefully orchestrated plan. Extensive research by Boll makes it clear that this was not the case. Affinities and grounds to expect future cooperation obviously existed—a coordinated strategy did not (Boll, 1984, pp. 56–61).

On the other hand, Boll has uncovered a wide range of plans, initiatives and *ad hoc* reactions which together amounted to a surprising level of sustained involvement by the United States in Bulgarian affairs. This activity began with the Office of Strategic Services (OSS) plan to detach Bulgaria from the Axis Pact in the spring and summer of 1943, which was undercut and effectively nullified by the secret agreement between Churchill and Stalin on 'percentages of influence' made in Moscow in October of 1944, and ended with the consolidation of the BCP government in December 1947. In the Moscow agreement Britain obtained Soviet acceptance of British and American primacy in Greece (90 percent) in exchange for acceptance of Soviet primacy in Bulgaria (75 percent) and Romania (90 percent), and even division in Hungary and Yugoslavia (Erickson, 1983, pp. 405–11; Kitchen, 1986, pp. 233–5, 255–7). At the same time Britain agreed to delay taking its seat in the Allied Control Commission for Bulgaria until the end of hostilities in Europe, and, apparently without informing the United States, undertook the same commitment in its name as well. This left the Soviet Union free to run the Commission as an extension of its military occupation administration and the US representatives to become enraged by the seemingly dictatorial way the Soviet Union dealt with its allies. In a breach of security for which he was excoriated by the Foreign Office, the British representative revealed the Moscow agreement to the US representatives in Sofia early in 1945, by which time bad feelings and personal animosities were well established (Boll, 1984, pp. 36–7, 49–50, 70, fn. 84). Conflict was inevitable, but the tone of US–Soviet interaction was poisoned from the very beginning. The sense of having been deprived of the fruits of its extensive diplomatic and bombing efforts by the sudden arrival of the Red Army contributed to a surprisingly substantial American investment of time and energy in attempting to reverse the growing power of the BCP–Fatherland Front government.

The extent and intensity of the US involvement in attempting to steer Bulgaria into the Western orbit is difficult to explain on the basis of economic ties or cultural affinities and it seems that

To a large degree, American involvement in Bulgaria was fortuitous, the result of accidental opportunities in combination with an abiding desire among both military and civilian planners to expand American influence wherever a possibility might present itself. [Boll, 1984, p. 2]

Boll places his valuable study of US–Soviet–British interactions in the context of a US commitment to the 'democratic reorganization in Eastern Europe' and more specifically to securing Bulgaria's 'democratic future,' 'reintegration within the democratic family of nations,' and so on. In light of the personal political histories of the allies the United States was prepared to work with and the clear expectation of 'relying upon the Bulgarian army as the basis of Western influence' (Boll, 1984, p. 3; see also pp. 46, 52), perhaps we could rephrase the US goal as being to produce a capitalist state not under strong Soviet influence. With that goal in mind it is easy to understand why the United States never made overtures of any sort to the BCP and seemed totally unaware of or interested in the real indigenous fascism that underlay the Bulgarian state after 1923 and was a core value of the leadership level of the Tsarist army.

Boll provides a very good and carefully documented account of the Allied interactions both at the foreign office level and between representatives in Sofia, but he does not seem to be aware of the personal and political history of the individuals whose behavior he carefully details during 1943–7. For example, Tsar Boris III is presented as having guided Bulgarian politics along a 'stormy path' in the inter-war period and the remark of OSS Director

William Donovan that Boris was 'an honest if confused idealist' (p. 8) is treated as a serious observation. But then, according to Oren (1973, p. 61):

Boris was not a dogmatic person. His natural wariness and endless patience gave him an advantage over his rivals. When the internal domestic quarrels had ended and the dust of battle settled, all eyes turned on him for guidance ... His tact, personal charm, and shrewdness helped immobilize many of his rivals at the most crucial junctures in the political development of Bulgaria.

Rivals in this case should be understood to mean those not dead, in jail or exile.

According to Boll the BCP was the only important participant in post-war politics that pursued a consistent set of objectives:

Forming the backbone of a small if determined resistance movement during the war and entering the coalition government of September with only four positions, the Communists waged an unflagging struggle for total control. Pushing themselves forward ... at a time when pacification of Bulgaria assumed importance because of the continuing military drive through Yugoslavia and Hungary, the Communists quickly entrenched themselves in key positions of military, political and economic control. It was to the Communists that the Red Army turned in its drive to reform the Bulgarian army into a reliable supporter of the war effort, and it was Communist direction that ensured mobilization of Bulgaria's declining economic assets. [Boll, 1984, p. 6]

When the unmentioned experience with domestic fascism after June 1923, with very large-scale murder of BCP and middle-to-left Agrarians, is taken into account, this orientation loses its mystery. Further, the BCP leadership which remained in Bulgaria saw its road to power as following an obvious three-part plan, involving mobilizing the army and economy for battle against Germany, securing effective internal control in the process, and earning Soviet respect as an effective and loyal ally worth preserving against internal and external adversaries. In contacts with the previous governments the Soviet Union had made utilization of the Bulgarian army a high priority and 'as late as September 1944, Stalin expressed interest in reaching an accord with the last bourgeois government in Sofia if only that cabinet would bring the Bulgarian army to the Soviet side' (Boll, 1984, p. 5). The army, quickly purified and reorganized as it was, remained a possible source of resistance to consolidation of power by the BCP, and by its commitment to the Red Army offensive through Yugoslavia it was physically removed from the country, leaving internal security largely in the hands of the newly organized militia which replaced the 30,000-member national police force which had simply been abolished in October 1944 (Boll, 1984, p. 71).

The Fatherland Front coalition was organized in 1943 under the leadership of the BCP. The strong underground structure of the BCP enabled it to dominate both the political developments within the umbrella organization and the partisan movement (the People's Revolutionary Army of Liberation) associated with it. The Fatherland Front was open to all anti-fascist groups and individuals, and in the first cabinet after the 9 September uprising, the BCP had four ministers (the crucial Interior and Justice Ministries along with Public Health and one minister without portfolio), the Zveno ('link') military group had four (including the Prime Minister), and the Agrarian Party had four. In the factional developments that followed the revolution, the non-Fatherland Front Agrarians revived and a consolidated Agrarian Party re-emerged first under G. M. Dimitrov (who eventually sought asylum in the US Embassy and moved to the United States) and then under Nikola Petkov (whose excecution on 23 September 1947 marked the effective end of resistance to the BCP-dominated Fatherland Front). The Fatherland Front itself developed many internal splits, but the BCP core group gradually purged the cooperating parties of incompatible individuals and groups and also purified the army and civil administration.

After a period of intense maneuvering and conflict between the Soviet Union and the United States within the Allied Control Commission, which included invocation of the provisions of the Yalta Agreement by the United States to postpone scheduled elections on two separate occasions, the BCP established control over the factions within the Fatherland Front, won a series of elections (see Table 2.6) including the election of 18 November 1945 in which the combined Front total was 88.2 percent of the vote, the 8 September 1946 referendum on the monarchy which led to the proclamation of a People's Republic by the National Assembly on 15 September 1946, and established its total domination within the Fatherland Front in the election of 27 October 1946 (see Table 2.7) for delegates to write a new constitution. Even this last-mentioned election was vigorously contested, predominantly by normal electoral methods, which in the case of the BCP involved mobilization of literally thousands of propaganda and education teams to concentrate on rural districts. Since there appear to be no charges of corruption in the counting of the secret ballot, this election is the point at which the BCP can claim to be a freely elected government. The Zveno group did so poorly that it shortly thereafter dissolved itself as an independent party, and the cooperating Obbov wing of the Agrarian movement settled into a permanently subsidiary role.

The opposition Agrarian faction under Nikola Petkov was shortly thereafter implicated in a conspiracy with an obscure group called the

Table 2.7 September and October 1946 election results

	Number	% of eligible	% of valid votes
8 September 1946 referendum on establishment of a Republic			
Eligible to vote	4,500,000	100.00	—
Did not vote	369,000	8.20	—
Invalid ballot	122,583	2.72	—
Total vote	4,008,417	89.07	100.00
Voted to retain monarchy	175,234	3.89	4.37
Voted for republic	3,833,183	85.18	95.63
27 October 1946 election to Grand National Assembly			
Elgible to vote	4,515,364	100.00	—
Did not vote	262,794	5.82	—
Total vote	4,252,570	94.18	100.00
Opposition	1,271,281	28.16	29.90
Fatherland Front	2,981,189	66.02	70.10
BCP	2,260,407	50.06	53.15

Source: Calculated from Ognyanov, 1981, p. 105.

Neutral Officers. On 7 June 1947, two days after the US Senate ratification of the Peace Treaty with Bulgaria, Petkov himself was arrested and twenty-three other Agrarian delegates were expelled from the Assembly. Petkov was tried, found guilty and executed on 23 September 1947 (Boll, 1984, pp. 184–8). Bulgaria was the first state to hold war crimes trials, which began in the spring of 1945 and resulted in almost 3,000 death sentences. These trials are part of a process described by Moore (1984, p. 194) as a 'particularly ruthless and bloody consolidation of power, which most observers agree was the most brutal in postwar Eastern Europe.' According to Holmes (1981, p. 141, citing Wolff, 1956, p. 293) 10,897 people were tried as war criminals and 1,940 received twenty-year sentences while 2,138 were executed. Oren observes

Proportionally, the war trials claimed more lives in Bulgaria than in any other German wartime satellite. The desire to prove to the world Bulgaria's determination to cleanse herself of pro-German and cryptofascist elements was undoubtedly the regime's primary motive in holding the trials . . . Even though the large majority of the victims probably deserved punishment, the arbitrary settling of accounts produced an atmosphere of terror and insecurity which affected the countryside more so than it did the towns . . . A sizeable segment of Bulgaria's tiny intelligentsia was exterminated. That most were people with rightist leanings and profascist sympathies did not alter the fact that many also were people of talent . . . a loss which a small peasant people could ill afford. [1973, pp. 88–9]

Although these trials resulted in the deaths of many ministers and other political figures of the wartime government, they do not appear to have been directed at the legal opposition of the post-revolutionary period, and are not connected to the Petkov case. Petkov had been deeply involved in secret arrangements with the United States throughout this period (and had a long established link to British intelligence), but the facts of the Neutral Officers plot are thus far not clear to Western writers. If the group existed, its links to Western participants in this struggle would be an interesting research path.

The period from 1944 to 1947 was marked by steady political turmoil, magnified by and to some considerable extent resulting from American efforts to undo the effects of the presence of the Red Army on the internal political balance. The prestige of the Red Army was extraordinarily high among the congenitally Russophile Bulgarian population as it closed in on Berlin and the BCP benefited directly from its close ideological and military association. The Red Army managed to avoid setting off any hostile public reaction to its presence in Bulgaria. The political behavior of the Russian military administration was circumspect and involved only a few direct interventions to facilitate BCP consolidation in power.

The numerous Soviet and Bulgarian memoirs and documents confirm the absence of detailed political objectives during the initial stages of the Russian occupation . . . [but] it was natural that the Soviet High Command extended full support to those indigenous political parties willing to sacrifice Bulgaria's pressing economic and social needs to the overriding military objectives. Thus an alliance soon developed between the Bulgarian Communists, who were fanatically committed to victory over fascism in all its forms, and the occupation regime, an alliance that complemented and transcended a natural ideological kinship. It would be naive to assume that this linkage was inevitable, and its logic must be sought within the dominant military objectives of the advancing Soviet army. [Boll, 1984, pp. 4–5].

The initial absence of a clear Soviet political program was soon supplanted by the natural attraction between the BCP and the Red Army based on the BCP's political and military reliability, historical and personal connections to the international communist movement, and obviously ardent anti-fascist commitment. The Soviet Union took steps at several different points which implied that it would accept less than total Fatherland Front control, but did not resist when the BCP will to power proved to be great and ultimately successful. Only after US refusal to allow Soviet participation in the post-war administration of Japan at the London Foreign Minister Conference in late September 1945 (Boll, 1984, pp. 152–5; Byrnes, 1947, pp. 102–8, as cited by Boll) did the Soviet position harden into unconditional support for total BCP control.

The US role in much of the immediate post-revolutionary political conflict was both morally ambiguous and, when it proved unsuccessful, fatal for many of the Bulgarians it had worked with both openly and secretly. The US representatives in Sofia, whose actions have been reported in great detail by Boll (1984), were prepared to work with 'any other' political forces. The expectation of controlling Bulgarian developments, in the event of a surrender organized by the United States, by means of the heavily fascist army has already been mentioned. The US representatives encouraged a series of Bulgarian political figures, including some who were originally part of the Fatherland Front government, to participate in political maneuvers which left obvious tracks and later were easily shown to be conspiratorial. The involvement went so far as to include editing of US Embassy dispatches by opposition figures before transmission to Washington. The effect of these relationships was to make opposition to the BCP seem to be the work of foreign powers (Boll, 1984, pp. 100–1, 141–6, 157–8, 165–9). Secretary of State Byrnes, responding to Soviet protests, on one occasion directly instructed the US representatives in Sofia to stop intriguing with the opposition (Boll, 1984, p. 152).

The US position was largely hopeless from the first, but was none the less played to the end at great cost to those Bulgarians who worked with it. They were undoubtedly led to place confidence in the potential for effective US action by the newly established US nuclear monopoly, the long period of US involvement dating from the first Donovan mission to Sofia in January 1941, and the initial lack of a Soviet commitment to control the details of the Bulgarian solution.

1947: The Year of Institutional Consolidation

In the course of the year 1947 the Bulgarian economy and society settled into forms and patterns which proved to be long-lasting and stable. After tentative attempts at planning during 1946 (Lampe, 1986, pp. 133–42; Jackson & Lampe, 1982a, pp. 560–1), a planning document covering the years 1947–8 was adopted in April 1947. This Two Year Plan is clear and straightforward in pointing to the adoption of Soviet-type institutions of directive central planning and state ownership of capital equipment of all significant scale (Bulgaria, 1947). On 4 December a new constitution (known as the Dimitrov Constitution) was adopted, which declared Bulgaria to be a People's Republic and detailed the institutions of a socialist state. An official history states directly that the 1947 Constitution was 'drawn up under the impact of the ideas and principles of socialist constitutionalism formulated by Lenin. The experience in framing the Soviet Constitution was widely used' (Spassov, 1981, pp. 191-2). Then on 23 December all private industrial and mining properties were nationalized, followed two days later by nationalization of all banks. These legal changes to some extent ratified already established government control of the economy. Although only 24 percent of industrial production came from government enterprises in 1947 (up from 5 percent in 1944), the remaining private firms had been under tight government control from 1944 on. The banking system, as a result of a process dating back to the 1930s, was under much more complete government control. At the time of the nationalization 91 percent of all bank capital was already held by government banks (Jackson & Lampe, 1982a, pp. 469-82, 554-61). The events of December 1947 thus ratified and formalized a process of cumulative change in the political, social and economic landscape. They were none the less significant in pointing directly to a future development process guided by the Bulgarian Communist Party in light of strong and explicitly acknowledged Soviet inspiration.

3 The Political System

The structure and mode of functioning of the Bulgarian Communist Party (BCP) are, in many respects, similar to those of the other Eastern European parties and above all to the Communist Party of the Soviet Union (CPSU) which has been directly emulated in many ways. Bulgarian political reality is complicated by the continued existence and distinctive functions of the Fatherland Front (FF) and Bulgarian Agrarian National Union (BANU). The Fatherland Front has carried over from its initial function as anti-fascist umbrella coalition to a major contemporary role, especially at the neighborhood, district and town level, as the mobilization and control (monitoring) organization for a wide range of economic, social and political programs. As suggested in Table 3.1, the Fatherland Front is a very large organization encompassing the membership of the BCP, BANU and the Communist Youth League (Komsomol), as well as 1,888,000 others from organizations like the trade unions and the Bulgarian Women's Organization. The Fatherland Front had membership equal to 87 percent of the working-age group and nearly half of the total population in 1984.

Table 3.1 Population and membership in political organizations in 1986

Total population	8,950,100
Working-age population (16–59M; 16–54F)	5,044,814
Fatherland Front	4,400,000
BCP	932,055
BANU	120,000
Komsomol	1,500,000
Other	1,888,000

Source: Statisticheski Godishnik, 1984, pp. 31–2; Bell, 1987, p. 275.

The Bulgarian Communist Party

The BCP itself qualifies as a mass party enrolling one of highest proportions of the population of any ruling Communist Party. Table 3.2 traces the

Table 3.2 Membership of the
Bulgarian Communist
Party

Year	Membership
1922	38,036
1932–33	30,000
1944 (9 Sept.)	25,000
1944 (31 Dec.)	250,000
1945	254,000
1948	495,658
1954	455,251
1958	484,255
1962	528,674
1966	611,179
1971	699,476
1976	788,211
1978	817,000
1981	825,876
1984	892,000
1986	932,055

Sources: Holmes, 1981, pp. 120, 131; Boll,
1984, p. 86; Bell, 1985, p. 263; 1987, p. 276;
FBIS, vol. 11, no. 9, 14 January 1986, p. C7.

membership history of the BCP from various intermittently available sources. The internal structure of the party is built up from the primary party organizations (which are mostly constituted on a workplace basis) along territorial lines, first at the municipal level, then at the city or regional level and then to the national bodies of the party. The fundamental pattern of party organization, including the subordination of each successive level through the principle of democratic centralism and the close interweaving of party and government personnel at each level, follows the CPSU pattern, as described by Hill (1985) and Hough & Fainsod (1979). The only significant difference from Soviet arrangements is the absence of the republic level in Bulgaria. The primary party organizations, which range from a minimum of three members to a maximum of several thousand, are the locus of the recruitment, control and mobilization activities of the party (Holmes, 1981, pp. 128–9). While such primary (workplace) organizations exist within state bodies such as ministries, they do not have the right to 'control' (monitor) the overall performance of those bodies. Party influence at this level of policy-making and administrative coordination is a central feature of the dual or parallel hierarchy form of government, but is exercised directly by higher party organs, not the basic organizations.

The highest decision-making body of the party is the Congress which meets for one week every five years when it elects the Central Committee. The Central Committee, which in April 1986 had 195 full members and 145 candidate members, elects a subcommittee (Politburo or Political Bureau) of varying size (generally ten–eleven full members and three–seven candidate members) to exercise authority between its formal meetings, and appoints the members of the Central Committee Secretariat which supervises and directs the administrative work of the various party administrative divisions. The Politburo and the Secretariat are the most important decision-making centers of the party between Congresses and by their position are able to heavily influence the agenda and policy perspective taken by the Congress itself. At irregular intervals national party meetings called conferences are convened to consider specific problems. This practice seemed to have been abandoned after 1950, but was revived with a conference 'Toward Higher Social Labor Productivity' in March 1974 (Staar, 1975, p. 15), followed by 'Improving the Socialist Organization of Labor and the Planned Manage-ment of the Economy' in April 1978 (Dellin, 1979, p. 13), and a March 1983 conference which focused on the interrelated problems of raising the quality of Bulgarian products and speeding the adoption of new and advanced technology (Bell, 1985, p. 267). The later theme was in the public eye for the entire period leading up to the XIII Party Congress in April 1986 and formed one of the two principal emphases of the campaign preparing for the Congress. The most recent conference in January 1988 was called to deal with the interconnected issues of constitutional amendment (and reorganiza-tion of the government structure), redefinition of property rights and categories and further extension of self-management at both enterprise and municipal levels.

Membership of the Bulgarian Communist Party

Membership in the BCP is a selective process beginning with the recommen-dation of a candidate by at least three established members of the party. The minimum age for membership is 18, but this is possible only for persons who have been Komsomol activists. If accepted by the primary organization and the next higher party organization, the individual immediately becomes a member. A one-year probationary period was eliminated in 1966. Membership may be withdrawn as the result of scandalous or criminal behavior, or during the house-cleaning process that sometimes accompanies the exchange of (that is, issuance of new) party cards before a party congress. The intensity of criticism of cadres' behavior (which seemed to include the highest levels) in late 1985 and early 1986 (*FBIS*, no. 181, 18 September 1985, pp. C1-6; no. 188, 27 September 1985, pp. C1-5; no. 189, 30 September 1985, p. C2; no. 228, 26 November 1985, p. C4) was the second major theme of the period leading up to the XIII Party Congress in April 1986 and suggested that an especially large number of members had been dismissed. However, statistics released at the time of the XIII Congress showed that only 8,545 members had been expelled since the previous Congress, far below the figure of 38,452 in the previous five-year period (Bell, 1987, p. 276). The changes in higher-level positions were generally judged to be the most extensive conducted by any Eastern European party during that year.

It is not possible to obtain comprehensive data on the age, sex and detailed occupational characteristics of the BCP membership. Over the last fifteen years it is known, for example, that there have been sustained efforts to recruit more industrial workers, young people and women as members. By 1978 roughly 40 percent of the membership was under 40 years of age, but slightly less than 30 percent were female (Holmes, 1981, p. 132). In the 1981-6 period 157,837 new members were recruited, roughly 50 percent classified as industrial workers, 70 percent under 30 years of age and 41 percent women (Bell, 1987, p. 276).

It is possible to obtain a somewhat fuller picture of participation in elected offices at different levels and also to trace trends through time. Table 3.3 shows the distribution by party, sex and occupational category of those winning election to local People's Councils. The sharp decline in the proportion of BCP members and the rise of non-party representatives is consistent with efforts to increase the role of the district level People's Councils in the resolution of local problems and in the management of small-scale economic (distribution and service) enterprises. Table 3.4 presents the occupational composition of the BCP membership over the period 1948-86, showing a rising trend in the proportion of industrial workers, white-collar workers and others, and a generally declining trend for agricultural workers (called peasants in earlier sources). Statistics of this kind are subject to considerable doubt, since in different sources and uses the term may refer to family background, first job or current position.

Table 3.3 Elections for local office (People's Council)

Date	Candidates elected	By party affiliation			By occupation		Women (%)
		BCP (%)	BANU (%)	Non-party (includes Komsomol) (%)	Industrial workers (%)	Agricultural workers (%)	
8.06.86	54,496	56					
4.12.83	54,475	54.9	14.6	30.5	31.9	25.2	37
25.03.79					34.1	21.7	31.4
30.05.76							
13.01.74	52,429	51.3	18.9	29.8	25.8	23.4	36.4
27.06.71	53,665	70.4	19.8	9.8	–	–	–

Sources: Bell, 1984, pp. 305–6; 1987, p. 279; Staar, 1975, p. 15; Pundeff, 1972, p. 11.

Table 3.4 Social class background of BCP membership (per cent)

	Industrial workers	Agricultural workers	White-collar workers		Others	Women
1948	26.5	44.7	16.3		12.5	
1954	34.1	39.8	17.9		8.2	
1958	36.1	34.2	21.7		8.0	
1962	37.2	32.1	23.6		7.2	
1966	38.4	29.2		32.4		
1971	40.2	26.1	28.2		5.6	
1976	41.1	23.1		35.6		
1978	41.8	22.4	30.3		5.5	
1981	42.7					29.7
1985	44.0					32.1
1986	44.4	16.3		39.3		32.7

Sources: Holmes, 1981, p. 132; Bell, 1986, pp. 266–7; 1987, p. 276.

The declining proportion of the membership composed of industrial and agricultural workers together is consistent with the expansion of the service, educational and other functions that make up the 'non-material' sectors of the economy. The BCP naturally presents itself as the party of the industrial working class and lays heavy emphasis on the role of industrial workers in the party. It has at times identified itself as the 'Party of all the Bulgarian people,' perhaps as an acknowledgement of the inevitable growth in size and importance of the various functions (many of which could be classified as administrative–bureaucratic) of the non-material spheres as the economy becomes more advanced and technically sophisticated. It should also be noted that despite the sharp decline in the number of party members who are workers in agriculture, their proportion in the total population has fallen even more rapidly, so their per capita representation in the party has risen over time.

The Government and Administrative Structure

The highest state body under the constitution is the *Narodno Sobranie* (National Assembly) which consists of 400 members elected on a unified Fatherland Front slate every five years, generally with 99.8–99.9 percent of the vote cast, which in turn reflects the participation of nearly all (more than 99 percent) of the eligible voters. In the 1986 elections the Fatherland Front slate was made up of roughly 276 BCP members, ninety-nine BANU members and twenty-five 'unaffiliated' members, most of whom belong to the Komsomol (Bell, 1987, p. 279). The National Assembly meets for three short sessions each year which generally involve approving, after some discussion, the actions, policies and legislation promulgated between sessions by the State Council and the Council of Ministers.

The State Council and the Council of Ministers

Until the adoption of the new constitution of 1971 the structure of the Bulgarian government had closely matched that of the Soviet Union, in which the government administrative functions were managed through a Council of Ministers appointed and supervised by an executive committee (Presidium) of the National Assembly. Under the new constitution the Presidium is replaced by a State Council, also elected by the Assembly, but including institutional representatives of the trade unions, Komsomol and other mass organizations. The Chairman of the State Council is the head of state, a position occupied by Todor Zhivkov since its establishment. The State Council combines executive functions, as it supervises the activities of the Council of Ministers, with legislative authority, since it is able to issue legislation directly as the representative of the Assembly when it is not in session. Legislation promulgated by the State Council requires the later endorsement of the Assembly, but the Council is able to pass decrees and resolutions without the participation of the Assembly. The possible abolition of the State Council was announced in July 1987, but the reality and implications of such a change are not known at the time of publication of this volume.

The Party in the Government

The role of the Bulgarian Communist Party within the separate govern-mental organs is comprehensive and profoundly important. The Council of Ministers should be considered to be the government proper and is made up of all ministers or officials of similar rank, numbering about thirty in 1984. An executive committee or bureau has existed since 1971 and both the Council and the bureau are under the chairmanship of Stanko Todorov, who replaced Zhivkov in the former role at the time of the constitutional change (Pundeff, 1972, p. 11). All of the members of the Council of Ministers are members of either the BCP or the BANU, and a number simultaneously hold important party and government posts. Table 3.5 shows the interconnections between the highest levels of the government and the party. The number of new appointments and dismissals at leadership levels was unusually large in the period leading up to the XIII Party Congress and has been reflected in this table.

Table 3.5 Party and government interconnections, January 1988

Full members of Politburo, BCP Central Committee	Other BCP positions	Government positions
1. Zhivkov, Todor	General Secretary	Chairman of State Council
2. Alexandrov, Chudomir	Central Committee Secretary	Chairman of Party–Government Commission on Energy Problems
3. Atanasov, Georgi		Prime Minister
4. Balev, Milko	Central Committee Secretary	Member, State Council Chairman, National Assembly Foreign Policy Commission
5. Doinov, Ognyan		Deputy Prime Minister
6. Dzhurov, Dobri		Minister of National Defense
7. Filipov, Grisha	Central Committee Secretary	Chairman of National Assembly Socio-economic Development Commission
8. Kubadinski, Pencho		Member, State Council Chairman, Fatherland Front Chairman of BCP Parliamentary Group
9. Mladenov, Petur		Minister of Foreign Affairs

Table 3.5 (*Cont.*)

Full members of Politburo, BCP Central Committee	Other BCP positions	Government positions
10. Todorov, Stanko		Chairman of National Assembly
11. Yotov, Yordan	Central Commitee Secretery	Editor of *Rabotnichesko Delo* Chairman of National Assembly Spiritual Values Commission

Candidate members of Politburo of BCP Central Committee

1. Dyulgerov, Petur		Chairman of Central Council of Trade Unions Chairman of National Assembly Commission for the Protection of Social Interests and Citizens' Rights
2. Lukanov, Andrey		Deputy Prime Minister Minister of Foreign Economic Relations Co-Chairman of Inter-government Bulgarian–Soviet Commission on Economic and Scientific Technological Cooperation
3. Markov, Stoian		First Deputy Prime Minister
4. Stoichkov, Grigor		Deputy Prime Minister, Minister of Construction, Territorial Structures and Architecture
5. Stoianov, Dimitur		Minister of Internal Affairs
6. Yordanov, Georgi		Deputy Prime Minister Minister of Culture, Science, and Education

Sources: *Rabotnichesko Delo*, 6 April 1986, p. 1; *New York Times*, 19 September 1987, p. A7; *RFER*, vol. 13, no. 2, part III, 15 January 1988, pp. 5–6.

Joint State-Party Decrees

Bulgaria has adopted a Soviet practice, although with a much lower frequency, of issuing announcements of special importance as joint decrees of the State Council and the Bulgarian Communist Party and sometimes separately mentioning the Council of Ministers. From a purely legal point of view the joint decrees are no different than ordinary decrees, so they may be amended or cancelled by the unassisted action of the Council of Ministers. According to the Bulgarian legal scholar Vulkanov (1979, p. 81, as cited by van den Berg, 1985, p. 64):

the Council of Ministers may give legal nature to the rules, but it cannot give them the socio-political meaning which is given to them by the Central Committee of the Bulgarian Communist Party. On the other hand, the Central Committee . . . is able to ensure a high degree of social mobilization of the addressees of the decision but it cannot give the issued acts a direct legal character.

A somewhat different form of joint decree is represented by the announcement of immediate increases in minimum wages and pensions and a draft plan for pension increases through 1990 which followed the 15 September 1985 price increases, and was presented jointly by the Council of Ministers and the Central Council of Bulgarian Trade Unions. This declaration ended with a 'proposal' that the State Council issue a decree 'in accordance with the adopted draft' (FBIS, vol. 11, no. 183, 20 September 1985, pp. C7–8). Why the State Council is required to do the one (raise future pension payments) and not the other (raise wages and pensions) is totally unclear.

The Party, the Press and the Water Shortage

An interesting example of the partly familiar parliamentary style in some aspects of Bulgarian political life can be seen in the handling of the water emergency issue in late 1985. As part of the dramatic price increases, mostly affecting energy and luxury food and drink products, the price of drinking water was raised sharply from 0.11 to 0.40 leva per cubic meter for commercial users and from 0.06 to 0.10 for households (Rabotnichesko Delo, 15 September 1985, p. 1; FBIS, vol. 11, no. 179, 16 September 1985, pp. C1–2). A number of newspaper columns answering questions from readers appeared over the next few weeks, and included information on Bulgaria's current use of water per day per person (at the upper end of developed

European countries), average water use per household (18–20 cubic meters per month), the implied increase of 0.80 leva per month in the typical water bill (0.16 percent of average family income, if no reductions in use occur), and other related issues (*FBIS*, vol. 11, no. 193, 4 October 1985, pp. C1–2). A week later, during live coverage of the opening of the session of the National Assembly, the announced agenda noted that the Minister of Construction and Territorial Settlements would answer the questions of deputy Boris Kochev (*FBIS*, vol. 11, no. 293, 4 October 1985, p. C9). The next day, reports of the session revealed that the questioning had been about water purification work, that following 'lively debates' the report of the Commission on Environmental Protection had been accepted by the Assembly, and that the report had included provisions for cutting off water to enterprises which violated water-use guidelines or failed to find alternatives to the use of drinking water in industrial processes. And finally, various organizations were invited to control (verify compliance) enterprise behavior on this score (*FBIS*, vol. 11, no. 195, 8 October 1985, pp. C4–6). While this was not treated as a major news story, the careful reader of the press would see multi-faceted attention to the issue coming from different quarters and to some extent directed by or at least involving 'parliamentary oversight.' It is possible to doubt the independent vitality of the National Assembly and still see it as more than simply a rubber stamp. It is interesting to note the increasingly substantial role of the analogous Standing Commissions of the USSR Supreme Soviet (Hill, 1985, pp. 105–6), and the extent to which the expanding role is depicted as a conscious party policy intended to increase the extent of 'socialist democracy' in Bulgaria.

The Fatherland Front

As noted earlier, the Fatherland Front serves to broaden the base of political and social activism beyond the membership of the BCP. The Fatherland Front has a dense network of independent offices and meeting rooms scattered throughout the cities as well as clubs, some organized for specific recreational or vocational purposes, and some for retired workers. These facilities are used for ballet, music and art classes, in addition to their more obvious use for political–social meetings. The Fatherland Front is the source of many of the rules of daily living, and for example issued the guidelines for energy conservation during the winter of 1985–6 in cooperation with the Movement of Bulgarian Women, an organization described as powerless by most Western commentators. The two women who have had a major impact on Bulgarian political life, Tsola Dragoycheva (one of the principal wartime leaders, head of the Fatherland Front in the crucial period after 9 September 1944, and long-time Politburo member) and Ludmilla Zhivkova (whose dramatic effects on culture and international relationships is discussed in Chapter 5) both worked through the mainline political institutions and had no special relationship with women's organizations as such. See also the discussion of Women and the State in Chapter 5.

The Trade Unions

The trade unions in Bulgaria occupy an ambiguous position analogous to like bodies in the Soviet Union. They have little or no ability to function independently at policy-making levels and in many respects serve as little more than a transmission belt to carry party and government decisions about the details of work life to the workplace level. Inevitably the local trade-union leadership develops some substantial advisory role in the details of enterprise management, the extent determined by the personality balance of trade union and enterprise leadership on the one hand and the specific link between the trade union leadership and the local party leadership on the other.

The role of the local (district) party committee and first secretary in guiding or controlling the individual economic organization is a vital but poorly understood aspect of Communist Party-led states as economically diverse as Yugoslavia and the Soviet Union, and it has important implications for almost all decentralizing reforms. In Bulgaria this is shown by the apparent tendency for the local party organization to take over and subvert the intentions of the counterplan. On this issue the relationship between the local trade union, local party and individual worker interests are extremely complex and may diverge.

With respect to the narrower issues of workplace discipline and the authority of management in staffing and manning decisions, the local trade unions have very great real power and can successfully protect individual workers from dismissal even under fairly extreme circumstances. The dichotomy between worker and manager interests is sharp under conventional central planning circumstances, and a fundamental question of the NEM is whether the use of the brigade method of organization and compensation will succeed in establishing a new relationship. The brigade method has the effect of establishing stronger group self-discipline because of the way compensation is determined. It also by implication opens the way to unconventional staffing and work patterns and thus conflicts with the established pattern of work rules the local trade-union organization has built up over time and perhaps has defended from managerial alteration. It is significant that discussions of the functioning of the 'brigades of a new type' and of the need to tap the creative potential of the counterplan concept tend to stress the contractual relationships that the work collective makes with the outside environment, leaving no direct role for the trade-union organization itself. It is too early to tell whether these brigade initiatives can influence significantly the realities of economic behavior. At the October 1984 Plenum of the Central Council of Trade Unions, the union, which had previously had a regional basis, was reorganized to match the reformed industrial structure of brigade, labor collective and corporation levels (Bell, 1985, p. 269). It is clear that the Bulgarian trade unions are anything but an empty shell and no less than draconian reforms can succeed without their actual cooperation at the workplace level.

The Komsomol

The Dimitrov Communist Youth League or Komsomol (*Dimitrovski Komunisticheski Mladezhki Suyuz*) has 1.5 million members and includes most of the school-age population. It has been criticized at various times for lack of imagination in inculcating proper values in Bulgarian young people. In addition to its directly political effects it is an important socialization and recreational feature of the school years in Bulgaria. It organizes youth clubs, dance, music and other social-recreational activities. Recently the Komsomol seems to be taking on a significant role in some educational and technology areas. The September 1984 Plenum of the Komsomol Central Committee was devoted to the problem of speeding the introduction of computer training as a part of general education. Goals of utilization of 3,500 and 30,000 classroom micro-computers were set for the end of 1985 and 1990, respectively, and Komsomol was instructed to organize and promote computer clubs and special night-school classes (Bell, 1985, pp. 268-9). The appointment of Andrei Bundzhulov (a 30-year-old sociologist) as Komsomol First Secretary in 1986 was accompanied by a promise of intensification of the struggle against the 'consumer mentality' and 'uncritical imitation of all things foreign,' thought to have developed among Bulgarian youth (Bell, 1987, p. 280).

Political Linkages and Relationships with the Soviet Union

The political, economic, cultural and military relationships between Bulgaria and the Soviet Union are extremely close for a variety of reasons outlined in Chapter 2. The Russian role in driving the Turkish state and army out of Bulgaria and of seeking to protect the territorial integrity of the new state against French and British efforts to assure continuation of a large Turkish presence in Europe are well known. In addition, much of the nineteenth-century Bulgarian revolutionary elite was educated in Russia and all were strongly affected by the revolutionary and Pan-Slavic movements which developed there. An autonomous Marxist tradition developed in Bulgaria which produced a strong and well-organized 'Leninist' party well before the October Revolution. After the defeat of the left and middle of the Bulgarian political spectrum in the military-royalist seizure of power in 1923, and especially after the unsuccessful counter-coup, the leadership of the BCP was sheltered in Moscow. They remained there until the arrival of the Red Army at the border in September 1944 permitted the overthrow of the Tsarist regime by the Fatherland Front, led initially by the underground NCP, which then, step-by-step, assumed power under the Soviet wing. The persistent efforts of the United States to resurrect the Tsarist army and political groups that had collaborated with the pro-German wartime government made BCP attachment to the Soviet Union in the Cold War unavoidable. The attachment to the Soviet camp was reinforced by fear of Yugoslav expansionism which was finally ruled out by the Stalin–Tito split of 1948.

The early years of the BCP have been characterized as 'a particularly ruthless and bloody consolidation of power, which most observers agree was the most brutal in postwar Eastern Europe' (Moore, 1984, p. 195). In part this represents a disputable interpretation of the 1944–5 war crimes trials. By March 1945, 10,897 persons had been tried as war criminals, with 2,138 executions and 1,940 twenty-year sentences resulting (Holmes, 1981, pp. 127, 141; Wolff, 1956, p. 293). These are certainly large numbers by the standards of other European countries, but I know of no evidence that these trials were used as a cover to destroy anti-fascist but non-communist political forces. The large number of individuals tried is to some extent explained by the precipitous German collapse in Romania and the speed of the arrival of the Red Army in Bulgaria, leaving no time for government and police officials to escape or conceal themselves. The BCP took revenge for both Gestapo-directed repression during the war and the massacres of the earlier decades by indigenous fascists and their allies.

The execution of Nikola Petkov, leader of the anti-BCP section of the Agrarian Union in June of 1947 was discussed in Chapter 2 and is very different from the immediate post-war trials. Two years later BCP leader Traicho Kostov was executed after a show trial on charges of 'Titoism' and many of his supporters imprisoned. This is part of what is probably correctly interpreted by Moore (1984, p. 195) as a power struggle between BCP members who had spent the war years in Moscow and those like Kostov, Yugov and Zhivkov who had been underground in Bulgaria. The tensions between Bulgaria and Yugoslavia over Macedonia, the discussions over a possible South Slav Federation of Yugoslavia and Bulgaria, and the direct effects of the Tito–Stalin split all played a role in the internal tensions that were manifested in these purges. Soon thereafter the two leading figures of the BCP, Georgi Dimitrov and Vasil Kolarov, died and almost immediately Vulko Chervenko was named both Party Secretary General and Prime Minister. Chervenko had spent two decades in Moscow, was a favorite of Stalin, and quickly consolidated a highly personalized and authoritarian rule.

The death of Stalin in March 1953 was followed by the adoption of a 'New Course' in Bulgaria which incorporated many of the economic and political features of the de-Stalinization period in the Soviet Union. The May 1953 protest by Plovdiv workers may have strengthened the case of Chervenko's opponents, but in any case as criticism of the cult of personality became more common in the Soviet Union the connection to the Bulgarian 'Little Stalin' was clear. In keeping with developments in the Soviet Union, government and party leadership were soon divided and Chervenko chose to remain Prime Minister (the reader is reminded that Stalin had severely reduced the role of the party and ruled through the government apparatus), while Todor Zhivkov was appointed General Secretary in 1954. In both the Soviet Union and Bulgaria the party position turned out to be the more powerful, but this marked a sharp reversal of form.

The famous April 1956 Plenum of the BCP featured the removal of Chervenko as Prime Minister and his replacement by Anton Yugov, and also marked the conclusive triumph of the 'home' Communists. The liberalizing and generally progressive 'April line' still figures strongly in the BCP image of itself and in the official picture of Todor Zhivkov as a Khrushchevian reformer. Apparently with the direct support of Khrushchev, Chervenko was removed from his remaining party posts in 1961 and at the VIII BCP Congress in November 1962 Zhivkov replaced Yugov as Prime Minister and Chervenko was expelled from the party (Moore, 1984, pp. 197–8). From this time on Zhivkov has been the apparently unchallenged leader. In 1971 he gave up the position of Prime Minister to become President of the newly created State Council, and continued to unite the chief government and party positions through 1987.

The transition to the institutions of Soviet-type central planning and agricultural organization was made easier by: the pre-liberation development of increasing government involvement in economic life (begun by the 1919–23 Agrarian government, but continued under the conservative regimes that followed); the poor and backward state of Bulgarian agriculture and the existing egalitarian pattern of landholding which on balance gave the peasantry less of a motive to resist collectivization; the extant cooperative traditions largely deriving from the organizational efforts of the Agrarian Party before World War I; the better (both short- and medium-run) treatment of the agricultural sector by state policy; and the absence of property jointly owned with German firms and subject to Soviet seizure at the end of the war. Soviet-type economic institutions have worked relatively well for Bulgaria from the first, producing rates of economic growth and structural change that are among the highest in the world for most of the period from 1945 to 1975. A contributing factor to this excellent overall economic performance has been sustained favorable Soviet treatment of Bulgaria on a number of levels, including provision of key raw materials on favorable terms, trade and investment credits, technical assistance, and what amounts to unlimited demand for many Bulgarian agricultural and industrial products. The last several years have seen some souring of this relationship, or at least the introduction of a more demanding Soviet approach to economic exchanges with Bulgaria.

Whether the Bulgarian–Soviet political relationship is as close and trouble-free as is stressed in all public pronouncements, and how generally popular this link is with the Bulgarian population is difficult to determine. It is widely observed that Bulgaria is the Eastern European country where the Soviet Union is most warmly and deeply appreciated. It is none the less possible that the incessant Soviet–Bulgarian friendship theme generates some resentment, especially if it is interpreted as a sign of Bulgarian inferiority. For example, Alexiev (1985, p. 90) suggests that the Bulgarians need not feel grateful or inferior to the Russians, since the liberation from the Turkish yoke can be understood as the simple by-product of Russian imperial ambitions. It is possible to cite nineteenth-century Bulgarian leaders who doubted the sincerity of Russian interest in Bulgarian independence, but none the less the dominant popular hope for over a century had been that 'Uncle Ivan' would finally come to liberate the Bulgarians. The conflicts and disagreements between the new Bulgarian state and the Tsarist and Soviet states were real and persistent until 1944. On the other hand the famous statue of the 'Tsar Liberator' Alexander II, which was erected in front of the Parliament building in 1907, still stands.

Mixed motives undoubtedly obtained at the time, but it is clear that the Bulgarian population does view freedom from Turkish control as a great historic gift from the Russian people broadly defined. While Bulgaria was allied with Germany in both world wars, as noted in some detail above in Chapter 2 (pp. 19–20, 41–5), the government believed that any decision to declare war on the Soviet Union, much less commit Bulgarians to fight against Russians, would lead to a mass uprising and destruction of the monarchy. These views were firmly held by Bulgarian ruling circles, despite their strong ideological and territorial attractions to the German cause, and long before such reticence could be justified by expectation of eventual German defeat or perception of the Eastern Front as a death trap.

It is obviously incorrect to judge mass opinions from the views of alienated *émigré* writers, but they often have considerable influence on Western opinion since we have no way of judging the relationship directly. Especially under the conditions (from 1984 on) of Bulgarian insecurity about its reputation in Moscow and the attendant massive efforts to demonstrate fidelity and comradely feelings, the propaganda flow has been particularly large and could be expected to elicit some cynicism from the Bulgarian population. In light of the widely advertised preference of Gorbachëv for the avoidance of flattery and ritual praise, and perhaps equally widely spread knowledge that the Soviet Union has real and substantial reasons to be unhappy with the Bulgarian government, popular resentment may focus more on the latter than on the Bulgarian–Soviet relationship *per se*.

Assassinations, Drug-trafficking and More

The close linkage to the Soviet Union has made Bulgaria a likely target for charges of involvement in various espionage and political crimes not obviously conducted by the Soviet Union but favorable to its interests. Especially well known are the cases involving Mehmet Ali Agca and the 1981 attempt to assassinate Pope John Paul II, the charges of official involvement in drug-smuggling to destabilize Western societies, and secret arms sales to destabilize the rest of the world. The Ali Agca case in particular has brought Bulgaria a sustained and unwelcome burst of international attention. It is a case that is never likely to be settled—the shares of reality and fantasy in the story told by Agca simply may never be clearly and conclusively resolved. The author, resisting the urge to caution in dealing with an issue so easily embarrassing, none the less states his view that the original Bulgarian government defense of 'all Bulgarians' has held up well. Even before the various flagrant forms of crazed behavior by Agca in public, the case he presented held together only for those analysts who intensely wanted to believe it.

Scepticism about this so-called 'Bulgarian Connection' was strong in even conservative European news sources from the beginning. American news organizations were much less cautious, with leading opinion-makers such as the *New York Times* presenting Bulgarian participation in the conspiracy as obvious, and the Italian investigating magistrates as paragons of morally elevated and scientific crime detection. The *New York Times* went so far as to present as independent news reports columns written by persons who had directly participated in the fabrication of the original 'theory' of the Bulgarian Connection. For an early authoritative dismissal of the logic, coherence and evidentiary basis of the case, see Hood (1984, 1985). Only as the courtroom behavior of Agca became so openly outrageous as to require a choice between a verdict of madness or conscious manipulation (for arcane and possibly changing reasons) did the major American news sources back off from the presumption of official Bulgarian guilt. The various connections between Ali Agca and a combination of Italian military, intelligence and underworld organizations, and Turkish, Italian and other rightist (and in some cases neo-fascist) groups were never given heavy emphasis in the English-language press. Even after the prosecutor had called for acquittal of the three Bulgarian defendants on the basis of 'no evidence' and the jury had found the defendants to be not guilty, the editorial response of the *New York Times* was to claim that they must be guilty of something and to propose drug smuggling and links to Turkish right-wing groups (*New York Times*, in the *International Herald Tribune*, 2 April 1986, p. 4).

The case is profoundly peculiar and cannot be said to have been resolved after several years of supposedly intensive inquiry and the formal acquittal of the Bulgarian defendants. The involvement of Agca in the attempted assassination itself and the existence of a conspiracy are without question facts. The involvement of Bulgarians of any stripe, much less those acting in the name of the Bulgarian government has not been demonstrated. The role of several Western intelligence services in the events that followed the assassination is now evident, and the apparently innocent role of the American CIA in planting the wildest of the conspiracy stories is one of the strangest aspects of the case. In the process of testing the credibility of the Polish military intelligence officer who had defected, doubt about his truthfulness arose. He was apparently fed a story from a famous (and virulently anti-Soviet) spy novel, which he proceeded to confirm fully.

Dismissed by the CIA as an unreliable fabricator, he toured the intelligence services of Western Europe telling his own stories and adding the assassination plot as newly discovered CIA information to be shared. This fable appears to have made its way to Agca by way of Italian intelligence sources, setting up an extraordinary synergism between fact and fancy when he adopted it as his own in the Rome courtroom. When the prosecutor summarized his case in February 1986, he was forced to defend the fundamental credibility of Agca, could offer no evidence to support claims of Bulgarian participation, and could only point to actions of Turkish nationals as having directly abetted the assassination attempt, one having given Agca the weapon and the other had given him cash, part of which was spent in travels which criss-crossed Europe and did include Bulgaria (*New York Times*, 9 March 1986, p. 8). Only the most careful reader of these end-of-the-trial reports would notice the distinction between 'a plot' and 'a plot with Bulgarian participation' in the stories which stressed that the acquittals came despite contradictory evidence. The treatment of this entire episode by Western journalists and editors is given a scathing appraisal by Herman & Broadhead (1986) and Cockburn (1984a, 1984b, 1985). The acquital was confirmed in December 1987. It should be noted that the wave of publicity surrounding the Bulgarian Connection case developed at the same time as the perhaps equally suspicious and persistent Yellow Rain controversy, and was fostered by many of the same sources.

Turkish Ethnic Groups and the 1984-86 Assimilation Campaign

The campaign to accelerate or finish the assimilation of the 'Turkish' sub-group of the population provides a more serious but still somewhat unclear case where Western reporting has parroted and accepted without independent verification stories and rumors (in this case largely emanating from the right-wing Turkish press). In these news stories Bulgaria is reported to have carried out mass executions of Bulgarians of Turkish background who have resisted government measures requiring or strongly encouraging replacement of Turkish-sounding names with Bulgarian names. The realities of this situation, even if *all* of the reports of deaths resulting from the actions of government security and regular army troops turn out to be false, is still intensely unflattering to the Bulgarian government and difficult to explain as a consciously selected state policy. Some consideration of this case, both the known and the possibly fabricated aspects, is also revealing of the problems of trusting reporting of interested parties about Bulgarian internal affairs.

There is a name-changing campaign and apparently related campaigns asserting that Bulgaria is now an ethnically homogeneous state. The question of whether the Bulgarian citizens in question are of Turkish ethnic extraction or only bear Turkish-sounding names is at the heart of the matter. This is not automatically and obviously a religious issue, but we will see that there are as well public campaigns directed at two religious practices which, though phrased in terms of their public health implications, could easily be seen as connecting the campaign against Turkish names with an anti-Islam campaign. The government has directly called for an end to the Ramadan fast and ritual circumcision, calling the former 'A Means of Crippling the Individual,' while describing the latter as 'Criminal Interference with Children's Health.' Collection of religious contributions (fitre) by village imams and selling religious 'relics' were also attacked (*FBIS*, no. 169, 30 August 1985, pp. C1–C7).

According to the official government explanation of the situation, the three major population exchanges of the last century have moved all ethnic Turks out of Bulgaria. Those remaining members of the population who bear Turkish-sounding names are ethnic Bulgarians who adopted or were forced to adopt 'slave' names by Ottoman rulers. Now more than a century later true Bulgarian names are being restored. This line of argument is in part true and cannot simply be dismissed out of hand as a cover story. When accused by a Turkish delegate at the October 1985 UNESCO Conference in Sofia of repressing its 'Turkish minority,' the Bulgarian delegate replied that 'Bulgarian Muslims have nothing to do with the Turkish nation. They are descendants of Bulgarians, who have been forcibly Turkicized during the five-century Ottoman yoke.' He was then able to quote the 1878 statement of Turkish Minister Midhat Pasha that

These Muslims have not come from Asia to settle in Bulgaria, but are descended from Bulgarians turned Turks, who were converted to Islam during the conquest and after. They are the sons of that country, of the same people, they come from the same social strata. There are some among them who speak only Bulgarian.

He also noted that the 1919, 1923 and 1925 treaties involving Bulgaria and Turkey had spoken of 'Bulgarian minorities' in Turkey, but of 'Muslim minorities' in Bulgaria (*FBIS*, vol. 11, no. 199, 15 October 1985, pp. C1–C2). A large number of more or less prominent Bulgarians who changed their names for these reasons have been presented as endorsing the government program. On the other hand the government argument has the kind of racial purity overtones that produce automatic discomfort and which are in any case a biological absurdity in the Balkans.

The question of extreme government actions directed at Turkish ethnic groups in Bulgaria is not new (Oren, 1973, pp. 120–2, discusses the forcible repatriation of perhaps 150,000 Turkish-speaking Bulgarians in 1947–8 and the ensuing Bulgarian–Turkish crisis). After the 1956 Census, official information on the ethnic composition of the population was no longer collected. After the X Party Congress in 1971 an emphasis on the existence of the 'single Bulgarian state' became common, and a campaign to 'Bulgaricize' the names of the Pomok Muslim sub-group that followed the Congress seems to be closely related to the 1984–6 campaign directed at Turkish Muslims. Acrimonious exchanges with Turkey reached a new peak in August 1987 after the Turkish Prime Minister Turgut Ozal was reported to have proposed dealing with the issue of Turks in Bulgaria like it had dealt with the Cyprus problem, that is, by invasion (Kamm, 1987c, p. 9).

The question of the extent and character of violent resistance or punitive state actions against recalcitrant villagers has been greatly confused by a mixing and retelling of several different stories. Initial reports spoke of peasants killed by regular army units, but these deaths appear instead to have been people killed in the explosion of a bomb planted on a train, possibly by Bulgarians and possibly to protest the name-change campaign. No one has ever claimed responsibility for the bombings. It was not until October 1987 that arrests were made in the bombing case (*FBIS*, 7 October 1987, p. C17).

In October 1985 the *New York Times* reported six killed, in February 1985 reported 100 killed, and in August 1985 reported claims by unnamed 'Turkish officials' that 'thousands' had been slain (*New York Times*, 10 October 1984, p. A1; 8 February 1985, p. A11; 7 August 1985, p. 10). The *New York Times* did report the May 1985 press conference in which the public prosecutor attempted to 'quell rumors' by explaining that thirty people had been killed by bombs from August 1984 until May 1985 (*New York Times*, 19 May 1985, p. 9). In December 1985 *The Economist*, reporting on 'The Other Side of the Moon,' claimed that 'hundreds of civilians had been murdered by security forces' (*Economist*, 21 December 1985, p. 16). In May of 1986 Amnesty International issued a report which claimed that 'hundreds of ethnic Turks in Bulgaria have been imprisoned or forcibly resettled,' and that it had the 'names of more than 100 people reported to have been killed by Bulgarian security forces since the campaign began' (Amnesty International, 1986 and 1987; *International Herald Tribune*, 2 May 1986, p. 2). The Bulgarian government then produced a number of individuals on the list for press scrutiny (Bell, 1986, p. 270).

We can conclude that there have been deaths and injuries, but the only confirmed deaths are civilians killed by bombs whose origin is unclear.

Allegations of Turkish villagers killed by Bulgarian army or security troops remain rumors or reports from unnamed representatives of hostile governments. Bulgarian–Turkish relationships have been sour for several years (or centuries if a longer-term perspective is adopted) on multiple grounds, and information from Ankara about Turkish groups within Bulgaria is obviously suspect. We must conclude that the case is unproved but possible, and is at best a very unflattering episode for the Bulgarian government.

Energy and Politics

Bulgaria is fundamentally dependent on the import of energy and energy technology, having only modest hydropower resources and deposits of very poor-quality (low calorie with high moisture and ash content) lignite that blights the air in other parts of Eastern Europe. Bulgarian lignite is burned in mine-mouth generating stations at East Maritsa and Bobov Dol (Dienes & Economou, 1981, pp. 46–7; Shabad, 1981, p. 127). Recently discovered high-grade coal in the Dobroudja region near the Black Sea Coast is very deep and complicated to remove. If technical problems are overcome, production from what would be the deepest coal-mine in the world may not begin until the year 2000, providing no immediate help to the energy balance (Makov, 1985, p. 5). Bulgaria was late in facing and even later in beginning to deal with the energy crisis of the 1970s, in part because it was able to count on yearly increments in the energy imports from the Soviet Union on very favorable terms. Bulgaria imports oil and Donbas hard coal by water across the Black Sea and electricity and natural gas by way of Romania. Generators, turbines and related equipment for conventional stations and entire nuclear power plants are imported from the Soviet Union as well.

In the face of a tightening Soviet oil-supply balance during the 1970s Bulgaria, along with other Eastern European countries, was encouraged to buy the still relatively inexpensive Middle Eastern oil. During 1981–5 total Soviet oil exports to Eastern Europe were held at the 1980 levels. Fears were expressed at that time that cut-backs would begin in 1986. Bulgaria at least seems to have been assured of maintenance of that same level until 1990. While oil imports have been stabilized, import of Soviet natural gas rose from 0.3 billion cubic meters in 1974, to 2.2 in 1976, and 4.6 in 1980. By 1978 Bulgaria was also importing 4.5 billion kWh Soviet electrical power. A new 700-km.-long, 750-kV line is being built connecting Bulgaria to the Konstantinovka nuclear station in the Ukraine (Stern, 1981, p. 112; Shabad, 1981, pp. 124–6).

The OPEC price rises made petroleum imports much more costly, since a five-year moving average of the world market price is thought to be used to set the price Eastern European customers pay for Soviet oil. The result was a delayed but none the less painful rise in those costs. The sharp decline in world oil prices in 1985 and 1986 raises the possibility of Bulgaria (and other Eastern European countries) paying more than world market prices if the formula is followed. The real price in these transactions is simply not known to outsiders. Even if it were known it would be hard to evaluate in light of the multiple and interrelated aspects of what is fundamentally barter trade. One price cannot be taken literally when it is part of a complex trade bargain between states.

The years after 1980 produced a number of changes or rumors of changes in the energy relationship with the Soviet Union which together seemed to place Bulgaria under much more pressure to find internal solutions to energy problems. In order to reduce the foreign exchange costs of energy, Bulgaria has moved to burning more local coal, but only undertook serious conservation measures in the fall of 1985. The winter of 1984–5 was extremely harsh in Bulgaria with sustained periods of unprecedentedly low temperatures sufficient to freeze solid the high-moisture local lignite, preventing mining or movement of already mined stocks. The Soviet Union is believed to have denied Bulgarian requests for additional shipments, possibly because of the high level of total demand on the Soviet energy supply system (in the conditions of a severe winter all across Europe and the mechanical fact that cold weather decreases the effective capacity of both natural gas and oil pipeline systems), but also because of anger over Bulgarian behavior two winters earlier. In that alleged but impossible to verify episode Bulgaria requested and received extra Soviet energy supplies and then resold them for hard currency (the ultimate recipient being either Austria or Turkey). In February 1985 Zhivkov is reported to have stated to the British Foreign Secretary Geoffrey Howe that 'Our first colony is the Soviet Union. It gives us raw materials, like your colonies gave you, and we sell it back manufactured goods and exploit it as a market for our exports' (*RFER*, Bulgarian Situation Report/11, 7 November 1985, p. 4). If true, these incidents may be a contributing element to the chilly economic interactions between Bulgaria and the Soviet Union before the 'friendly visit' of Mikhail Gorbachëv to Sofia in October 1985. This climate is illustrated by an unusual interview in July 1985 in which the Soviet Ambassador criticized the work habits and residual peasant attitudes of Bulgarian workers and pointed to the low quality of Bulgarian exports to the Soviet Union. While these remarks were balanced and included substantial self-criticism, they were none the less remarkably direct (*Pogled*, no. 26, 1 July 1985; *RFER*, Bulgarian Situation Report/10, 10 September 1985, pp. 3–6). Soviet criticism of exports from Eastern European countries had been voiced on other occasions (e.g., *RFER*, Czechoslovakia Situation Report/15, 24 September 1985, p. 51) over the last several years but the explicit negative appraisal of worker attitude and 'work culture' in Bulgaria was unprecedented.

Western observers have noted the unusual signs of Soviet displeasure with Bulgaria, and some have drawn the conclusion that the former is attempting to push the latter to adopt comprehensive economic reforms (Diehl, 1985, pp. A33, A42), in some ways an odd conception given how much further reforms have been carried in Bulgaria. It is, however, obvious to any observer that Bulgaria coasted along for several decades with Soviet energy support on very generous terms (including provision of large amounts of crude oil for Bulgaria to refine and re-export to hard-currency buyers) and even in the early 1980s had taken few steps to economize and rationalize its use of energy. In addition to real complaints about export quality the Soviet Union may have felt a comradely obligation to assist Bulgaria in understanding the new energy-cost realities. A more detailed discussion of energy policy in Bulgaria is provided in Chapter 5 (pp. 156–61). By 1986 relationships with the Soviet Union had 'resumed their traditional harmonious appearance' and Zhivkov addressed the CPSU XXVII Party Congress in the name of all the non-Soviet members of the Warsaw Pact (Bell, 1987, pp. 281–2).

Bulgarian Foreign Policy

Some would doubt the existence of an autonomous category of foreign policy behavior for Bulgaria, the links between Bulgarian and Soviet international policy and conduct being so strong. We have had the opportunity in the Ali Agca trial to observe the absurd conclusions that can be based on this difficult to test hypothesis. We none the less must basically adopt it as a working description of Bulgarian foreign policy in its broad themes and directions. We cannot settle the question of whether this is a thoroughgoing identity of interests or a Bulgarian capitulation in one realm in exchange for support in another. That is a less provocative question in the Bulgarian case than for other Eastern European countries since fundamental differences in interests are hard to find. It is possible to note different emphases and regional concentrations in the foreign policy orientation of the Bulgarian government, in particular the direction of substantial diplomatic and economic attention to immediately adjoining European states and African and Middle

Eastern countries. Some authors such as Aspaturian (1984, pp. 23-4) have suggested that this type of pattern may be the result of a pre-arranged 'division of labor' between the Soviet Union and the various Eastern European states. That is both possible as an explanation of the Bulgarian foreign policy concentration on adjoining states and at the same time is not inconsistent with attention to simple geographical proximity and the obvious importance of Middle Eastern and African energy inputs for both Bulgaria and its CMEA trading partners.

It is also important to remember the pattern of cultural and diplomatic assertiveness during the 1970s, associated with Ludmilla Zhivkova, which stressed development of strong relationships with major Third World countries such as Mexico and India. One interpretation, which I judge to be hare-brained, saw this period as a threat to Soviet foreign-policy interests sufficient to explain her murder by the KGB or its Bulgarian agents. Those familiar with Zhivkova's earlier, near-fatal, automobile accident did not find her death at age 40 (of what was announced to be a brain hemorrhage) to be biologically difficult to explain.

In general the concurrence between Bulgarian and Soviet foreign-policy conduct is very close, but there are several cases where divergences may have occurred. The first instance was in the late 1950s when some real enthusiasm seems to have developed within the BCP for a Maoist 'Great Leap' approach, and which indeed had major (mostly positive) effects on Bulgarian development in the 1959-62 period. As Aspaturian has noted (1984, pp. 17-18), the Sino-Soviet split and aggressive Chinese diplomacy had the effect of providing the European socialist states with a sense of greater room for maneuver in their relationships with the Soviet Union. This could be part of the explanation for the Bulgarian Great Leap experimentation, which could also be traced to Soviet experience in the early 1930s. Lampe (1986, pp. 149-53) denies important Chinese influence in this case. A second example involves somewhat greater Bulgarian enthusiasm for the first Erhard proposals for improving German relationships with Eastern Europe in the mid-1960s (Holmes, 1981, p. 138). A more recent example of foreign-policy divergence may be found in the willingness of Todor Zhivkov to pay a friendship visit to the Federal Republic in September 1984 at a time when the Soviet Union was attempting to apply maximum pressure to prevent Pershing deployment (Bell, 1985, p. 270).

Bulgarian Foreign Political-Economic Relationships

While the Bulgarian economy is unusually heavily involved in foreign trade, it cannot be considered to be an open economy in the traditional sense because so much of its trade is within the framework of official state-to-state barter and countertrade arrangements with other socialist CMEA countries. These arrangements are fundamental sources of stability in both export and import relationships, but are subject to 'fraternal' renegotiation in times of climatic or other stress on one of the trade partners. For a country like Bulgaria, these inter-CMEA links provide a large and stable market for food and manufactured exports and a generally favorable source of raw materials and energy supplies. Using figures for Bulgarian foreign trade in 1985 (in millions of convertible leva), it is clear that within CMEA the Soviet Union is overwhelmingly important, taking 56.5 percent of exports and providing 56.1 percent of imports, followed at a great distance by the GDR, Czechoslovakia and Poland. In normal years the Federal Republic of Germany is the only capitalist country to play a large role in Bulgarian trade, predominantly as an exporter. In poor agricultural years (like 1985) other agricultural exporters temporarily play a significant role.

Table 3.6 Bulgarian exports and imports in 1985

| | Exports | | Imports | | Deficit (−) or surplus (+) |
	leva m.	%	leva m.	%	leva m.
Total	13,736.0	100.0	14,002.3	100.0	−266.3
Socialist	10,558.9	76.9	10,783.5	77.0	−224.6
USSR	7,754.3	56.5	7,849.3	56.1	−95.0
GDR	714.3	5.2	735.4	5.3	−21.0
Other	2,090.3	15.2	2,198.8	15.6	−108.5
Non-Socialist	3,177.1	23.1	3,218.8	23.0	−41.7
FRG	199.2	1.4	544.2	3.9	−345.0
Other EEC	642.1	4.7	721.6	5.1	−79.5
Libya	619.7	4.5	400.9	2.9	+218.8
Other	1,716.1	12.5	1,552.1	11.1	+164.0

Sources: *Statistecheski Spravochnik*, 1986, p. 163; *The Statistical Reference Book of Bulgaria*, 1986, pp. 69–70.

Table 3.7 Bulgarian short- and long-term
external debt (current US$ millions)

	Bank claims	Other trade-related credit	Total
31 Dec. 1983	1,838	571	2,410
31 Dec. 1984	1,685	441	2,126
31 June 1985	1,841	462	2,303

Sources: OECD/BIS, 1986, pp. 5, 9, 13.

Previous Cases or Signs of Instability or Unrest

There have been no significant popular manifestations of opposition to BCP rule, although there have been several minor incidents which are worth mentioning. In 1953, shortly after the death of Joseph Stalin, an unknown number of Plovdiv tobacco workers engaged in a work stoppage that may have had an explicit political aspect. In the Zhivkov period several cases can be cited, although often with little certainty of the reality of the alleged events. Shortly after the removal of Nikita Khrushchev as CPSU First Secretary, there appears to have been some kind of attempted but unrealized conspiracy to force the removal of Zhivkov. Zhivkov had risen to power in close association with both the person of Khrushchev and the spirit of the thaw in political and cultural life associated with his name. The Vratsa Conspiracy (named after the region north of Sofia where it centered) involved a number of active and retired military officers in what appears to have been discussions of ways of removing Zhivkov. The intended program and basis for unity of the small group of conspirators is the subject of opposing Western interpretations and is ultimately a mystery. They are described in various sources as neo-Stalinist, anti-Khrushchevian but pro-Soviet counter-reformers, pro-Chinese, and outright Maoist. The best Western discussion of this episode is provided by Brown (1970, pp. 173–89). Although called anything from an abortive military coup to a coup attempt, an attempted conspiracy, and a *putsch*, the Vratsa Conspiracy does not appear to have amounted to much of a serious threat to the regime. It is notable mainly because something did happen to roil the otherwise smooth Bulgarian political waters.

From time to time Western analysts have speculated on the significance of the ideas and policy direction that appeared under the sponsorship of Ludmilla Zhivkova. Her brief but dramatic period of public importance, first as Vice-Minister of Culture and then Minister of Culture, raised speculation that she was being groomed for the highest leadership position. She is associated with the active use of nationalist historical themes, historical restoration projects on a grand scale, and a very active and personalized foreign policy. Special attention was given to fostering relationships with Mexico, India, and a variety of Third World countries. Bulgaria took a leading role in establishing the 'Banner of Peace' children's peace campaign. Some Western commentators have hypothesized the existence of what they have called the 'Zhivkova effect' as a continuing element in Bulgarian political life, displeasing to the Soviet Union because of unspecified but possible adverse effects on Soviet geo-political interests. The demotion of Alexander Lilov and several others who had been closely associated with Zhivkova, was interpreted as an attempt to rein in this incipient tendency. One of the wilder and apparently totally baseless explanations of the early death of Zhivkova (in 1981 at age 40) offers assassination by the KGB as the resolution of the mystery, which is then used to explain the obvious coolness between Todor Zhivkov and Yuri Andropov (erstwhile head of the KGB) when the latter was briefly CPSU First Secretary (*FBIS*, vol. 11, no. 207, 24 October 1985, p. C2, from AFP, 23 October 1985). This bizarre possible relationship is something like the Vratsa Conspiracy in the vagueness of its presumed political motives and their foreign policy implications.

Again in 1986 there was a report, difficult to evaluate, of open opposition to the Zhivkov government, involving a petition purported to have been circulated by workers at 'a Sofia locomotive works.' This could only refer to the Gyorgi Dimitrov Works, and indeed the petition was signed 'Dimitrov.' This story is only supported by a document available in Paris and which appeared in an *émigré* journal there (*RFER*, Bulgaria Situation Report/5, 27 May 1986, pp. 3–7). No such petition is known to have been seen by anyone in Sofia. The Paris text is long (2,500 words) and complicated, and is marked by flights of socio-economic absurdity (such as 300 percent across-the-board wage increases). This could be disinformation (perhaps spread in anticipation of a succession crisis at the XIII Party Congress) or a manifestation of an internal political development of a new type.

Future Stability and New Leadership

The question of leadership succession was not resolved at the XIII Party Congress, to the surprise of many Western observers. If the present author is correct in seeing *de facto* government-by-committee as the reality of the last decade, then the question of when Todor Zhivkov relinquishes the positions of Party First Secretary and President of the State Council is not important in its effect on system stability. Clear divisions within the party leadership are not readily visible and there does appear to be something of a consensus supporting continuation of what has been described as a 'moderately reformist course.' As Terry suggests,

> what we are least likely to see in Bulgaria is instability in the form of overt popular unrest. No organized focus of opposition exists, whether within the church, the intelligentsia, or the working class, moreover, the regime has shown itself quite capable of maintaining domestic order and, especially in the last 10 to 15 years, sensitive to the need to elicit an acceptable level of popular support through incremental material gains. [Terry, 1985, pp. 523-4]

Thus the future course of Bulgarian political and economic life is likely to be determined by the internal political processes of the BCP. During the course of the BCP Plenum of January 1986 a major clarification of the lines of the likely future leadership evolution did occur. Grisha Filipov, the logical older candidate (66), stepped down from the positions of Prime Minister and chief economic manager, while remaining a member of the Politburo. He was replaced as Prime Minister by Georgi Atanasov (born 1933). Ognyan Doynov (born 1935) became head of the Economic Council, which is in effect a super-ministry. Stoyan Markov (born 1943) became First Deputy Prime Minister and head of the State Committee for Scientific and Technical Progress. Chudomir Alexandrov (born 1936) became the Central Committee member in change of party organization and cadres, and supervises the affairs of all social organizations. These four Politburo members appear to divide most operational responsibilities among themselves. Todor Zhivkov remarked in March 1985, possibly disingenuously, that 'I think that the younger ones in the Politburo keep me there as a kind of decoration. I've been head of state for nearly 30 years—no other country would have me' (*RFER*, Bulgarian Situation Report/1, 17 February 1986, p. 4). Zhivkov's will and ability to retain the leadership position should not be underestimated. He has been counted out a number of times, most recently in January 1986 when some Western newspaper confirmed his impending resignation. It none the less appears that the long predicted 'revitalization' in Bulgarian party and government leadership has already occurred in his continued presence. The implications of dissolution of the State Council for the succession to Todor Zhivkov are unclear. The present author is among those who find Alexandrov to be the likely next party leader. Alexandrov has been Minister of Machine Building, head of a special commission on energy problems, and is by training a mining engineer. In the wake of the latest round of economic reforms in July 1987, at least some Western sources have taken to describing Alexandrov as the 'Bulgarian Gorbachëv.' The party and government leadership positions can obviously be held by different persons.

Decision of the BCP Politburo on the 'Attributes of Power'

In addition to the further flurry of economic reforms, an interesting and unusual Politburo decision was released in August 1987, dealing with the development of a 'system of norms and regulations for manifestations of power' in order to eliminate 'attributes of power which contradict the principles and norms of socialism.' This statement called for a series of fundamental changes in the ceremonial aspects of Bulgarian life, which is described as being 'marked by hypocrisy, vanity and formalism' and suffering from 'excessive pomposity, airs of grandeur [and] unnecessary staging in advance.' It requires an end to the public display of portraits of living leaders, the end of empty ceremonial occasions or parades that have little meaning to their participants, the opening of major events like May Day and 9 September to more spontaneous and participant-designed activities, restriction of military parades to once a decade, and the elimination or sharp reduction of the posting of exhortatory slogans and proclamations. These wide-ranging measures were described as necessary to give room for expression of the authority to be devolved to 'self-management bodies' as part of a 'gradual transition from power exercised in the name of the people to power implemented through the people.' Some elements of this policy can be seen as emulation of recent Soviet practice. The possible implications for internal political life or more pointedly the succession to Todor Zhivkov are not obvious, despite the statement that 'Manifestations glorifying leaders should be eliminated, regardless of their rank' (BBC Transcription Service, 12 August 1987, pp. EE/8640/B/1-4). The day the decree was announced the statue of Zhivkov was reported to have been removed from his birthplace in Pravets (Kamm, 1987b, 3 October 1987, p. 3). Also announced during the summer of 1987 was the intention of abolishing the State Council, which has been the highest organ of government since the promulgation of the 1971 Constitution. How the Constitution will be amended is not clear, but the re-emergence of the leading role of the Council of Ministers is the most obvious possibility.

4   The Bulgarian Economy

The only means to emerge from this pernicious backwardness is to industrialize and electrify the country and modernize the whole economy of the nation.

We believe in the strength of our people, in their abilities, that they will realize this plan and will not feel ashamed before our Soviet brothers and the other Slav peoples, who proved that they are able to realize great plans.

First Bulgarian Two Year Plan
[Bulgaria, 1947, pp. 7, 43]

Bulgarian Economic Development in Historical Perspective

Bulgarian economic evolution and history has considerable importance as a sub-case of the European development experience, as a variation in its post-World War II form on the Soviet development model, and lastly as a possible mixed model for application in developing economies. We will return to the last two themes in the final chapter of this book, but begin here with brief consideration of the historical evolution of the Bulgarian economy in comparative perspective. Following Alexander Gerschenkron's classification (1962a, pp. 5–30), Bulgaria at the time of its liberation from Ottoman rule can be fearlessly assigned to the category of absolute backwardness—so far removed from the standards and qualifications of the advanced countries of the time as to be in need of the systematic intervention of powerful external forces if economic growth in the sustained and qualitative sense was to be achieved. While England and the United States, due to a combination of resource, cultural, technological and relative wealth (high average living standards already in the eighteenth century which made mobilization of resources for investment relatively painless) reasons, entered the era of modern economic growth through a largely spontaneous and market-driven pattern of development, everyone else (including what are generally thought to be long-established powers such as France and Germany) has had to rely on some combination of guidance and direction involving either the banking system or the state at least to start the process.

There is no doubt that Bulgaria experienced some economic change in the Ottoman period and drew some considerable advantage from the close proximity of the large Constantinople market (Gerschenkron, 1962b, pp. 223–4; Lampe, 1975a, p. 58; 1982, pp. 141–5, 280–4; 1986, pp. 22–3). Despite some expansion in total agricultural output and exports and some manufacturing development, there seems to be general agreement with Gerschenkron's early conclusion (based on analysis of statistical fragments drawn from the presumably far-above-average 'state encouraged' industries) that Bulgaria failed to achieve sustained economic growth and modernization prior to World War II (Gerschenkron, 1962b). He concludes that what output increase was achieved was the result of greater use of inputs not the structural change generally associated with modern economic growth. Pottery and electrical power are the exceptions, the latter being fully explained by Belgian financing and capital equipment. He observes that

the consumer-goods industries ... accounted for most of the growth of output that did take place [and] relied to a surprisingly small extent upon domestic raw materials, and particularly upon raw materials produced by Bulgarian agriculture. [1962b, p. 213]

Even the leather, wool and wood pulp produced in Bulgaria were not of great help, since 'agriculture ... [was] much too backward to be able to produce materials suitable for industrial processing' (1962b, p. 215). The technological level of Bulgarian agriculture was extraordinarily low and the economic logic of technological choice was affected by the combination of the 1878 land settlement, the BANU land reforms, the migration of refugees from Macedonia and Serbia, and population growth so that the size of the average holding was quite small and fragmented and did not invite machine methods. Yields did not rise, land per agricultural worker fell steadily and so did income, with the result that agriculture also failed to create any significant demand for manufactured goods. Gerschenkron sees a political dimension looming behind the backwardness and inertia of agriculture, since

no government ... before or after Stamboliski could afford to pursue an economic policy that involved placing, for the sake of industrialization, major burden on the peasantry. It was not merely the immediate economic interests of the peasantry, but their whole system of social values—the ethos of equality—that opposed itself to large enterprise ... [creating] aversion from industry, and particularly from foreign capital. [1962b, p. 226)

While the state may have been inhibited in drawing maximum revenues from the countryside, it none the less did raise great amounts of money to be spent on maintaining a very large and well-equipped army and let the classic opportunities, such as were offered by large-scale railroad construction, slip away with very little developmental effect on the local economy. The state-encouraged industries were given aid in many forms but in very small overall amounts, as compared with more successful development stimulation efforts in Romania and Hungary (Lampe, 1982, pp. 264–72).

Some private wealth accumulated from merchant and small manufacturing enterprises and modern production methods were introduced in some places. The building boom in Sofia gave the illusion of a more general and broadly based prosperity, but there was little change in the countryside where centuries-old equipment (such as wooden plows) and cultivation practices persisted. The efforts of the Agrarian Union to transform the life and work culture of the Bulgarian peasantry had barely got under way by the time of the June 1923 coup and though some aspects of the Agrarian program survived, the coordinated and persistent government support necessary to break through the inertia of conventional forms and methods died with Stamboliski. Economists in particular are inclined to think of economic growth as always waiting in the wings, ready to blossom at the slightest opportunity. Systematic study of the growth process in all of the more or less backward areas of Europe (every country that followed after England and Scotland), shows that matters are not so simple even for culturally sophisticated areas with favorable resource endowments such as France, Belgium and Germany. The Balkan countries as a group were disadvantaged in both regards and only Romania seems to have achieved sufficient momentum really to benefit from what Lampe has characterized as the 'golden age of unprocessed exports' in the decades before World War I. Bulgaria lacked most of Romania's advantages of favorable transportation and market location, soil quality, mineral endowment, large-scale immigration of entrepreneurial and technical skill from Austria and Germany, considerable flows of Western European investment funds, and state economic stimulation measures that were both timely and strong enough to have an effect (Lampe, 1975a, pp. 73–82), while suffering from the disadvantage of a remote and economically poorly located capital city placed to reinforce Bulgarian claims to the Macedonian areas lost in the revision of the treaty of San Stefano in 1878 (Lampe, 1975b).

Gerschenkron notes that the 'poverty and economic backwardness of the country effectively precludes its industrial development upon the pattern of more advanced countries.' Even though the banking system was augmented by connections to large Western European financial institutions it was unable 'in conditions of extreme backwardness such as prevailed in Bulgaria' to mobilize successfully long-term capital resources in the face of low, short-run rates of return. It was left to the state to shoulder the 'twin tasks of covering the balance of capital needs and providing, for a number of years, the demand for the products of the new industries' (1962b, pp. 232–3).

Despite the opportunities to use railroad building as a leading sector to pull into existence a supporting industrial and technical structure, and the extremely favorable conditions in world credit markets, the Bulgarian government took no effective action. Although ornamented with more than a touch of Cold War rhetoric, Gerschenkron's conclusion captures the sense of the lost opportunities for relatively easy growth:

Bulgarian statesmanship left the task of economic development to a much less favorable situation and to a regime which, unperturbed by such changes as may have taken place in technological determinants, was willing to do the job without counting the price or weighing the burden it imposed upon the people and without envisaging an end to the years of sacrifice and deprivation . . . [1962b, p. 234]

The World War II period had little net effect on the capital stock as some infrastructure improvements were offset by sabotage (Erickson, 1983, p. 373). Since Germany paid for the large supply of foodstuffs and raw materials it drew from Bulgaria in a currency that ended up having no value, the Bulgarian economy may fairly be said to have been exploited during this period. One of the arguments made within the Fatherland Front against joining the Soviet war effort was the need to remedy disastrous conditions within Bulgaria and concentrate on internal revival—an opinion forcefully opposed by the BCP which successfully mobilized the Fatherland Front to provide 340,000 troops to the Red Army, 200,000 of whom served at the front and 32,000 of whom died (Boll, 1984, p. 61, fn. 42).

Bulgarian Economic Development Strategy and Soviet Precedents

The circumstances under which the new post-war economic system of Bulgaria took shape could not have been clearer, and the initial forms of economic organization have been remarkably durable and persistent in the face of vast changes in technology and world market conditions, as well as efforts over more than two decades to reform and restructure the behavioral core of the system. These initial conditions consisted of the Soviet-assisted accession to power of a party with strong historical, doctrinal and personal links to the Soviet state, at a time when the prestige of the Soviet economic system (after the rapid industrialization drive of the 1930s and the extraordinary accomplishments of the wartime relocation and production effort) nearly matched that of the Red Army. Western governments had invested all of their efforts in the attempt to prevent consolidation of the BCP in power and showed no interest in the probably hopeless task of attracting Bulgaria to some other development path. The Soviet Union also provided a large amount of economic aid during these first few years, including oil, technical assistance and credits. Despite claims of harsh Soviet exactions which have been reported steadily but without evidence by a number of sources, it appears that the long-standing pattern of net Soviet subsidies was established almost immediately after 9 September 1944.

From the time of the adoption of the Two Year Plan on 25 March 1947 (Bulgaria, 1947) and in particular the nationalizations of 25 and 27 December 1947, the movement to Soviet-style economic organization and centralized materials balance-planning was clear. In addition to a well-developed and highly competent statistical service, it was possible to draw on some tentative wartime planning experience under the Directorate for Civilian Mobilization (Lampe, 1986, p. 126). A preliminary attempt at central planning had been made during 1946. The adoption of collectivization of agriculture was similarly settled at an early point, although carried out in stages and not completed until 1958. Already in 1943-4 there were fifty-eight producer cooperatives in existence (Lampe, 1986, p. 112). The first plan called for expansion of labor cooperative farms to 560 in 1947 and 800 in 1948, with 250,000 and 400,000 hectares, respectively (Bulgaria, 1947, p. 53).

Bulgaria adopted the Soviet model of state ownership and central planning of industry, collectivization and central direction of agriculture, nationalization of all but the smallest service units, and party guidance of economic affairs in its classical form and has, despite several more or less substantial reforms and development of a number of distinctly idiosyncratic features, maintained it with considerable fidelity for nearly four decades. Bulgaria has followed a development path that has in many ways paralleled the articulation of Soviet institutions at similar political–economic points. Despite periods of emphasis on agricultural development during and immediately after collectivization and the reputation for impressive agrarian achievement, it is none the less true that the agricultural sector has generally been accorded a relatively low investment priority. The rise over historical levels in mechanization, technical sophistication and productivity is indeed impressive, but does not indicate sustained emphasis on agriculture as a source of overall economic growth. If use of agriculture to generate a surplus (product and labor force) to fuel a predominantly urban industrial growth process and socialization of the agricultural production process are together the hallmarks of the Soviet development model, then Bulgaria must clearly be assigned to this category of development experience. Yet Bulgaria has followed the Soviet pattern at an accelerated pace, at least in part as a result of learning directly from experience in the 1930s, and by 1965 had begun to evolve in its own directions. It is notable that with all the organizational change and real innovation in the intervening two decades, during which the degree of emphasis on agriculture as a positive source of and direct contributor to economic growth is widely believed to have risen, the proportion of investment funds allocated to agriculture (reported in Table 4.2, p. 110) has steadily declined.

Industrial Development and the Soviet Model

Bulgarian post-war economic development has occurred through use of the classic institutions and organizational methods of the Soviet-type centrally planned economy. This approach to industrial development may be summarized by the following attributes:

1. State ownership of almost all significant capital equipment and related structures, excluding the tools of self-employed repair and craft workers (and in agriculture the tools used to cultivate personal plots).
2. Physical planning of both the relationship between producing units and between producers and the outside world (domestic customers, retail distribution network or foreign customers) through the method of *material balances*.
3. Communist Party predominance in the setting of broad economic and social priorities, with administration of actual performance through a separate governmental structure (partly overlapping in membership with the party but none the less forming a parallel hierarchy), headed by a Council of Ministers consisting of the chief officers of the major industrial ministries. The 1971 Constitution created a State Council supervising the Council of Ministers and having the ability to exercise the legislative functions of the National Assembly when it is not in session.
4. Direction and control of the individual production facility by the provision of a central plan which carries the force of law, but is strongly supported by an incentive and reward structure which combines material incentives (wages, bonuses and various premiums) and moral incentives (prestige and status) which together establish a very strong relationship between plan fulfilment and manager/worker income.
5. Plans organized into five-year blocks, but having reality and directive force to the enterprise in the form of successive One Year Plans, which themselves are generally subdivided into quarterly or monthly subplans. The Five Year Plan is a statement of policy perspective and direction, but it is not an action plan.

6. A state supply network to organize the flow of inputs between firms and outputs between firms and marketing organizations to match the requirements of the plan.
7. Use of taut planning (planner's tension) as a conscious incentive strategy, calling for very high and stressful efforts and hoping to mobilize extra energy and effort as a result.
8. A ratchet-like relationship between the achievements of lower-level units each year and what is expected of them in the following period. Very high output (and hence large bonus payments for overfulfilling the plan) in one period tends to result in sharply increased targets for the next period (and much greater difficulty in meeting the target, not to mention receiving bonus payments), but exactly meeting the plan produces a small bonus. Enterprise managers thus operate in a complex decision-making environment in which they can be seen as trading off present for future income in deciding how far to go beyond planned output.
9. An incentive structure that judges enterprise and especially managerial performance in terms of multiple success indicators such as the gross output plan, the assortment plan, the quality plan, the labor productivity plan, the profit plan and so on, but which in practice emphasizes the gross output measure. Gross output is fundamentally a physical measure of output (by tons, number of units, volume or other appropriate dimension), even if it is clothed in value terms when the physical output is multiplied by fixed 'price weights.' These prices are an accounting device which often remain unchanged for many years and ignore changes in quality. The primacy of the gross output measure insures little attention to the quality of the goods produced, a feature which was reinforced by the tendency to define output *per se*, and not as output accepted by customers or users.

And, based on the interrelated effects and implications of (4), (6), (7) and (8) a pattern of managerial and enterprise behavior (described as 'seeking the safety factor') occurs, involving defensive measures to protect current and future bonus-earning capacities against the possibility of supply irregularities, technical problems or accidents by hoarding inputs (raw material, labor and capital) and attempting to negotiate the lowest possible plan targets by concealing the extent of current working abilities. The resulting relationship between planners and enterprise managers is complex, marked by a variety of contradictory and coinciding interests, differential bargaining power and familiarity with the technical realities of production, all carried out in a temporal context where past events can be used as grounds for current actions and the current advantage of one party undone by the learning behavior of the other.

Behavioral Implications and Economic Policy Problems of the Soviet Model

The pattern of economic performance that results from use of the Soviet-type model is able to produce rapid growth and extraordinarily rapid structural transformation in backward economies like the Soviet Union in 1928 or Bulgaria in 1948, but this growth is generally regarded as being *extensive* in nature (resulting from rapid increase in the number of economic resources deployed, rather than increased 'efficiency' in their use) and the ability of such an economy to continue to perform well in a situation requiring *intensive* growth (steady qualitative improvement in the use of inputs) has been widely questioned. In Bulgaria the exhaustion of reserves of underemployment in agriculture and unemployed (outside the home) women combined with the low birth rate (Chapter 2, pp. 26–8) to raise the problems of labor shortage just a few years after the absorption of the remaining open unemployment in 1958–60. This concern has been behind much of the pressure for intensification (productivity-raising) reforms since the mid-1960s.

Within the high total flow of investment funds mobilized to fuel extensive growth, emphasis is devoted to the 'structure-determining' heavy industrial sector (Group A, following Marx's name for capital goods industries) with special attention to metal-working, electrical and chemical branches over the consumer goods sector (Group B), and services. Services are not counted as contributing to the material production sphere (not included in gross or net social product). It is sometimes suggested that this statistical invisibility has encouraged their neglect once emphasis on measured rates of growth became a common political practice.

High investment levels do not imply falling current consumption as long as there is relatively rapid overall output growth. Similarly, emphasis on investment in heavy industry does not require or logically imply absolute decline in either the total or per capita production of Group-B consumption goods. Such absolute declines did occur in the Soviet Union during the Civil War and World War II (and for the rural population at times during the 1930s), but in general it is either the relative rate of growth that is being referred to or ignorance when 'declining consumer welfare' is identified as an automatic characteristic of growth under the Soviet Model. The Bulgarian economic development experience provides evidence that this same set of institutions can be used in the service of somewhat different policies and priorities than were pursued in the original Soviet case.

Reform and Rationalization

Without changing the overall structure of the economic system described here, performance and efficiency could be improved by redesign and rationalization of the various performance measures. Much of the discussion, experimentation and implementation of economic reform in the Soviet Union and Eastern Europe after 1962 has taken this fundamentally conservative path. Improvement of the functioning of the existing system has been sought on the one hand by partial decentralization of authority on small-scale production questions to the enterprises, and on the other by rationalization and simplification of the central directives and supporting incentive schemes that remain. This approach was expected to improve the performance of the planning function itself by freeing the central authorities from the need to exercise petty tutelage over the details of enterprise behavior, thereby allowing them to devote more coherent attention to questions of strategy and coordination and actually *increasing* their control over the behavior of the system. An overlapping perspective, sometimes called 'perfect computation,' saw the adoption of mathematical optimization techniques as the path to improvement in the quality of planning, regardless of the comprehensiveness of central control attempted. These optimization techniques were nevertheless expected to have a latent decentralizing bias, since they would allow planners to calculate measures of input values which were price-like. Qualitatively improved input prices would make it possible to guide enterprise behavior indirectly through the use of 'synthetic' success indicators such as profit.

During the discussion and implementation phases of these reforms a possibly contradictory pattern of industrial amalgamation was simultaneously carried out in countries as different as Bulgaria, Hungary and the Soviet Union. The powers handed down by central authorities came to rest at a production level now made up of larger units, called production associations or combinats. The association brought a number of previously independent enterprises under the control of a single management, somewhat like branch plants of a large modern Western corporation, and thereby permitted concentration and possible economies in the use of skilled managerial workers.

This pattern of simultaneous devolution from the top to more concentrated units at the bottom has been quite typical and makes the use of single terms like 'decentralization' misleading in describing the various Eastern European reform measures. Likewise, describing the reforms as being market-oriented or aimed at creating a market economy is often misleading unless very carefully qualified. Frequently reforms have aimed at more real and effective central control over the important elements of enterprise behavior by freeing planners from responsibility for unimportant details that had been absorbing their time and attention. Clearly and consistently in Bulgaria, and even to some extent in Hungary, reform has been viewed as a way of perfecting and refining the planning function and not replacing it. Only Hungary has made the further step of greatly reducing the directive role of the central administrative body in 'planning' individual enterprise worklife; these changes are smaller and less fully realized than is generally reported in the West, but they are accompanied by an official explanation of their goals which does directly speak of market relationships replacing many of the planning functions. The German Democratic Republic has taken a different reform path, carrying out substantial decentralization of details but engaging in almost no talk about markets or the replacement of planning functions (McIntyre, 1986b, 1988b, c).

While there are Bulgarian economists who advocate even more substantial movement 'toward the market' than has been undertaken in Hungary, this opinion is in a distinct minority and has had little or no effect on the actual course of reforms, beyond providing the enemies of change with an illustration of the horrors that might lie concealed within otherwise innocent looking measures. Bulgarian evolution has followed an intermediate path between the Hungarian and GDR alternatives, generally much closer to the latter. Whether this is by accident or design is not clear. Given the considerable success of the GDR in achieving intensification of resource use (Cornelson, 1987) and a good record of productivity improvement within a fundamentally unchanged Soviet-type economic structure, one would expect great interest in that experience by Bulgarian (and Soviet) economists. A tendency to explain this experience by superficial cultural analysis, which asserts that Germans are *ipso facto* more efficient, has to some extent prevented constructive comparative use of the GDR experience.

The five principal elements of the more modest Liberman-type reform are obvious, but have proved to be very difficult to introduce in both Bulgaria and the Soviet Union. *First*, a reduction in the number of success indicators used to evaluate the conformity of enterprise behavior with planners' intentions. The advantages of removal of redundant, inconsistent or simply time-wasting requirements is obvious. *Second*, use of a definition of production that only counts output that is acceptable to the customer. Use of realized output or sales as the measure of the amount produced raises the incentive to meet quality standards and the leverage of buyers, as long as buyers have alternative sources of supply or can do without the specific product. Persistence of the conditions of a suction or seller's market mitigate against this reform having much effect on actual behavior. *Third*, increase the weight of the net revenue or profit target. Even in the early days of Soviet central planning, enterprise managers were expected to produce an excess of total revenues over costs and were formally expected to meet a profit plan. Much of the substance of the reforms after 1962 in the Soviet Union and elsewhere has involved simply giving greater weight to the profit indicator and defining output in a more subtle fashion so as to raise the bargaining power of customers and make the quality of output a visible characteristic to producers. This 'synthetic' indicator summarizes many actions that are hard to plan in detail from above. A faulty initial price structure may pose problems, but almost regardless of the efficiency implications of a given set of relative input prices, the effect of a price change (e.g., for energy) will none the less be to push managers in the desired direction. *Fourth*, reduce the extent of planners tension and thereby reduce the level of dysfunctional frenzy about being able precisely to achieve the planned output. And *fifth*, increase the rewards for meeting the plan precisely while de-emphasizing overfulfilment. The emphasis on overfulfilment causes a number of types of dysfunctional behaviour by way of the ratchet effect and probably has hidden costs in terms of capital longevity and performance, quality standards and work culture.

The effects of adopting this interrelated set of reforms is in no way to create enterprise independence, much less to move towards abandonment of central planning. The reforms simply meant reduced central control of the details of economic life, clearer guidance to the enterprise as to what is really important, and more room for enterprise-level initiative and flexibility.

The core institutions and behavioral patterns of the Soviet-type planned economy as well as the troubled history of economic reform efforts are treated thoroughly in Gregory & Stuart (1986) and in less detail in Gregory & Stuart (1985, pp. 232–69) and Zimbalist & Sherman (1984, pp. 115–329). An earlier work by Sherman (1969) remains extremely satisfying in its explanation of the full administrative structure and intricacies of the Soviet economy. Wiles (1977) has an excellent discussion of the motives and perspectives of individual actors within planned and other systems and is insistently comparative in treating the various economic, social and political subsystems. The common emphasis on the Soviet Union in these works does not detract from their relevance to the Bulgarian case in light of the strong institutional commonalities of the two systems. Works devoted solely to the Bulgarian economy include Dobrin (1973), Feiwel (1977) and Lampe (1986).

Economic Reform Measures in Bulgaria

The economic reform process in Bulgaria dates from 1963 and remains to this time partial in both its effects and in the seriousness with which it has been implemented. After the XIII Party Congress in April 1986, the reform agenda remains to a considerable extent the same as what was described in the Central Committee Theses on economic reform in late 1965. The specific reform measures introduced in 1963, 1965, 1968, 1970–2, 1978–9, 1982 and 1985–7 are all efforts to find concrete forms to embody the generally expressed desire for greater enterprise flexibility, autonomy and responsiveness to both world and domestic market conditions.

Jackson observes that the recent Bulgarian developments echo familiar themes (1986, pp. 47–9), and it should be stressed that they are old indeed. The classic discussion of the implications of strict economic accounting within the centrally planned environment (*khozraschet* in Soviet usage, *stopanska smetka* in Bulgarian) is Campbell (1961). The obvious questions are whether this is something progressive in the Bulgarian case that was not found in the Soviet original or whether it is new in the Bulgarian case itself. Taken literally, the answer to both questions must be negative. Charitably interpreted we could view the entire NEM process, at least as it affects the large state organizations, as simply the assertion of the desire to take the *existing* mechanisms seriously and apply their established incentive 'levers' with real force.

The inertia of the existing central planning institutions should not be underestimated and operates at a number of different levels. Managers and workers who have adjusted to the rhythm and incentive characteristics of the classical planned mechanism cannot be expected automatically to accept different rules, uncertain outcomes and general unpredictability in exchange for the promise that higher earnings are possible. Similarly, ministerial and planning officials charged with implementing reforms are often not enthusiastic about loosening their control over the conduct of lower-level bodies. Party and government policy-making bodies are often similarly conflicted—fond of the prerogatives or values that are threatened by the reforms at the same time that they proclaim their sincere and deep commitment to those reforms. This pattern has been evident in all economies where central planning has had any time at all to take hold, and in Bulgaria the core of the Soviet-type planning system has been in place for almost four decades.

The relatively good performance of the Bulgarian economy has served to deflect serious criticism and prevent the movement for conventional economic reform from gathering real momentum. The combination of factors that emerged during the last years of the 1981-5 plan—extraordinarily bad and sustained weather problems which had both agricultural and industrial effects, energy stress heightened by changed and possibly damaged economic relationships with the Soviet Union, and problems in adjusting to rising quality standards in both Western and CMEA markets—may have finally pushed economic reform to the top of the political agenda.

Agricultural Experience and the Soviet Model

The pre-existing conditions of relatively even land distribution, general poverty, and the absence of modern methods of all kinds, combined with considerable historical foundation for cooperative forms of organization, were not strongly unfavorable to the collectivization process in Bulgaria. The collectivization itself was coercive, but avoided violent methods and was not so systematically resisted as it was in the case of the Soviet Union, with the long-term result that Bulgaria avoided permanently alienating and embittering the rural population. Part of this relatively favorable experience with the collectivization process is the result of the investment and social welfare policies pursued during and in the first decade after collectivization. Bulgaria in effect reversed the Stalin-model investment priorities, by providing sufficient capital to newly collectivized agriculture to allow substantial output growth, and making the terms of sale to the state (procurement prices) relatively favorable. Together with the inclusion of the rural population in the social security and pension systems, these measures resulted in a real, obvious and sustained rise in rural living standards.

The result of all these differences in detail is to produce a very different agriculture system in Bulgaria from that found in the Soviet Union, despite nearly identical core institutions. These institutional similarities allow a comparative analysis which yields extraordinarily powerful insights about the pure structural and organizational characteristics of the Stalin model of socialized large unit agriculture, as distinct from the particular methods used to establish the Soviet collective farms and the investment and rural living-standard policies adopted in the Stalin period. In effect Bulgaria has the organizational parts of the model, without the political tactics and economic policy features of the Soviet original. This is not to imply that in Bulgaria agriculture has been viewed as a leading sector deserving more than proportionate investment emphasis, but only that during and after the collectivization process the sector was not systematically impoverished. While the overall emphasis on heavy industrial investment was high, it was not pushed to the levels which required declining peasant living standards, as occurred in the Soviet Union in the 1930s.

In the immediate post-war period the Soviet agricultural model was adopted to some extent in all of the Eastern European countries. The roots of problems and policy dilemmas of contemporary communist agriculture can generally be traced to the distinctive organizational forms and correlate state policies of the Stalin period. As a result there have been important common themes in the agricultural policies of the Soviet Union and all of Eastern Europe after the death of Stalin in 1953. Emphasis during that quarter-century has been on raising agricultural productivity and improving rural living standards, both to remedy the existing social–demographic–cultural weakness of the rural sector and to respond to the rapidly expanding demands of the urban population for higher quality foodstuffs. The rising income of the urban population, in the context of moderate expansion of the supply of consumer goods, and the negligible amounts of household income spent on housing, health care, savings for retirement and education results in a very high income elasticity of demand for foods seen to be of higher quality and meats in particular (Wädekin, 1982, pp. 102, 122, 125-6).

The unifying themes of decentralization, higher technology, more adequate investment financing, and stronger performance incentives for rural workers and managers are found in every country, not solely in Bulgaria. Yet with the exception of Yugoslavia, and to a considerably lesser extent Hungary, the decentralizing tendency has coexisted with a continuing desire by the state to maintain strong central macroeconomic control over the behavior and performance of the agricultural sector. One may justify less pessimism than some writers such as Wädekin (1982) regarding the possibility of ever reconciling these goals, but nevertheless agree that easy success should not have been expected.

An examination of the evolution of the Bulgarian agricultural model in comparative perspective can provide many insights into the difficulties of reconciling these potentially contradictory goals. Reforms generally thought to have failed in the Soviet Union have sometimes survived or even flourished elsewhere and Bulgaria serves as the source of a whole series of assaults on the conventional wisdom about inherent vs. purely Soviet characteristics of socialized agriculture. Of course, if socialized agriculture is inherently inefficient and not subject to remedy, these examples must be temporary abberations. I take the view that there are grounds for a less categorically negative long-term assessment of socialist agriculture and find broad implications in several aspects of Bulgarian agricultural development, in particular the agro-industrial complex (AIC) form of organization and the institutional arrangements that have successfully made the personal plots of individual farm families into an effectively integrated part of the overall socialist agricultural system. At the immediate level of effects on average diet, Bulgaria has done very well over the last several decades (see Table 4.5, p. 124). As Hajda (1980, pp. 296–302) has pointed out, the overall agricultural performance of Eastern Europe since 1960 (especially from 1965 to 1975) has been quite good when compared with the rest of the world, so Bulgaria is not unique, but is different in its methods and emphases.

Agro-Industrial and Industrial-Agricultural Complexes

Development of the Agro-Industrial Complexes (AIC) and Industrial-Agricultural Complexes (IAC) has carried Bulgarian agriculture to levels of concentration and enterprise size extraordinarily large even by Soviet standards. It has done so without a collapse of agricultural performance, with rising quality standards and successful penetration of Western markets for premium fresh and preserved produce, while at the same time successfully and somewhat abruptly transforming its collective farms into state farms. This experience is intriguing to students of agriculture in Soviet-type economies especially in light of the parallel developments in Soviet Moldavia which have remained experimental for quite some time. In both Bulgaria and Moldavia the state farm has been the dominant form for the new types of activities, and indeed Bulgaria eliminated cooperative farms as autonomous units by 1977.

It is important to note that the Agro-Industrial Complex represents at least a partial rejection of the decentralization impulse and greater market orientation which appeared to be major themes in most of the 1960s' reforms (Wädekin, 1982, pp. 233, 259). The AIC units are very large and closely connected to the central plan, although they have considerable micro decision-making autonomy. According to Deutsch (1986, p. 78):

Of all the CMEA countries, Bulgaria operates with the least centralization in agricultural decision making . . . Despite a framework of centralized planning, the Bulgarians have seemingly been able to combine cooperative ownership with high labor productivity by closely linking the personal income of the producers with the final result of their work.

While many of the Bulgarian agro-industrial complexes reflect only horizontal integration and are thus extraordinarily large but not qualitatively different versions of the standard state farm, some of the best-known and most successful AICs are vertically integrated organizations, charged with achieving regional self-sufficiency in basic foodstuffs.

Historical Development of the Agro-Industrial Complexes (AIC)

There has been a complicated feedback between changes in the agricultural and industrial sectors, with agriculture first borrowing and then serving as an example to the industrial sector. The initial decision to form large agricultural units came in 1970 and reflected the application of lessons of the industrial management reforms of the period after 1963. These reforms set up the large DSO organizations, and simplified planning at the center by shifting many of the details to the DSO, under a system characterized by Wiedemann (1980b, 1983) as the Streamlined Centralized System with Decomposition (SCSD).

Announced in 1969 as an experimental program, the AIC concept was quickly implemented nationwide. In the period 1970-2, the 800 existing state and collective farms were grouped into 170 very large AICs. According to Wiles (1977, p. 109) the Bulgarian style agro-industrial complex is

surely the most promising of all paths to agricultural socialism, and has been widely copied. Such vertical integration has long been progressing under capitalism; it corresponds to system-free technological trends.

The state farms and collective farms initially maintained juridical autonomy, but eventually this was lost and they became operating sections of the AIC. While losing their autonomy the organizational divisions were continued and made it possible to keep separate economic accounts, management evaluation and worker bonus calculations on this basis. Some AICs were simply groupings of multiple units producing the same crop, but others combined diverse crops and others were vertically integrated, including, along with direct agricultural production, fertilizer production, packaging and marketing, agricultural research and possibly retail sales of the finished products. Certain agricultural units integrated from an initial involvement in manufacturing into farming and these organizations (the most famous of which is the DSO Rodopa near Sofia) were called Industrial-Agricultural Complexes (IAC).

A full explanation of the evolution of these units is provided by Wädekin (1982, especially pp. 238-56) and Wiedemann (1980a, b) who also provides

(1983) a rather negative appraisal of their overall performance in Bulgaria. As proposed above, the Bulgarian development emphasis has been on industry, with agriculture treated generously in terms of incomes and social conditions, but basically viewed as a holding action (with the exception of some particularly promising export crops), rather than a leading sector. Thus investment and mechanization sufficient to free the large workforce needed to support urban industrial expansion and to provide for the improvement of the domestic diet have been considered appropriate. The result has been an industrialization of agricultural worklife, virtual disappearance of urban–rural income differentials and a separate, highly effective policy of channelling rural workers' spare-time energies and activities into market-directed production by way of special arrangements between the AIC and the personal plot operators.

The size of the AICs may have been too large initially and after falling to a low of 153 units in 1974, some redivision occurred, with the result that roughly 340 separate units made up the agricultural sector in 1979 (Wädekin, 1982, p. 243). The transfer back to the industrial sector has come more recently in the form of reinforcement of the belief in the effectiveness of very large managerial units and demonstration of relatively successful use of the 'brigade' methods of work-group organization and remuneration. The latter was selected as one of the themes for emphasis at the April 1986 Party Congress and industrial enterprises were instructed to adopt the brigade methods that had proved successful in agriculture. Some mention was also made of more widespread use of the practice of electing first-line supervisors, which is claimed to be a normal part of AIC work organization.

Integration of Personal Plots into Socialized Agriculture

A fundamentally new relationship has been established between the state agricultural sector and the household garden-plot sector in several Eastern European countries. Careful study of developments in Hungary suggests that the success of its private-plot component can only be understood as working through rather than in competition with the socialized agricultural sector. One of the most interesting and seldom noticed similarities in the relatively successful agricultural development of Hungary and Bulgaria is in the organizational forms adopted to embody the household–plot sub-economy firmly in the socialized sector. This relationship is so deeply symbiotic and reciprocal that the citation of productivity figures of one sector against the other, as though there is a competitive or adversarial relationship between them in which they can be viewed as competitive models or alternatives, had become fundamentally false. In both Bulgaria and Hungary the state sector provides inputs and services to the personal-plot sector in return for contractual sales of much of the resulting output to the state for final sale through the state distribution network. What appears in public farmers' markets is only a part of the marketed output of the plot sector and a smaller proportion yet of its total production.

Fodder, seeds, fertilizer, piglets, plowing, veterinary seeding and harvesting services, and technical advice move in one direction and are met by a return flow of finished output. According to one Bulgarian economist the personal plot

is not identical and differs in principle from the petty private farming; it is not a separate sector but develops as a continuation of the public farming; it is, therefore, a supplement to the socialist agriculture ... [which is able] to satisfy the personal needs of the farmers and to contribute to the self-sufficiency ... of the urban systems. [Ivanova, 1985, pp. 13, 19]

Since the early 1970s the state has been eager to expand the output of the rural personal-plot sector because it represents a vast reservoir of untapped labor power in a labor-short economy. This official attitude is expressed clearly by the party newspaper *Rabotnichesko Delo* (19 September 1985, p. 2, in *FBIS*, 26 September 1985, pp. C3–C5).

The specific characteristic trait of private plots and auxiliary farms is the fact that they are developing on their own basis and are organically linked to the agro-industrial complexes which are providing them with land, fodder, seeds, fertilizer, insecticides, and other means of plant protection, as well as animals for breeding and fattening. [These measures are] ... a new expression of the great care and attention that are constantly devoted to the further development of the private plot sector and to its transformation into a natural extension of the public sector.

This is a new and interesting relationship that has been noticed by few foreign observers (Brucan, 1983), though many have been struck by the relative agricultural abundance of these two countries.

The auxiliary farms mentioned above represent another potentially interesting development in Bulgarian agricultural policy. The term is sometimes used to describe the personal plots of non-agricultural workers (Cochrane, 1984, p. 17), but in Bulgaria these plots are simply called personal plots, while auxiliary farms are in effect market-gardening activities run by industrial and other non-agricultural enterprises to supply vegetables and meat inputs for the factory and office canteens which provide workers with midday meals. Roughly a third of the supplies required for these kitchens was drawn from the auxiliary farms by 1985. This is an unusual adjunct to the previously mentioned emphasis on regional self-sufficiency. It is possible that some of the output of the auxiliary farms is sold directly to non-agricultural workers through the factory *gastronom*. According to Brucan (1983, p. 71), several thousand of these units have been established in Bulgarian factories, allowing workers to place orders at the beginning of the day and simply pick up pre-assembled grocery orders at the end of the workday, thereby avoiding the large-scale waste of time involved in shopping in the peak period after the end of the workday. The auxiliary farm is difficult to evaluate as an economic tactic without more information. It could be a source of waste and inefficiency (if workers are diverted from regular production duties), but also offers some possibilities for fuller use of retired workers and regular workers who are temporarily underutilized to raise the quality of one of the important workplace incomes-in-kind (canteen meals).

Development of Personal Plots

Leasing of small garden plots for personal use began in Bulgaria in the 1950s as a form of compensation to farm families that had become part of collective farms (a process that was completed during 1956–8). Development of legal, small-scale kitchen- and market-gardening follows the practice of Soviet collective farms from the time of the 1935 Model Charter to the present, although the symbiotic relationship described in the preceding section for Bulgaria and Hungary is scarcely visible in the Soviet Union. Plot size varies depending upon the character of use, ranging from 0.2 hectares (0.49 acres) for intensive cultivation of fruit and vegetables, to 0.5 hectares (1.23 acres) for grain, and 1 hectare (2.47 acres) for poor-quality land. A further 0.1 hectares is provided for each head of cattle raised (Ivanova, 1985, pp. 5–6; Binder, 1985; Lampe, 1986, p. 210).

The right of collective farm members to these plots was reaffirmed in 1963 and 1967, but it was not until after the adoption of the AIC form in 1970 that government policy began actively to encourage plot production and support measures to raise the scope and efficiency of their exploitation. In 1971 restrictions on the number of livestock kept were removed and leasing of additional plots was authorized. In 1974 loans were provided (and 1974 income taxes were remitted) to encourage more people to cultivate plots, and provision at zero or very low cost by the AIC of machine services, equipment, seed and fertilizer was guaranteed. The simultaneous cut in the standard work week freed city-dwellers for work on the plots of relatives, and in 1977 direct leasing of plots to urban residents was introduced.

Adoption of market-gardening as a full time occupation was prohibited and new plots were only assigned to those who already had and agreed to continue full-time positions. There are also strict limits on the size of farm implements that may be privately owned (Ivanova, 1985, pp. 15–16; Petrov, 1984; Hristozov, 1984; Lampe, 1986, p. 210). There have been reports (Binder, 1985) that strict size limits are no longer being enforced, but removal of size limits is not the same as allowing plots of any size. The natural limits imposed by prohibition against the use of any hired labor and the discretion of local government authorities who face a basically fixed supply of land and many applicants combine to prevent 'large' farms from emerging. Lampe notes that by 1982 the personal plots produced (or participated in the production of) 33 per cent of all vegetables, 51 per cent of potatoes, 30 per cent of milk, 40 per cent of meat, and more than half of eggs—together one-quarter of both agricultural output and farm family income (Lampe, 1986, pp. 211–12). The problems of interpreting this all as 'private' activity have been duly stressed in the previous section, but regardless of how we choose to classify the activity, the 'plots sales to town markets resolve the paradox of overall rates of agricultural growth, which have been low during the past decade, and an urban food supply which has undeniably improved' (Lampe, 1986, p. 212).

While the role of the personal plot is indubitably important, much of this output is marketed through the AIC channels (many sales people in what appears to be 'peasant' markets are AIC employees working regular shifts), thereby taking on something of a subcontracting character within the business universe of the AIC. According to Ivanova (1985, p. 17–18), the role of explicit subcontracting is already large and is expected to grow as a part of the intended process of placing personal plot output 'on planned rails'. It is also important to avoid suggesting that plot output is a new and rapidly growing quantitative feature of the Bulgarian agricultural situation since, as Wädekin (1982, p. 97) points out, the personal plots were already in the late 1960s producing 21 per cent of farm income and 25 per cent of gross farm output. What Bulgaria has done is temporarily reversed an inevitable downward trend (Turgeon, 1983, p. 40; Wädekin, 1980, pp. 316–17) in the quantitative importance of the personal plot in a way that has made a probably permanent qualitative change in both its relationship with the state sector and the character and refinement of foodstuffs available to the urban population. All of this has occurred without any significant shrinkage in the size, or degree of central control over the behavior, of the state agricultural institutions.

The greater importance of qualitative than quantitative factors in the new

Table 4.1 Personal plots: size, animal stock and output as percentage of total agricultural production

	1956	1960	1970	1978	1980	1983	1984	1985
Total land	21.9	8.4	—	—	10.7	13.2	13.2	12.8
				(9.7)	(9.7)	(9.8)		
Cultivated land*	25.2	9.8	10.7	13.6	13.5	14.4	14.4	13.8
				(12.7)	(12.8)	(13.0)		
Cattle‡	—	—	—	—	21.0	21.4	21.3	19.4
Milk cows‡	—	45.7	34.4	31.0	29.3	28.2	27.8	25.8
Pigs‡	—	35.8	27.4	25.7	27.2	29.4	28.1	26.3
Chickens†‡	—	—	—	—	41.1	38.1	36.9	37.0
Meat produced	22.3	27.7	—	—	42.5	44.8	45.4	46.5
Milk produced	18.6	20.3	—	24.0	26.1	27.0	26.9	27.4
Eggs produced†	58.7	50.4	—	53.7	55.0	55.5	54.8	53.1

* Apparently reported as land-use for personal plots plus other non-APC uses. Figures shown as ( ) are calculated based on irregularly available data on personal plots alone.

† Includes laying hens and eating chickens so this figure cannot be directly compared with egg output.

‡ End of year.

Sources: *Statisticheski Spravochnik 1985*, pp. 113, 130, 132; *1986*, pp. 117, 134, 136; *Statisticheski Godishnik 1965*, p. 178; *1968*, p. 171; *1978*, p. 279; *1982*, p. 267.

role and relationships of the personal plot is underlined by the figures presented in Table 4.1. Total cultivated land-use by the personal plots has risen from 9.8 per cent in 1960 to 13.8 per cent in 1985, with most of the increase in the late 1970s. There was a sharp increase (although private plots are a *smaller* proportion of the total land than cultivated land) in uncultivated land assigned to individuals after 1980 as the result of measures to increase private livestock holdings. Production of those crops (grains, sunflower seeds, red peppers, etc.) and animals (chicken, pigs and cows) that enjoy clear cost advantages in large factory operations (Turgeon, 1983, pp. 36–7) have become progressively more concentrated in the large socialized production units. Production of the personal plots has been particularly strong in specialty vegetables and fruits, eggs, sheep and goats, and the fattening and preparation for market part of the cattle-raising cycle. It is clear that the state has decided to actively support and indeed foster the development of this integrated relationship.

False Measurements of Efficiency in Socialist Agriculture

When a study of Eastern European economies cites the percentage of several specific agricultural products grown on private plots and the percentage of total agricultural land in private use, and draws conclusions about the inefficiency of socialist agriculture, the serious reader is entitled to draw one of two conclusions: Either the author is ignorant of both the rudiments of causal analysis and the meaning of the word 'efficiency' or the author has a conscious desire to deceive and mislead. The analytical point has been noted a number of times, most recently by Durgin (1982), but the practice continues. Perhaps since we know socialist, or at least Soviet, agriculture is plagued by numerous micro inefficiencies and snarls we are less critical in appraising this type of seemingly innocent evidence.

It is worthwhile to use agricultural production data for Bulgaria to illustrate in some detail the flaws in this type of reasoning. The experience of Bulgarian and Hungarian agriculture is then used to illustrate a further point—that the meaning of 'private' has itself been altered by little-noticed organizational changes that have created a deeply symbiotic relationship between the socialist agrarian enterprises and the garden-plot production of their employees and members.

An example of this approach is Moore (1984), who while noting that the performance of Bulgarian agriculture compared favorably to other Eastern European countries, attributes this performance to some mixture of the traditional peasant commitment to hard work and to the role of the private plots in making total output look good. He concludes that

the inefficiency of the collectivized system, in Bulgaria as elsewhere, is shown by the fact that although private plots constitute only 12.5 per cent of the total arable land, they account for 39.9 percent of meat production, 55.7 percent of eggs, and 28.5 percent of vegetables. [Moore, 1984, p. 205]

The objections to this form of reasoning can be summarized by six principal points, the first five generally suggesting that the output ratios are misleading measures of the relationship they seek to illucidate. *First*, an incorrect land measure is used, since much of the privately managed livestock is grazed on or supported by forage collected on uncultivated land. A similar problem results from the legal and intentional supply of forage grown on state land for this same use. *Second*, the ratios cited are generally the extreme values from a divergent set of possible comparisons. If one selects instead sunflower seeds, peanuts, cotton, hemp, fiber crops, tobacco and sugar beets from the same page of the statistical yearbook cited by Moore (*Statisticheski Godishnik 1982*, p. 281) the opposite conclusion would appear—cultivation on garden plots is totally insignificant. Even within the vegetable category that Moore cites, the state sector totally dominates the red pepper segment (98.6 per cent of output), while the private production of green peppers is 31.8 per cent of the total. *Third*, if the figures on yield per unit of land devoted to specific crops are consulted (*Statisticheski Godishnik 1982*, p. 285), they show quite a surprising picture, with yields on state lands frequently higher even within the vegetable category emphasized by Moore.

It is salutary to emphasize that comparisons of the type cited are often irrelevant to the point they appear to support. They are either simple propaganda or evidence of a lack of familiarity with agricultural data and causal analysis. However, this is just the first level of causal confusion. What if the yield-per-acre figures had generally (contrary to fact) showed higher ratios of output to land utilized on garden plots than on the state agricultural lands? We would not have the evidence we require because we are still using a transparently incorrect definition of efficiency. *Fourth*, over time many of the ratios cited, whatever their value, have moved in a direction unfavorable to private agriculture. This is true of many of the most commonly cited figures for the Soviet Union, and is true for several of the cases cited by Moore for Bulgaria. *Fifth*, the measure of efficiency is not correct. The microeconomic conception of efficiency assumes that if two different production processes are to be compared, either the resource endowments are identical so that different outcomes are self-evident proof of different levels of skill in resource management, or that some statistical method (generally regression) is used to establish a synthetic standard against which to judge actual performance. So, even in their corrected form (output/unit of area), the ratios were wrong as a measure of efficiency because they provided only a single-factor conception of efficiency—land was all that mattered. This is similar and equally incorrect to associating efficiency solely with output per unit of labor input. Both single-factor methods are misleading, except when all of the other factors in the production process are identical.

Specific objective circumstances that need to be considered include the fact that the private plots are worked by children and retired persons during regular working hours and by otherwise fully employed state agricultural employees (after 1977, urban residents as well) during their off-hours and days. If high output were to occur it would not prove high efficiency but would simply be the result of enormously high but unacknowledged and uncounted labor inputs (Turgeon, 1983, pp. 39–40). What is really shown here is different factor proportions in the state- and private-plot sectors, tending to make land productivity look good in the latter because the productivity of labor is so low (once its amount is correctly calculated). This situation, reminiscent of Gershenkron's paradox, is not bad or good, but is certainly no longer powerful evidence of the efficiency of private-plot agriculture. And as we noted above (pp. 101–2), a wide range of mechanical, technical and marketing services are provided directly to the private-plot sector by the state sector. High inputs of capital services into state-managed agricultural production, of course, cut in the opposite direction.

Last and most important is the fact that the ritual repetition of misleading ratios of the type under discussion have the effect of concealing (by making it appear that there is nothing worth studying) the development of a fundamentally new relationship between the state agricultural sector and the household garden-(private-) plot sector in several Eastern European countries.

Bad Weather and Socialist Agriculture

Over the period from 1970 to 1985 there has been a great deal of bad weather in Eastern Europe and the Soviet Union. Since many observers are prone to assume that perpetual crisis is a definitional feature of socialized agriculture, it is necessary to consider the possibility that unfavorable weather during any specific year is simply an excuse to cover failures mostly induced by other motivational and planning problems (Wadekin, 1982, p. 262). This cynical evaluation is most common and perhaps most appropriate in dealing with Soviet agriculture, even granting high rates of overall growth during the post-war period and the special problems created by a commitment drastically and rapidly to raise the proportion of meat and dairy products in the Soviet diet. Bulgarian agriculture has used fundamentally Soviet-type institutional and organizational forms (and has even carried some of what are generally thought to be the most dysfunctional features, such as large farm size, to even greater extremes), but appears to have found ways to make these institutions function successfully over a considerable period of time.

While the agricultural performance of the Bulgarian economy detailed below is sufficient to dismiss the charge that climatic abnormalities are simply used as a cover for general agricultural incompetence, it is still possible that these Soviet-type organizational characteristics make Bulgarian agriculture inflexible and inefficient in dealing with crisis situations such as occurred most recently in 1984–5. That particular year was marked by a winter so severe that it caused output losses in several agriculturally important industrial sectors (chemical and fuels), followed by the most severe and sustained drought for at least thirty and perhaps eighty-five years in the spring and summer of 1985.

There is speculation that bad judgment by energy planners contributed to the magnitude of the effects of the weather. Winter conditions were so severe that working surface deposits of high-moisture soft coal and moving already mined supplies became impossible. Cut-backs in domestic use of energy may have been more extreme than required by the relationship between available capacity and domestic needs because of a decision to continue to meet export commitments which produced convertible currency earnings. It is also suggested that resale for convertible currency of emergency energy ship-ments received from the Soviet Union earlier in the decade played a role in the Soviet decision not to provide extra supplies during 1984–5. Some well-founded plans failed in the face of extreme conditions that could and should not have been anticipated; nevertheless, the disruption to the domestic economy was quite substantial.

Reform and Performance in Bulgarian Agriculture

After the adoption of Soviet-type collective and state farms in a collectiviza-tion process completed in 1957–8, the ensuing reform and organizational restructuring has involved an intensive search for optimal (or closer to optimal) forms of organization, management and worker remuneration, while holding back from any overwhelming commitment of capital resources to the agricultural sector. As Table 4.2 reveals, fixed investment in agriculture was raised to a very high level during and for several years after the completion of the collectivization process. The capital stock in agricul-ture had therefore become quite large by the early 1960s when the movement toward comprehensive economic reform first appeared in Bulgaria, but the failure to achieve proportional productivity gains from this sustained investment campaign seems to have planted firmly the presumption that it is the style of use of the existing capital stock rather than its dramatic increase that is the place to look for improved agricultural performance. Human capital investment in the form of both managerial and technical specialists has been stressed, and the (real) amount of investment in agriculture has continued to increase, but as a proportion of total investment agriculture has dramatically declined. From a peak of nearly 30 per cent in 1961, the share of investment resources flowing into agriculture declined slowly but steadily to less than 10 per cent of total fixed investment in the mid-1980s.

Table 4.2 Sectoral distribution of fixed investment, 1949–85 (per cent)

	1949	1956	1960	1965	1970	1975	1980	1985
Industry	31.4	36.8	34.2	44.8	45.2	39.9	41.9	48.4
Agriculture								
and forestry	12.4	22.9	29.7	19.7	15.8	14.7	12.4	8.2
Construction	2.2	0.5	1.6	2.7	2.9	4.1	2.5	3.8
Transport	16.5	6.2	5.4	6.1	7.8	12.0	9.7	8.4
Housing	22.9	23.8	19.2	16.9	15.8	15.3	20.2	19.0
Other	14.6	9.8	9.9	9.8	12.5	14.0	13.3	12.2
Total	100.0	100.0	100.0	100.0	100.0	100.0	100.0	100.0

Sources: Calculated from *Statisticheski Godishnik, 1971*, p. 51; *1982*, pp. 138, 146; *Statisticheski Spravochnik 1976*, p. 14, as cited in Lampe, 1986, p. 165; *Statisticheski Spravochnik 1986*, p. 61.

It is puzzling to try to reconcile characterizations of the Bulgarian government policy as having finally adopted agriculture as a leading sector and a good reputation for agricultural exports, with statistics which show a low and relatively steady flow of investment resources into the agricultural sector and which suggest a very low effectiveness in use of that capital. It is worth mentioning three points here: first, the inherent slipperiness of statistical measures of capital productivity (which show low dynamic efficiency for implausible pairs of countries like Japan and the Soviet Union); second, the failure to account for either the quality of material inputs or output (if prices are not a reliable indicator of quality); and third, the absence of any consideration at all to the role of non-material inputs.

Efficiency and Productivity: Real and Apparent Meanings

The common-sense use of the words 'productivity' and 'efficiency,' and to some extent their conceptual definitions when employed in standard microeconomic treatments, are not entirely appropriate to the needs of comparative studies of systems behavior. Productivity is frequently erroneously conflated with intuitive ideas about 'efficiency' and is regularly measured for purposes of popular discussion by the ratio of output (O) to labor input (L). It is important to note that variation in the O/L ratio across countries is subject to enormous influence from the factor endowments of the countries in question. Investigation of differences in O/L reveals that countries which, by the combined effects of 'original circumstances' and capital accumulation over time, possess very large capital stock produce current output by the economizing of their *relatively* scarce factor (labor) and using their relatively abundant factor (physical capital) with considerable liberality. The automatic result of this pattern is that the individual unit of work effort appears to be very 'productive' compared to the effects of a comparable work unit in a capital–poor society. Almost every public use of measured 'labor productivity' and most efforts to capture in numerical form differences in 'efficiency' founder on this logical error.

By implication, efficiency might also be reflected in the skill and intensity with which capital was utilized. Calculation of output per unit of capital (K) employed (the parallel concept to labor productivity) leads to the conclusion that societies that are relatively 'capital–poor' will often use that capital intensively and support its contribution to output by generous application of the resources that are *relatively* abundant. Countries which would be ranked low in terms of O/L would be ranked high in O/K, so which measure is the true indication of what we intuitively mean by 'efficiency'? It appears that neither measure is adequate to the question posed, but one measure (O/L) is in fact almost universally used when efficiency or productivity are considered in popular economic discussion, whether lay or professional in inspiration. For Western students of comparative economics this is a powerful form of preconditioning, since we live in a capital–abundant society and have become accustomed to defining the polemically powerful concept of efficiency in a logically inconsistent way which at the same time makes the performance of our own society look highly attractive. This is not an argument that should be interpreted as implying that there are no measures that can usefully be applied to the questions of efficient and intelligent resource utilization, but only that almost all common comparisons are logically flawed and misleading. We will give serious weight to the incremental relationships (the effects on output of changes in the use of specific inputs), but the measurement and conceptual problems remain. An example of the former is the result of such measures applied to Japanese post–war economic growth. Capital productivity is found to be negative, suggesting that it is implausible that L, K or technical change has been measured correctly. Yet this is the result of work with unusually good and clear data. An example of the latter is the difficulty in judging the extent to which unemployment is converted into low productivity employment by a social policy decision. The strong emphasis on wiping out unemployment which was built into Bulgarian economic life at the time of the so-called Great Leap in 1958–60 (Oren, 1973, pp. 144–6; Lampe, 1986, pp. 149–53) has yet to be undone and so measured low productivity appears to have a continuing social policy rather than a purely economic root. Kuttner (1983) offers a revealing analysis of different responses to this social–economic choice in otherwise quite similar capitalist economies. In most centrally planned economies there has been an ancient systemic decision to absorb open unemployment at any cost (Granick, 1987). The accretion of employment rights and guaranteed stability in these economies is now widely viewed by Western economists as a source of vast inefficiency and inflexibility (Lane, 1987). This is of course a far cry from the situation once imagined by Western critics of these same arrangements who charged the trade unions in command economies with total powerlessness and presented the worker as totally subject to management whim. We note here the contrary effects of empowerment of the individual worker and both negative measurement and incentive effects on 'productivity.'

Economic Reform, the NEM and the Bulgarian Model

The Bulgarian experience with economic reform dates naturally from the beginning of the so-called Liberman discussions in the Soviet Union in 1962 and has gone through a cycle of changes, reversals and revival typical in some ways of all Eastern European countries. It has, however, pursued economic reform with a degree of unrelenting public attention that perhaps justifies Lampe's characterization of its unique commitment to reform (Lampe, 1986, p. 200). Despite nearly constant talk of 'reform of the economic mechanism' there appears to have been very little impact on the management and planning system as it affects the daily behaviour of the large socialist organizations, unless their sharp increase in scale (and assumption of the operational prerogatives of their previously autonomous sub-units) is treated as a decentralizing reform. The relatively sharp favorable changes in consumer living standards observed over the last decade have occurred as a result of the great improvement in food supply under the new form of integration between the AIC and the personal plot (discussed pp. 100–5), and the foundation and effective performance of relatively autonomous small and medium-sized units generally *within* existing larger state enterprises (which are considered below, pp. 119–23).

Steady and self-conscious use of the name New Economic Mechanism for what is now a decade-old reform process should not be taken to imply actual or intended direct use of market forces in the style of the Hungarian reforms. While the extent and linear development of the Hungarian reforms have often been exaggerated in the West, they none the less go far beyond what happened under the same name in the large enterprise sector of the Bulgarian economy. Similarly, in those small service and trade categories where Hungary (and the GDR) have been fostering a modest and tightly controlled privatization, no such Bulgarian policies appeared until 1987.

The large enterprise management and planning reforms known as the New System of Management were introduced on an experimental basis (mimicking the famous Mayak and Bolshevicka experiments in the Soviet Union) in a few consumer goods enterprises in June 1964, then were extended to the rest of the industrial sector following the Central Committee Plenum in December 1965. Ministries were instructed to pull out of the detailed tutelage of individual enterprises and deal with the industrial associations (DSO) instead. The number of types of planned targets are detailed in Table 4.3. Beyond the six targets provided to the DSO by the Central Planning Board, which the DSO could pass through to the sub-units (enterprises), the DSO was authorized to utilize two additional indicators to direct their behavior. The industrial association thus asborbed many of the tasks previously carried out by the central planners (Feiwel, 1977, p. 91–102).

The reversal of this 'decentralization' move in 1968 is often attributed to the chill that followed the Warsaw Pact intervention in Czechoslovakia. However, Bulgarian discomfort with and second thoughts about the coherence of the reform and the acceptability of the results had emerged as early as 1966 when Todor Zhivkov called for a reappraisal of the adequacy of the new methods. Renewed centralization began at mid-year 1968 and took the form of creation of additional success indicators and abandonment of a brief experiment with independent decision-making by the investment bank. This recentralization of management was accompanied by new confidence in the ability of mathematical methods and optimization techniques drastically to improve the quality of central planning and make centralization more effective. Wiedemann (1980a, 1983, pp. 126–30) has characterized the new system as a Streamlined Centralized System with Decomposition (SCSD). First mention of plans for massive concentration in the management of agriculture through establishment of the Agro-Industrial Complexes was also made at this time (Wiedemann, 1980b, p. 102).

A decade later it was argued that such 'administrative' measures had failed to achieve their intended results, so that a return to consideration of questions of incentive redesign was in order. Under the new set of reform measures that were finally announced in 1979, the number of success indicators was again cut and ministries were again instructed to stay out of the daily affairs of enterprise management. Despite some small changes and continued discussion of reform, matters of economic management appear to have gone on

Table 4.3 Success indicators under first and second reform regimes

1965—to the enterprise	*1979—to the DSO*
1. quantity to specified production in physical units	1. realized production in physical units
2. maximum investment outlay	(a) exports
3. volume of raw materials and intermediate inputs	(b) cooperative deliveries and spare parts
4. import or export target	(c) deliveries to domestic market
	2. net product in value terms
1968—recentralization	3. foreign exchange earnings or expenditures
5. specific volumes of specific good under contractual delivery	4. maximum supplies of raw materials, intermediate goods, labor, energy, a certain shortage machinery and equipment
6. maximum wage-bill	5. payment to the state budget
7. installation of new technology	
	1979—DSO to its subdivisions
	1. & 5. as above are 'passed through' to the constituent enterprises
	6. normed cost of production per unit of output
	7. tasks for the application of technological change

Source: Kaser, 1981, pp. 86, 88; Feiwel, 1977, pp. 93, 101–2.

with little change in the large state enterprise sector. Institutional innovations such as the Small and Medium-Sized Enterprise Program and removal of tight controls over some part of the banking system were begun at this time, but their effect on the fundamental patterns of behaviour was quite limited. The small enterprises established were semi-autonomous units within the administrative structure of the large DSOs, without major effect on the balance of their operations.

Only with the sustained economic difficulties of 1983, 1984 and 1985 did the reform movement again take on serious weight. Energy disruptions and very poor agricultural production made 1985 the worst year of the entire post-war period for overall economic performance. While consumers were largely shielded from the consequences, except for the indignities of the regime of interrupted electrical services, the events of the year undoubtedly had powerful effects on popular confidence in the performance of the economic system (which had for two decades provided an essentially unbroken period of rapidly rising living standards). The intense self-criticism and substantial personnel changes in early 1986 can be viewed as providing scapegoats to blame for the set-backs of the last several years, while sending the message that this time the pressure for improved and 'intensified' work methods was really strong.

The 1986 Reorganization

During the National Assembly meeting in March 1986 a series of apparently dramatic personnel and administrative structure changes were announced. Grisha Filipov was relieved of the position of Prime Minister and replaced by Georgi Atanasov, but Filipov remained as a member of the Politburo and a Central Committee Secretary. At the same time it was simply announced that the Mechanical Engineering, Power Engineering, Metallurgy, Chemical, Communications, and Woods and Forestry Ministries had been 'closed down.' The Committee for Culture and the National Agro-Industrial Union were both stripped of their ministerial rank, the former reconstituted as a committee 'with the Council of Ministers,' and the latter replaced by a new Ministry of Farming and Woods (*FBIS*, vol. 11, no. 56, 24 March 1986, p. C1). The appearance of drastic reduction in the extent of the hierarchical control structure of the economy created by the elimination of six major ministries is evidently misleading. Within the Council of Ministers an Economic Council, Social Council and a Council on Intellectual Development have been established, with at least the first having what appear to be super-ministerial coordinating responsibilities which include direct supervision of the work of the State Planning Commission. Then in May 1986, a series of five 'voluntary associations' were formed—a Construction Association, a Trade Association, a Light Industry Association, an Electronics Economic Association, and a Food and Tobacco Industry Association (*FBIS*, vol. 11, no. 94, 15 May 1986, pp. C2-3). There is obvious support for the idea that only names are being changed without alteration of real behavioral and structural relationships—a practice sometimes called semantic organization theory. The passage of several years will be required to determine what if any change is introduced by these superficially substantial reform measures.

The ambitious tone of the new reform measures under the slogan 'For Qualitatively New Growth of the Economy' is reflected in the Council of Ministers implementation decree which asserted that it would

carry out in a timely manner a profound reorganization of its own entire activity and bring it into conformity with the new tasks. Special attention was given to the practical measures for eliminating the bureaucratic atmosphere and departmental approach toward work, and for raising the level of initiative and responsibility of the economic organizations and their sub-divisions, while the economic levers and dialogue are to ensure the unity of collective and public interests.

The principle is to be applied unconditionally that questions should be solved basically at the appropriate managerial level under whose competence they are . . . A radical reduction is envisaged in the vast flow of reports and proposals presented to the government, as well as an increase in efficient and businesslike attitude and unity between words and deeds.

The quotation thus far suggests an uncompromising decentralization intent, which is then called into question by the concluding sentence

Special importance was attached to tightening control and increasing responsibility in relation to the execution of decisions at all levels, down from the Council of Ministers to the individual labor collective. [*FBIS*, vol. 11, no. 82, 29 April 1986, p. C1]

Obviously the relationship between words and practice in this reform can only be revealed in practice.

At the same time that the imperfections in the operation of existing economic arrangements were discussed, another theme emerged which emphasized the need to create new and stronger individual and group rewards for better effort. At the group level this consisted of suggestions that the brigade method be extended and thoroughly applied. The shorthand phrase 'brigades of a new type' seemed to have been adopted to signify actual application of the techniques of small group self-direction (with flexibility in job assignments, work methods and scheduling), separate financial accountability and perhaps election of team leaders. The individual incentive emphasis was concerned principally with stimulation of innovative managerial and entrepreneurial activity, by means of systematically allowing larger rewards for successful performance. As perceptively noted by Wiles (1977, pp. 443–5), many Eastern European advocates of 'incentive reforms' and performance-based payments are actually advocating overturning the 'socialist' wage structure that produces high cash incomes for manual workers and modest incomes for managerial and technical workers at all but the highest levels.

Again and again . . . members of the [Eastern European] socialist intelligentsia . . . tell you that 'incentives' must be increased. Pressed, they admit that Stalinism . . . was a highly incentive system. It emerges that Eastern European Stalinism, unlike Soviet, was highly egalitarian, and that they mean that their own salaries, as professional workers, researchers, teachers, etc., are only a very small multiple of the average wage . . . There is in the whole recent reform movement an element of 'rebourgeoisification.' [They] have quite simply wanted to re-establish the income differentials their fathers enjoyed; and they have tried it on in the name of incentives. [1977, pp. 444–5]

Wiles finds these arguments to be totally unconvincing, reasoning that the relationships between non-competing groups are quite malleable and indeed arbitrary, while the incentive relevant differentials are within competing groups. This 1977 commentary on the spirit of the reform movement is cited at length because it emphasizes a point that is seldom noted in Western analyses of developments as diverse as the Hungarian NEM and (economic reform aspects of) the Prague Spring, and because it so perfectly characterizes the opinions of Bulgarian economists interviewed by the author in 1985 and 1986. The April 1986 reforms appear to have been strongly affected by this tendency, which takes on special importance in light of the great degree of equality and compression of wages scales of the various non-competing groups in the contemporary Bulgarian economy.

The new set of reforms which were announced at the XIII Party Congress in April 1986 had been preceded by an extensive series of personnel changes (including the discharge of the chief of the Central Planning Board, Stanish Bonev) and an unusually direct and intense press campaign which called into question the competence and seriousness of the work efforts of a broad range of political and economic leaders. The condemnation of the performance of 'top leaders' was so strong and unqualified that it produced widespread speculation that it presaged the resignation of Todor Zhivkov, First Secretary and Chairman of the State Council. This did not occur, but instead the Party Congress witnessed strong attacks by Zhivkov on the performance and management of the economic and social system which he had presumably managed for the last three decades. It must be stressed that the criticism directed at the planning mechanism assumed its permanence at the core of the system, denied none of its prerogatives, and focused exclusively on the insufficient wisdom and competence with which it had been operated.

The reforms themselves managed to be at the same time daring in apparent scope and in almost every specific detail connected to already existing elements of tendencies in the system. The dual themes of heightened *party* control and strategic direction in economic decision-making and reduced *government* interference in the details of economic life are not, as is sometimes implied in Western discussions, logically inconsistent. They may, however, turn out to be contradictory in practice. The decreased central control of the details of economic life has been a theme in the Bulgarian reforms dating back to the formation of the DSOs after 1963 and formally described in the late 1960s as the SCSD. The agro-industrial complexes established in 1969–72 were also a manifestation of this tendency, which had both centralizing and decentralizing aspects. The unifying centralizing element in all of these changes was the progressive reduction in the number of separate decision-making units in the economy and the concentration of productive activity in very large units. In agriculture literally all land was in the hands of 320 separate AICs and IACs by 1975. The number of DSOs covering the entire industrial sector of the economy had fallen from 120 in the mid-1960s to only sixty-four in 1971 (Zwass, 1984, p. 19). At the same time these new units were granted many of the powers over their constituent parts (enterprises) that had been previously exercised by the industrial ministries and the Central Planning Board.

The most radical-sounding change of the spring 1986 reforms was what was described as the 'abolition' of the industrial ministries themselves. If both true and behaviourally meaningful this would establish a new and direct relationship between the central planning board and the DSO in which both would seem to have gained new power and leverage over their environments. The reservation here is that the new supervisory 'councils' established to replace the ministries may simply make the old ministries into subsections or bureaux, scarcely altering the operational realities of DSO life, but adding another layer to the existing administrative structure. Other policies which have the possibility of making important changes in the functioning of the society and economy, but which also can only be evaluated after their actual implementation details become clear, include the spread from the agricultural to the industrial sector of the process of electing first-line supervisors, intensified efforts to apply 'brigade' methods in the industrial sector, the introduction of some degree of direct competition between producers of the same consumer goods (with specific reference to allowing some decentralized control over pricing), and increased rewards for outstanding managerial, technical or inventive activities.

In July 1987 a further and in some ways contradictory series of economic reform measures were introduced. The various super-ministerial councils created two years earlier were eliminated and the ministry structure was largely reconstituted. A further enigmatic change was the transformation of the State Planning Commission into the Economy and Planning Ministry under the direction of Stoian Ovcharov. It is reasonable to suspect that these are further examples of 'semantic organization theory,' changing the names but not the underlying organizational structures or patterns of behavior. Some of the new ministries simply returned to their pre-1985 form when the various short-lived super-ministerial councils had been established. Examples of the Bulgarian capacity for institutional ingenuity (such as the Small Enterprise program) suggest that it would be wise to wait and not reflexively dismiss these recent moves as vacant bureaucratic exercises. A parallel theme in the summer 1987 reform discussions was a renewed emphasis on movement towards more vital and real 'self-management' at all levels of economic and political life, and strong statements of intentions to devolve real power to self-managing bodies in both realms. While these words have an ambiguous meaning, along with a clear non-correspondence with Yugoslav-style uses of the terms, they too could have substantial effects on actual behavior. Changes in property laws that come out of the January 1988 Party Conference will apparently make the enterprise collective the formal owner of what is now state productive property. The behavioral implications of this change are unclear. In the economic sphere self-management may mean no more than enterprise self-financing, but even so real movement in that direction would be a significant economic change. If it goes beyond that to meaningful elections of supervisors and any degree of real intra-enterprise democracy, it could have wide implications.

The BIA, Banking and the Small Enterprise Initiative

The organization of the Bulgarian financial system is part familiar and part unusual. The bulk of credit extension and the monitoring of transactions between enterprises are carried out by the Bulgarian National Bank (BNB) which functions much like Gosbank in the classical Soviet model. Long-term investment financing for projects included in the annual plan is thus administered by the BNB, which also makes short-term working capital loans. In addition to functions of central banking and currency control, the BNB has acted like the Gosbank in the Soviet Union in monitoring the financial aspects of plan fulfilment and the financing of investments included in the plan. In 1986 it was decided to separate the central banking and investment functions, creating a new Investment Bank to handle the latter. A similar separation was introduced in the 1960s and then reversed. The functions of the BIA and MB have not been altered by 1985-6 economic reforms.

There is another source of credit to enterprise that is less familiar and that, while not free of connections to the BNB, can be viewed as coming from a separate financial decision-making center. The Mineral Bank–Bank for Economic Initiatives (MB) plays a major role in financing credit for two quite different categories of projects: (1) investment projects of large enterprises which are above or beyond those called for in the plan; and (2) the foundation and expansion loans for Small and Medium-sized Enterprises. The Mineral Bank is a joint-stock company owned 50 percent by 'other banking institutions' (meaning the BNB) and 50 percent by some 200 large economic organizations. It is closely linked to the BNB (the Chairman of the MB is the First Deputy Chairman of the BNB) and to the Bulgarian Industrial Economic Association (the Chairman of the BIA is Chairman of the Expert Council which appraises individual applications for credit to the Mineral Bank).

The Bulgarian Industrial Association was founded in 1982 as a 'voluntary membership organization.' It is in some ways like a Chamber of Commerce since it is actively involved in trade promotion, but it engages in a unique set of very different activities which range from provision of management and technological consulting services to foundation of new enterprises. The BIA both directly stimulates enterprise formation in areas where its studies have discovered gaps in the domestic or export market and provides a kind of venture capital support to new projects developed by existing enterprises (Mishev, 1985, 1986). In some ways the BIA operates like a national 'Ministry of New Methods and Products,' despite having no such statutory standing. Its power and latitude for independent action seem to be very great, and it is able to work outside (or at least is able to transcend easily) traditional organizational channels. The special role of the BIA in stimulating the foundation of new, small-scale production units is one of the intriguing features of the New Economic Mechanism period. These new enterprises have played a major role in the rapid improvement in the quality and supply of a large range of clothing, small appliance and specialty foodstuff products. After Jackson's excellent discussion of the possibilities contained in the 1982 law (1986, p. 52, written in 1983), the actual development of these arrangements has received almost no attention in the West (McIntyre, 1986b, 1987b, 1988a, b, c).

The link between the BIA and the Mineral Bank has been very strong and the Mineral Bank is sometimes referred to as 'the bank of the BIA,' although that seems to be something of an exaggeration. The lending policies of the Mineral Bank are different for its two different categories of borrowers. Four times each year competitions are held for funds to be distributed through the Small Enterprise program. Applications are reviewed and ranked by an outside Expert Council (made up predominantly of economists and strongly influenced by the BIA) and are then funded until the allocated funds are exhausted. As of the beginning of 1986, sixty projects had been put into operation, 400 more had been approved and were in the process of construction, and a total of 1,500 such small plants were planned to be in use by the end of the Ninth Five Year Plan in 1990 (Mishev, 1986). About 5 percent of total capital investment is to be allocated in this fashion. Despite the use of the term 'competition,' this is not formally equivalent to the late-lamented Yugoslav investment auction (Neuberger, 1959), since in the Bulgarian case the interest rate is determined by the bank *after* the loan is approved and is not itself an element in the bidding. Projects are ranked on the basis of their effectiveness (which most likely amounts to their payback period), modified by any special characteristics, such as high energy saving or large foreign currency generating potential. The interest rate on these loans is generally 4 percent (2–15 percent) with a repayment period of up to thirty-six months.

Loans to established enterprises for projects beyond the dictates of the plan (projects which are designed to facilitate achievement of the planned results in most cases, but in ways not foreseen in the plan) are handled in an entirely different manner. Appraisal of projects is done on a year-round basis by the professional staff of the bank and approved projects are normally charged interest rates around 4 percent, but the bank has the authority to lower rates as far as 2 percent when there is a special desire to stimulate the sector or the investor has a particularly good credit history. Rates as high as 15 percent may be charged to investors with a bad credit history or whose work on a current project (initially funded at a lower interest rate) has been unacceptably prolonged. The MB may also request that the BNB impose salary penalties up to a maximum of 20 percent in cases where long delays in completing investment projects are due to managerial incompetence or inattention. As much as 5 percent of the loan may be assigned to cover start-up costs and raw materials for up to seventy-two hours of testing, but additional working capital must be borrowed from the BNB (Boichev, 1985). A number of Bulgarian economists have suggested increasing the share of investment funds allocated through the MB–BEI, especially through the Small and Medium-sized Enterprise program. Perhaps the new Investment Bank announced in late 1986 will move in this direction (Daviddi, 1987b).

It is important to be clear about the character of the Small Enterprise program, which has been erroneously cited as an example of movement toward private ownership. These units are not private in any respect and reflect a management experiment within the general pattern of state ownership. They are best viewed as semi-autonomous divisions of existing larger enterprises which remain responsible for coordination and general supervision of the small enterprise activities. Still, the managerial staff of the Small Enterprises appear to have much more autonomy and room for independent action at all levels of business behavior, including product design, production methods and practices, marketing and pricing. The divisions generally have a separate brand name and some have tied retail outlets operating under that name and selling only their own output.

Examples of consumer-goods-producing units include, mayonnaise, rubber sports shoes, Italian ice cream, various clothing and small appliance items, and injection-molded polymer furniture (for a more detailed discussion, see McIntyre, 1988a). After initial concentration on consumer-good products the BIA emphasis seems to be shifting toward an increased attention to research and technology applications on the one hand and high-level computer services on the other. It has stimulated the formation of the first three Bulgarian science parks (the first being scheduled to open in 1987) in conjunction with university research facilities. Separate organizations to develop and/or produce small batches of newly developed speciality products will be established under the personal direction of the chiefs of university research sections. The BIA has stimulated the formation of several consulting and technical service enterprises. One example of the surprising developments under this program is provided by IKO, an 'Information and Consulting Complex' which consists of nine small enterprises that have grown up around the leading Bulgarian management journal *IKO*. This is in effect a consortium of nine distinct computer consulting and information service units operating under a single general manager, but with separate financial accounts (McIntyre, 1987b, 1988b).

The Small Enterprise program is an important and authentically innovative form of decentralizing reform which has developed enclaves within the otherwise unchanged large state enterprise. It is a move 'closer to the market' in the limited sense that the enterprises: have been set up as a result of research or observation suggesting their usefulness in light of market conditions; are much freer to respond to small shifts in consumer preferences and are able to do so more rapidly; have somewhat stronger performance bonus and reward arrangements for their managers; and appear to have some small price-setting latitude. They are none the less state enterprises in a system where the role of classical central planning, materials allocation and price formation have changed very little. They reflect an effort to improve the supply of services and simple consumer goods outside the existing large enterprise channels and it is useful to compare them with measures adopted in other Eastern European countries having the same purpose.

In Hungary the existing structure of very small private retail outlets (basically booths rather than stores) and services has been augmented by a program of renting out state-owned premises (small restaurants in particular) to the highest bidder for five-year periods. In the German Democratic Republic a complex private sector has continued to exist, despite the widespread Western belief that nationalization of all such enterprises was completed in 1972. Many small private businesses were either not nationalized at all or were partly nationalized, leading to the existence of enterprises jointly owned by private persons and the state. The GDR has recently and without fanfare expanded the number of small, privately managed restaurants and retail stores, possibly on the same basis as the Hungarian program. In Bulgaria a number of unpublicized experiments along these same lines were established in 1985 in remote corners of Sofia. It should be noted that purely private, one-person (no hired labor) repair, tailoring and personal service shops have always existed in Bulgaria, although they do not bulk large in the overall service sector of the economy (McIntyre 1988b, c). The personal agricultural plots mentioned above are the other 'private' element in the modern Bulgarian economic system and their integration with the socialist sector is heavily stressed above (see pp. 101–5).

Clearly the BIA Small Enterprises have played a role in testing some of the economic accounting and financial discipline provisions of the long-delayed NEM. The BIA appears to be actively involved, at least in an advisory role in the process of 'reform design.' With the intensified emphasis on acceleration of technological change after the February 1986 Plenum of the BCP, the BIA has played a role in the distribution of the special fund for adoption of particularly efficient or high-quality processes (Tonkov, 1986).

In addition the BIA seems to have a competition philosophy, which, while not running in the direction of adoption of a full market system, seeks to increase the extent of competition between socialist units. BIA also seems to favor a systematic revitalization for poorly managed or ill-equipped existing enterprises that in effect creates a two-stage process in which after consulting and evaluation firms are either revitalized under their existing management or are (in something colorfully called 'socialist bankruptcy') put in the hands of another group or organization which wishes to take it over. This effort to convince the government to apply such an 'ultimate' financial punishment was under serious consideration in 1986 and may be a part of the detailed 1986–7 reform provisions.

Physical Standard of Living in Bulgaria

The physical standard of life in Bulgaria has risen rapidly and steadily over most of the post-war period, but especially in the period following 1965. The sharp changes in the stock of major consumer goods and diet are detailed in Tables 4.4 and 4.5. The range and availability of domestically produced consumer goods has expanded, with clear improvements in quality and style, though not reaching West European levels in many areas. Imported consumer goods have appeared on a significant scale, although often from other Eastern European countries. These changes are most obvious in the dramatic rise in the style and taste of everyday dress and in the emergence of

Table 4.4 Various consumer goods per 100 households, 1965–85

	1965	1970	1975	1980	1985
Radio	59	62	76	88	97
Television	8	42	66	75	93
Electric washing-machine	23	50	59	71	89
Refrigerator	5	29	59	76	94
Private automobile	2	6	15	29	37
Telephone	—	7	12	24	42

Sources: Statisticheski Spravochnik 1986, p. 226; Lampe, 1986, p. 194.

Table 4.5 Food production and consumption, 1956–85

Production (1956 = 100)				Consumption (kg. or liter per capita)				
	Crop	Animal	Total	Meat	Fish	Milk	Eggs	Grain prod.
1956	100	100	100	26.6	1.1	81	69	257.0
1960	147	130	141	29.1	2.2	92	84	261.4
1970	196	195	196	41.4	5.5	117	122	238.8
1975	212	250	226	58.0	6.2	143	197	217.8
1980	204	288	236	61.2	6.9	169	204	216.0
1984	229	315	262	71.0	8.2	190	236	197.0
1985	182	309	233	71.3	8.3	191	239	197.4

Sources: Statisticheski Spravochnik 1986, pp. 121–2, 196; *Statisticheski Godishnik 1974*, p. 73.

the custom sewing and cleaning services necessary to support these new patterns, but are thoroughgoing and profound.

Some observers, the present author included, would suggest that the pace of change in the physically obvious signs of higher living standards has been greater in Bulgaria (noting of course very different initial levels) than in countries such as Hungary whose development has been regularly and approvingly noted in the West. The failure to appreciate fully Bulgarian developments undoubtedly has manifold roots, including the geo-political filter applied with opposite effect to countries perceived to be close to versus moving away from Soviet forms of organization. Favorable attention can be secured by either domestic of foreign policy deviation. Although there have been important economic changes in Bulgaria, they have not thus far been in the direction of significantly greater use of market forces and so they have been largely ignored. Although it is suggested above that the extent and significance of the Hungarian changes have been exaggerated, they have included increased use and even more talk about use of the market as the key coordinating force, explaining the generally uncritical Western response. See, however, Hare (1987) and Marer (1987) for a balanced and critical evaluation of the NEM.

When comparisons are explicitly or implicitly made between Bulgaria and countries such as Hungary or Czechoslovakia, it is important to note that very large differences in living standards existed prior to the socialist period. Rapid Bulgarian progress has closed much, but far from all, of this historical and cultural gap.

There has been a drastic improvement in the quality, style and range of domestically produced consumer goods and a large increase in the availability (for local currency) of imported consumer goods in Bulgaria during the last decade. A great expansion has occurred in the variety of domestically produced food and drink products. Butter now appears in convenient packages in four grades differentiated by butterfat content, mayonnaise has appeared for the first time and in several varieties, numerous sub-types (by region or grape) of wine have been introduced and beer is now produced in three grades with roughly a dozen different varieties produced regionally and available nationally. Milk now appears in several grades, flavored fresh milk for children is available in plastic single serving bags, and flavored varieties have been added to supplement the famous Bulgarian yogurt (*kiselo mlyako*). The original popularity of soft drinks based on imported licenses has peaked and the Bulgarian carbonated apple drink *yablaka* has come back into favor, supplemented by new pear and raspberry variants. Bulgaria has as well a remarkable variety of bottled fruit *nektars* (with sugar added) including apricot, peach, apple, cherry (three varieties), quince, raspberry and others, often in combination. Juices (which are filtered and unsweetened) cover the same range, plus carrot, tomato and various mixed vegetable combinations. The variety of routine choice in this sector of the market is quite remarkable.

Another area of rapid proliferation of product types is specialty meats and cheeses. The great increase in fresh meat supplies (even in bad agricultural years) has already been noted. A number of new types of hard sausage have been introduced and produced in relatively large quantities. Smoked pressed goat and veal (*pasterma*) have appeared in new forms and smoked whole chicken and pork loins are now more readily available than in the past. The variety of domestically produced cheese has expanded, packing in smaller units has been introduced for the traditional white and yellow cheeses, and Hungarian specialty cheeses have become available.

The specialty items mentioned above have become standard items and are more or less regularly available. The irregularity in the distribution and stocking of individual products, suggested by the last qualification, has decreased but not disappeared. These specialty items are more expensive than standard products, and were singled out for sharp increases in the September 1985 price reforms. It is none the less true that the price of the most expensive specialty product is only three times the least expensive cut of meat (18:5 leva per kilogram or 8.05:US$ 2.24 per pound at the official 1986 exchange rate), which is a very small differential.

Other imported specialty items have begun to appear and are available for local currency (such goods had long been available through the convertible currency store CORECOM), including Western-produced whiskey, cognac and liqueurs, French and Dutch mustards and other spices. Some items such as first-quality French butter are likely to be temporary (accidents of the Common Market agricultural policy), but oranges and grapefruit from Cuba, bananas from Colombia and Venezuela, and specialty oranges from Greece seem to have become a regular if not constant part of Bulgarian life. It is worth underlining the fact that these products did not disappear during the semi-crisis of 1984–5.

Aggregate Measurements Do Not Reflect Improved Quality and Broader Choice

Measurements of the volume of consumer-goods production implicitly assume constant quality of a given product through time and a given set of goods produced. The addition of new products or quality changes in existing products create practical and theoretical problems for economic statisticians even in capitalist economies which have relatively competitive market structures. In Soviet-type systems prices have generally been set administratively and changed infrequently (the rouble prices of a kilogram of meat or a subway ride in Moscow, for example, are the same in 1956 and 1986). Western analysts have often noted that unavailability of goods may make even these prices misleading. Little attention has been given to the opposite phenomena of increasing availability within a given price structure, a rise in the quality of existing products, and an expanding range of consumer products. All three favorable developments have been occurring over the last decade in Bulgaria, making the measured rate of increase in consumer-goods consumption a considerable underestimate of the real rise in private living standards. Further, this discussion only takes account of goods that pass through the market, and during the last decade the state has been systematically encouraging rural and urban dwellers to take up cultivation of personal plots on APK land. While the immediate goal is to raise the supply and quality of agricultural products marketed by the AIC, a side-effect is improvement in the living standard of the participating households from direct consumption of their output.

The Disappearance of 'Lines,' Lines and Retail Distribution

If defined literally lines are a feature of retail distribution in all economically vigorous enterprises both East and West. The special meaning of the word in the context of socialist countries refers to the manifestations of the perennial seller's market for consumer goods in the Soviet Union and the situation that has arisen elsewhere (for example, in Poland and Romania) in times of economic crisis. One way that Western observers acknowledge the improvement in consumer-goods availability is to note the decrease or disappearance of lines in their pathological form, where people spend many hours per week in lines which may lead to nearly empty or poorly stocked stores and in which people buy products they do not want simply because they are available, hoping to be able to trade them later for needed goods. Bulgaria made the transition to nearly complete freedom from these dysfunctional aspects of line behavior sometime in the 1970s, and despite widely reported economic difficulties in 1983–6 has not reverted to the earlier pattern.

Supply Inconsistencies and Irregularities

Despite the general good availability and improving quality of various consumer goods (foodstuffs and other light consumer goods), Bulgaria still suffers from irregularities and inconsistencies in the pattern of supply. Even at times of maximum availability, the full range of types of a particular product will seldom be found in the same place. In a December 1985 speech, Pencho Kubadinski, who is a Politburo member and chairman of the Fatherland Front, noted that

the alarming facts and unresolved problems are mainly the result of slipshod attitudes and the underestimation by many state and economic organs of this exceptionally important issue (which people use) as a yardstick to judge the work of party, state, economic, and social organs and organizations.
(especially in settlement systems of the 4th and 5th functional types) the level of services is particularly unsatisfactory . . . one must not underestimate the fact that the population continues to be offered goods in insufficient quantities and low quality. In the shops of many populated areas essential goods, such as sugar, cooking oil, cheese, rice, etc., are on occasion not available. This produces the anomaly that many shops are overflowing with goods, but the people cannot buy what they need. [*FBIS*, vol. 11, no. 4, 7 January 1986, pp. C2–C3]

For several reasons Westerners, especially short-time visitors, often see lines where there are none, at least in the pathological sense. Some of these perceptions are reflections of the manifold eccentricities of the retail distribution system in Bulgaria. While they might well be criticized on a variety of grounds, they do not reflect congenital shortages and a specific hunger for consumer goods. First, there are several structural features. Because nearly all Bulgarian households are made up of two adults with full-time jobs, and living with grandparents is no longer a standard pattern, there is an unavoidable 'peaking' of retail activity during the lunch period and at the end of the workday. Second, lines frequently form waiting for shops to open after the common two-hour mid-afternoon closing. Third, the physical premises of many shops are very small and the staff frequently prefer to conduct business outside, thus moving a small group of shoppers out onto the sidewalk where they become mixed with pedestrians. Fourth, many shops establish 'outposts' to sell a special product, away from the immediate premises of the shop and on the already narrow sidewalks.

Three other explanations for lines derive from the nature of the products themselves and cultural patterns in food preparation. Fresh bread and sweet coffee cakes are baked on the premises of hundreds of small shops and some people gather to wait for the newest batch to emerge from the oven. Second, many Bulgarians buy certain food product (grapes, peppers, onions, leeks) in enormous quantities, sometimes 50 kilograms at a time, for once-a-year wine-making, home-canning, or curing. Finally, some tropical food products (such as bananas, mandarin oranges and pineapples) are available only at certain times during the year and when they arrive do produce lines. Each of the factors enumerated produces the appearance of a classical shortage line, but only the last fits the category after more careful thought. When lines are observed it is generally too few people available to sell the available product at that point and time, or localized distribution problems, rather than evidence of generalized scarcity.

It is of course possible that even when the extent of the rise in private household living standards, as marked by the disappearance of lines and the great expansion of the variety and quality of goods available, is fully understood, it is still too slow to satisfy the expanding aspirations and expectations of the population. The point to be emphasized is that Bulgaria has undergone a decade-long process in which the real and tangible quality of life of private persons has systematically risen more rapidly than reflected in the calculated measures of the output of consumer goods.

Income Distribution and the Visible Standard of Living

A major structural factor which clouds the comparative vision of occasional visitors results from the relatively egalitarian character of the Bulgarian development process. This is in part the result of a particularly rapid rise in the living standards in the countryside which has eliminated the historical imbalance, even before non-monetized amenity benefits and costs are brought into the question. As a result Sofia lacks some of the glitter of certain other Eastern European capitals that include more real poverty. Sofia suffers many of the growth pains of capitals world-wide, intensified by the highly centralized governmental structure of Bulgaria. The supply of rewarding and attractive jobs in Sofia feeds population growth so rapid that construction of new apartment blocks on the city edge is selected as the short-term response to the housing crisis. As a result much of the housing stock in the central city, as well as the supporting infrastructure, waits its turn for the allocation of scarce construction resources. The construction of a series of impressive public and cultural facilities in the late 1970s and after, along with systematic refurbishing of adjoining neighborhoods, has only begun to remedy the run-down and worn-out look of much of the central core of the capital city. The physical condition and design standards of public and residential construction are considerably higher in cities such as Plovdiv, Varna, Ruse and Turnovo. This is possibly an effect of the 1959 territorial reorganization (discussed in Chapter 5, pp. 150–2) and the ensuing decentralization of control over municipal affairs.

Part of the construction quality problem in Sofia results from the constant emphasis on speedy completion of many projects at roughly the same time, leading to pressure to ignore details and a constant shifting of specialist construction brigades from site to site. The failure to complete construction projects on time has been a steady element in public criticism of economic performance for much of the post-war period, but the pressure for improved results has been particularly intense in recent years. This pressure has mitigated against any effort to stress quality in the details and finish of construction work. It is common to see work on the intermediate stages of one aspect of a project damage adjoining finished work with no apparent concern by the workers involved to avoid destroying already accomplished work. Whether this is a carry-over of peasant work habits ('Bulgarian work') or the original product of forty years of forced draft construction with no salient quality measure is unclear. The results are worst in the capital and are quite unsettling to anyone with a Northern European sense of craftwork. Despite this pattern of unnecessary error the average quality of the finished work has been rising even in Sofia and projects such as the mammoth Ludmilla Zhivkova National Cultural Palace have been both planned and executed at a high level.

This discussion of quality in construction has obvious connections to both the strong stress on raising quality levels (and accelerating the adoption of new technology) under the 8th Five Year Plan and again at the XIII Party Congress during the first months of the 9th Five Year Plan (1986–90) and to the consideration of the problems of redesigning the incentive and reward system that are at the core of the New Economic Mechanism.

'Rational' Pricing and Actual Eastern European Practice

It is often stated that the structure of relative prices in contemporary socialist systems is irrational. Since individual product prices are arbitrary and not related to the cost of production, vast subsidies are required to cover the gap between input 'costs' and the sales price of the item. Western economists in particular are inclined to become exercised at the thought of a buyer being denied the price information necessary to make a decision of what to buy by reflecting on the true costs to society of producing the various alternative products.

Recognizing that the socialist price system could indeed remain 'irrational' after introduction of qualifying information, the following qualifications are offered:

(1) There is a conscious pattern to the subsidy policy which has been adopted for clear social policy reasons that reflect an alternative structure of rationality. The intention is to avoid allowing a market price for vital supplies and services to balance supply and demand forces at some definite but unspecified level which inevitably strongly reflects household income. An active desire to use non-market allocation tools is quite different for the ignorance of the force and logic of the market that is often ascribed to the practitioners of such market manipulation. Prices of the biologically essential elements in the household budget, as well as those especially relevant to the young or infirm, have been held below costs of production so that a minimally acceptable floor level of consumption is available to all. The specific products receiving such subsidies are staple foods, bread, milk products, children's clothing and educational supplies, health services, housing rentals, heat and electrical services, public transportation, and so on. Use of social criteria for pricing can be corruptly or incompetently managed, but is not by itself evidence of irrationality.

(2) A related but not identical point is seen in the price policy for meat. In Japan the market clearing price is in the vicinity of US$35 per pound and there are no lines and no reports of shortages. In the Soviet Union, there are lines and constantly reported shortages, but the price of meat is around US$5 per kg. In Bulgaria the price is the same, but there are no lines. We note that the Soviet price is unchanged over several decades, that there were shortages at earlier times, but that per capita meat consumption has risen from a very low to a very high level over that period. Obviously the presence of a shortage at a given price is not enough information to reveal the actual supply conditions to the population. Hard though it may be to explain the Soviet pricing practice, there is no 'shortage' of meat in relative or historical perspective. Meat was viewed as a symbolically important luxury good and allocation was made on a willingness to wait rather than willingness to pay basis. A large increase in the amount of meat available and consumed has occurred in the Soviet Union, but there is still excess demand at the fixed price, though the market clearing price is now probably considerably closer to the actual price. In Bulgaria a conceptually similar pricing policy has been

followed, but output has risen so rapidly that the market clearing and actual price more or less coincide.

(3) Completeness of product information provided to the consumer: although very limited in certain areas, due to the lack of a commercial consumer testing service for the determination of physical performance characteristics, information is remarkably extensive in other directions. All food products, for example, appear with both a specific date of production and a shelf life-span.

(4) In some product areas there is an infinite variety of sizes available because of the persistence of very small retail outlets and very limited prepackaging.

(5) In many products there is a separability of various subcomponents of the consumption process, with at least in some respects more clearly marginal cost pricing and less use of average costs. Tea and coffee bear one price with sugar and another without. The amount of bread actually consumed with the meal determines the charge. The price of ice cream is higher in warm weather when it requires much more refrigeration. (This last example is also consistent with the idea of revenue maximization by taking account of different price elasticities in different 'markets.')

The foregoing suggests that the pattern and structure of distribution in Bulgaria has grown in somewhat unique ways, embodying both disadvantages and advantages to the citizen as consumer. Social policy considerations lie behind many of the situations where state subsidies are required to fill the gap between selling costs and costs of production. Evidence that the price structure does not automatically adjust to changes in foreign market prices and that unintended subsidies do develop can be found in the extraordinary set of price increases introduced on 15 September 1985.

The decree of the Council of Ministers explained the need for price increases on luxury goods, energy (electricity and liquid fuels) and water as a further measure to 'compensate for the losses caused to [the] national economy by the natural disasters in 1984 and 1985.' Explicit reference was made to the dual role of prices in encouraging economy and efficiency in the use of scarce resources by households and business enterprises and in providing incentives for greater production of certain goods.

Prices for basic foodstuffs, milk products including standard cheeses, meat (except pork), and centrally supplied heating services remained unchanged. Price rises for some products were quite remarkable: for electric power, 58 percent to enterprises and 41 percent to households; gasoline and diesel fuel, 35 percent; drinking water, 364 percent to enterprises and 67 percent to households; telephone rates by 250 percent for enterprises and 50 percent for households; and a whole set of 'luxury' foodstuffs—coffee beans, specialty sausage, cheese and beer, and so on were raised by 35–42 percent. Prices for fresh pork were raised from 4.5 to 5 leva per kilogram ($2.01–$2.24 per pound at the official exchange rate). Prices of construction supplies, household appliances and paint rose from 20–38 percent and automobiles by 12 percent (*FBIS*, no. 179, 16 September 1985, C1–2).

According to the chief of the Price Administration Office, the rising world market prices for energy and raw materials had not been felt internally, because only 'administrative and organizational–technical' measures had been undertaken to encourage conservation. Since these measures had had no effect, 'economic regulators . . . first and foremost, prices' would now be used. Special emphasis was laid on reducing energy consumption, but higher rates were offset by reduced charges for power consumption during the 'off-peak load' evening hours. Local government units were instructed to supplement directly the incomes of any low-income households which would be sharply affected by the new energy costs (*FBIS*, no. 183, 20 September 1985, C4–7). Several days after the price announcements the Council of Ministers produced a decree raising the minimum payroll wage from 110 to 120 leva per month, adding 5 leva to the wage of workers close to the new minimum, increased the minimum pension from 50 to 60 leva per month, and detailing yearly pension increases from 1 January 1986 until 1 January 1990 (*FBIS*, no. 183, 20 September 1985, C7–8). Although the connection is obvious, the wage and pension decree did not mention the price increases.

The relationship between world energy market developments, the special supply relationship with the Soviet Union and the internal price and production situation in Bulgaria has already been considered (pp. 75–7). The dramatic domestic price rises of September 1985 serve to underline how long the Bulgarian sense of invulnerability to the effects of the world energy market revolution in the 1970s persisted. When these price shocks finally arrived, they were amplified by the simultaneous occurrence of a string of real natural disasters.

Comparisons with other Balkan and Eastern European Countries

It is obviously desirable, despite the difficulties, to attempt to compare Bulgaria with Greece, Romania and Yugoslavia, as well as countries outside the Balkans. A very unusual and interesting study by Apel (1975) and Apel & Strumpel (1976) contains a detailed multi-level comparison of Bulgaria and

Greece. The excellent and comprehensive volume by Jackson & Lampe deals with the entire area but is quite brief in its consideration of the post-World War II period (1982a, pp. 520–99). The study by Gianaris (1982), contains some useful information and includes Turkey and Albania, but slips back and forth between reference to specific countries and the clump of countries called 'Balkan planned economies.' The Balkan planned economies described here bear so little resemblance to Bulgaria (at least any time after 1970) that interpretation is difficult. Even in the unusually stressful years of 1984–5 the anecdotes and images (empty stores, bare shelves and interminable lines), Gianaris quotes have no connection to Bulgarian reality. It is difficult to tell whether this is projection of the Soviet spectre (with a little recent Romanian and Polish leavening), very old information, or disinformation.

Certain of the aggregate level statistical comparisons are useful and appear to be based on accurate and current data. In particular the picture of Bulgaria generating reasonably high annual rates of investment but steadily achieving very moderate results from what is cumulatively a very large investment program is strongly underlined. I have suggested above (pp. 88–90, 97–101, 109–10) that the agricultural program has involved a middle course with enough investment to generate high output and living standards for those who stay in agriculture, while freeing large numbers of workers for the rapidly expanding urban industrial sector. But the question of why the efficiency of use of that capital was not higher in both agriculture and industry remains. Gianaris calculates incremental capital output ratios (ICOR) for several periods and shows quite clearly the poor performance in the use of industrial capital that seems to be a sustained performance feature. Jerome (1985) provides a detailed estimation of the aggregate productivity measures for the 1950–80 period for Bulgaria, Greece and Yugoslavia, along with the standard results for a number of other countries. In general I agree with Wiles (1977, p. 589) that econometric estimation of productivity relationships based on various production functions and what are basically guesses about the factor share weights 'rests on bad data and over sophisticated theory.' For our purposes it is also important to note Wiles's observation that Bulgarian results are the most strikingly improbable of any of the twelve countries he included in his agnostic study, and that the calculated rate of growth of the overall efficiency of resource use (even restricted to industry and the short period 1960–72) varied wildly (0.8–4.5 percent per year), depending on the assumed factor share weights (pp. 591–3). The study by Jerome, like most others of the type, uses only one set of weights, reducing the confusion but veiling the volatility and weakness in explanatory power of the calculated results.

Lampe (1986) provides a more detailed explanation of the behavioral roots of these problems, which seem to have been scarcely affected by the various reform measures in the two decades since the Eastern Europe-wide 'Liberman' discussion and ensuing economic experimentation took hold. I have argued above that the application of the reforms has been half-hearted and very gradual, with real and strong pressure being felt by enterprise managers only after 1 January 1982. The semi-crisis of 1984–5 veils any positive macrolevel effects that may have emerged since then, but on the other hand it has created a deeper and more serious party and government commitment to quality- and efficiency-enhancing reforms as a way to reduce future vulnerability.

It should also be emphasized that there is now a powerful institutional momentum towards more careful use of the levers already provided by the NEM to refine qualitatively behavior within those contexts. It is this very partial commitment to reform, mixed with an intense desire to improve system functioning that makes the Bulgarian case so close to and relevant for students of the Soviet economy. On the other hand, it may be argued that slack behavior allowed by the reforms that have come into force contributed to the 1984–6 energy embarrassment, and this may have resulted in a reduction in blind faith in reform *per se*. The new reform measures introduced at the XIII Party Congress, despite 'abolition' of ministries, are not clearly decentralizing because of the creation of a new set of supervisory councils that could conceivably operate like super-ministries. With reference to the Soviet case, Berliner (1983, pp. 44–7) has argued that a reassertion of conventional planning authority along with improved workplace discipline (which together he calls the 'reactionary model') may well provide the best short-run approach to reviving economic performance. Clearly elements of this approach can be found in the brief Andropov period and in the first year of the leadership of Mikhail Gorbachëv, although obviously accompanied by more straightforward 'liberalizing' tendencies in the latter case.

5 The Social System

Efficiency, Order and the Less-Than-Fully-Modernized Village Culture

The social system interacts with and to some extent forms and limits the behavior and performance of the political and economic subsystems of any society. The features of the contemporary social system that are most characteristically Bulgarian are frequently rooted in the agrarian past and village culture that were still dominant and scarcely changed by modern industrial, commercial society as late as the end of World War II. In the ensuing four decades Bulgaria has urbanized and industrialized at a breathtaking and perhaps excessively costly pace. The population working full-time in agriculture has plummeted in response to rapidly expanding industrial employment opportunities, aided by a sustained program of investment in elaborate and labor-saving agricultural technologies. At the same time the strong family traditions and attachment to the land have been maintained by a very high proportion of the newly urban population.

The advantages of this continuing tie to the land, in terms of access to fresh fruit and vegetables and vacation weeks or weekends without commercial arrangements, were evident even before the recent measures to encourage urban dwellers to take up cultivation of personal plots on AIC land (generally well away from the cities). The rapidly spreading ownership of private automobiles and the shortening of the workweek occurred in parallel, both facilitating and encouraging the new weekend return migration. The negative features of this relationship involve difficult to quantify problems of persistent careless peasant attitudes towards machinery and, as was ungenerously pointed out by the Soviet ambassador in his famous *Pogled* interview (see p. 76-7), an incomplete 'proletarianization' of the workforce—which presumably thinks too much of the state of the pear trees and too little of the plan.

Bulgaria has an oddly mixed reputation with assumptions about strictness and tight state control coexisting with references to a lackadaisical popular approach to worklife and a predominantly self-satisfied attitude at policymaking levels. Talk of economic reform in Bulgaria (renewed most recently in March 1987) has been taken seriously in the West because of the reputation for toughness, and also because, unlike the Soviet Union, we have little of the kind of informal information about how things really work to lead us automatically to call into question the relationship between announced reforms and actual behavior. As we have seen above in Chapters 3 and 4, the political system has failed to act effectively against egregious economic malfunctions. Little action was taken against profligate use of energy and water, in a society very short of both, until something close to a systems crisis occurred in the winter of 1984–5. The room for increased efficiency within existing institutions is very large, so if the fall 1985 'intensification' initiatives are pursued with real seriousness they could have very dramatic positive effects. The parallel Soviet campaign for improved efficiency and discipline in the workplace would seem to increase the possibility for effective Bulgarian actions, both from the tendency to emulation seen in many post-war turns of social, political, cultural and economic policy, but also because it seems to be a call for a sign of seriousness from an ally obviously displeased with many aspects of recent Bulgarian conduct.

The countervailing inertial forces within Bulgarian society are well summarized in the lament of the price administrator (see p. 133), as is the tendency to adopt drastic administrative remedies after sustained failure to produce cooperation or compliance through the standard control channels of the system. Examples of these resolutions include the threat to cut off all water to firms which failed to rationalize water use and the total shut-off of all electrical power for multiple hours per day (and restricted appliance-use hours thereafter) over the period from June to November 1985. The latter is a seemingly desperate measure, the need for which has never been convincingly explained. Although the costs of this measure were high in terms of popular faith in the competence of government economic managers and energy planners, it may have been in part an attempt to shock the population into at last taking austerity measures seriously. While drastic by the standards of the placid and progressive 1965–83 period, it should be noted that these measures (and indeed the entire tone of policy making and administration) bear little resemblance to the more extreme developments in Romania. Energy rationing measures were again introduced for the winter of 1987–8, despite the arrival on line of the new 1,000 MW reactor at the Kozloduy (*Financial Times*, 21 October 1987, p. 4).

In some seemingly trivial areas there appears to be an absence of either legal restrictions or *ad hoc* control efforts directed at obviously socially destructive practices (e.g., the mass open air burning of garden wastes and leaves in the middle of cities with intense air pollution, or the burning by clean-up crews of wastes in parks and residential area garbage containers).

Examples such as these on the one hand suggest the absence of rational social control, but on the other are evidence of cultural traditions carried over from peasant agriculture and untrammelled by the modern urban state.

Reform of the Educational System

Reforms in the last several years have attempted to reduce the total number of students enrolled at the university level (with special emphasis on reducing the number who spend many extra years before graduating) and increasing the number of students who are able to go directly to work at the end of their formal studies. In addition to the existing four-year technical schools which enroll about half of the students 14–18 years of age, a two-year vocational module (called the 'educational-vocational complex') has been inserted into the curriculum of all academic and special language high schools. This is a fact rather than a plan, although the history of curriculum experimentation suggests grounds for doubt about its permanence. Students in the 11th and 12th grades receive some Bulgarian language and social problems courses, but spend the bulk of their time on course work clearly linked to their future workplaces. Students in schools that have an electronics emphasis, for example, will study direct and practical aspects of the subject, possibly including some work experience in a cognate enterprise.

The Bulgarian Orthodox Church

The role of the Bulgarian Orthodox church is complex, combining formal toleration and extensive subsidization on the part of the State along with restriction on the range of permitted activities and public role. Like all other religious groups it is strictly prohibited from undertaking any activities with even indirect political or social policy implications. Operation of schools, except for the Theology School (which is in the center of downtown Sofia) and the internal instructional functions of the many remaining active monasteries, is prohibited. While the Russian Orthodox church was so deeply involved with the Tsarist State that for many its moral authority was destroyed, in Bulgaria the Orthodox church bore the double burden of close association with successive unpopular foreign and domestic ruling groups, the former through the Ottoman millet system which made the church a fundamental administrative channel of colonial rule. Perhaps for these or other more subtle reasons the Orthodox church has been a minor political, social and cultural force over the entire post-Ottoman period. Individual priests played a role in the various anti-Turkish insurrections leading up to 1878 but the role of the Orthodox Church is minimal in contemporary Bulgarian life.

Leisure

The remaining attachment to the village and the widespread practice of cultivating rural garden plots even when no direct family tie to the countryside remains, together constitute a major explanation of the use of leisure time, and simultaneously provides a considerable volume of specialty food stuff to the urban population. It seems that almost every urban family has some sort of pipeline to the countryside or a well-cultivated garden plot closer to the center. Members of AICs receive in-kind distribution of goods produced from the common fields, which, along with the personal plot production, are often shared with city relatives and friends.

Other important recreational activities include family and group hiking which is something of a national avocation. Beyond the predictable set of mass sports activities, a relatively wide participation in downhill skiing has developed during the 1980s and the beginnings of a tennis boom are evident. Subsidized vacation and spa trips arranged through the place of employment are organized very much on the Soviet model. Travel to other Eastern European countries is easily arranged (no visas are required for several countries) and widely pursued. In 1985 for example 533,000 Bulgarians went abroad (6 percent of the population), but Eastern European destinations dominated this flow (*Statistical Reference Book of the People's Republic of Bulgaria, 1986*, p. 83). Measures that will make acquisition of passports for foreign travel easier were announced in 1987.

Research on Bulgarian Attitudes Toward Social Life and Well-being

An interesting and unusual study by Apel (1975) and Apel & Strumpel (1976) contains some direct evidence about how Bulgarians view their social-economic system. They have directly gathered survey data from the early 1970s, in the middle of a long period of rapid growth, and make a comprehensive effort to compare the development experience and economic-social achievements of Greece and Bulgaria, reaching conclusions favorable to the latter on almost every score. This study combines the use of aggregate data with an extraordinary comparison of the responses of 500 citizens of each country (a stratified example of randomly encountered Bulgarians and Greeks) to a long list of direct attitudinal and objective questions about economic, social and personal conditions, views about the future, and quality of health care and other important measures of the quality of life. Because of the unique character of the materials contained in this study (there are literally no other works which address these questions from a social science perspective) and the insightful and accurate observations about the inner workings of the Bulgarian social system, it is quoted in some detail here.

In the course of evaluating the strongly positive Bulgarian response to questions about past, present and future living standards and social mobility, Apel and Strumpel noted a consistent connection between the responses and objective measures of the average (viewed both in terms of the mean and standard deviation) conditions of the Bulgarian population. They offer a number of hypotheses as to why the response was so strongly favorable. According to Apel (1975, p. 17):

Alienation due to the repressive tendencies of a centrally directed system tends toward the vanishing point when this system provides for marked and continuous improvement of living standards and keeps the limitations of personal freedom in line with the basic requirements for its functioning. Successful implementation of egalitarian tendencies is a particularly strong factor in keeping alienation at a very low level.

Since the income distribution was really extraordinarily compressed (especially when viewed in terms of household income, which is better than individual income as an indicator of how individuals live in a nearly universal two-earner culture), very little optimism was required for a Bulgarian citizen to view themselves as average or above:

even a modestly optimistic perception of one's own situation would be sufficient to place oneself above the middle; while in Greece, there is probably less uncertainty about one's place in society, since the concomitant differences in social and economic status are more pronounced. [Apel & Strumpel, 1976, p. 176]

Income Distribution and Inequality

Even after deletion from the sample of the wealthiest 1 percent of the Greek population, the ratio of the family income of the 95th percentile to the 5th percentile was 11.11:1 in Greece and only 4.9:1 in Bulgaria. Detailed comparison shows a much more uniform income pattern in Bulgaria, without the wealthy upper edge of the Greek distribution and totally lacking the lower end which amounts to real destitution in Greece.

With the exception of incomes of independent shopkeepers, mean work incomes are ranked in the same way in both countries. White-collar workers earn the most, followed first by blue-collar workers, then by agricultural workers/farmers. However, the effect of income differentiation upon consumption and welfare is mitigated, actually almost washed out, in Bulgaria, but remains a serious source of inequality in Greece. First, the differences in earned income between the three labor groups are much smaller in Bulgaria than they are in Greece . . . Second, the dispersion around the mean is much higher in Greece, which indicates more heterogeneity in incomes within this society. And finally . . . individual incomes in Bulgaria are supplemented more frequently with (the earnings of) other family members . . . In Greece, there are larger initial differences in work incomes between occupational groups, and they are reinforced in the distribution of family incomes. [Apel & Strumpel, 1976, pp. 173–4]

Urban-Rural Differentials and the Spectacular Rise in Rural Living Standards

A major element in this overall pattern of relative equality has been the reduction of large differences in standard of living between rural and urban residents. The ratio of rural to urban income was estimated at 77 percent for 1962 and had risen to 93 percent by 1970 (Apel, 1975, p. 6), even before the intensification of government efforts to stimulate production from personal plots discussed above in Chapter 4 (pp. 101–5). Apel notes that

incomes [of employed individuals in 1972–3] average slightly higher in Greece, but family incomes are markedly higher in Bulgaria due to the fact that the number of gainfully employed person per household is slightly over 2.0 for Bulgaria compared with only 1.3 for Greece. For the older people in Greece, as well as for those employed in agriculture, individual incomes are also strongly lagging. Most noteworthy in Bulgaria is the opposite trend along the occupational ladder and in regard to family income, where Bulgarian white-collar earners range behind the blue-collar workers, with agricultural families at the top. [Apel, 1975, p. 10]

As early as 1972 it appears that household living standards of rural residents are at least at the level of city dwellers. This is a reversal of a long established pattern of differentials, which has undoubtedly intensified since the early 1970s. There does not appear to have been a reverse migration back to the countryside by full-time residents, as may have occurred recently in Hungary (Brucan, 1983, p. 77), but it has made the life of those who have remained in agriculture, or have been recruited as technical specialists, much more pleasant and less cut-off from the developments elsewhere in society. According to Kiuranov (1975, p. 281) this equalization has been the result of an 'overt closing-of-the-gap policy [embodied in]: the Socioeconomic Plan of Bulgaria until 1980.' The foundations for this policy were laid in the 1956 decision to include rural residents on an equal basis in the social insurance system and by a succession of minimum-wage increases which have had a great effect in agriculture. Whatever the intrinsic status of agricultural work at the moment, it no longer brings assumptions of relative poverty and deprivation in Bulgaria:

family incomes exhibit a conspicuous stability across occupational groups, so that the family incomes of agricultural workers are even higher than those of the white-collar group, presumably because there are more workers in rural families. [Apel & Strumpel, 1976, p. 173]

Clearly these objective conditions are reflected in the way occupational groups assess their social status and sense of absolute and relative well being. While there are drastic interoccupational differences in the sense of well-being in Greece, they are almost entirely absent in Bulgaria. While the collectivization process in the Soviet Union resulted in bitterness and nearly permanent rural morale problems, the peasants and children of peasants who moved to the cities enjoyed a dramatic positive change in status, life style and material living conditions, which to this day remain a fundamental source of popular support for the existing system of government (Zaslavsky, 1982, pp. 136-9). In the absence of such a traumatic collectivization, equally rapid social change, urbanization and mobility have built powerful legitimacy and support for the Bulgarian party and government, exactly in parallel with objective developments. The rural sector has itself enjoyed such sharp and obvious increases in living standards that it cannot be viewed as an 'internal colony' as is sometimes suggested to be the case in societies with agriculture collectivized and centrally controlled. Bulgarian agricultural workers seem to be integrated into society and are positively affected by its changes, while showing none of the dissaffection or sense of being cut-off from progressive developments elsewhere in society found in Greece (Apel & Strumpel, 1976, p. 177).

Indeed, the living standards of the workers on the large state agricultural complexes have attracted the attention of many observers ranging from Western economists to the Soviet ambassador to Bulgaria. From very different perspectives Turgeon (1983, pp. 38-9) and Brucan (1983) both stress the sharply higher quality of rural housing (and apparent levels of wealth and well-being) in Bulgaria than in the much more widely discussed Hungarian countryside. As noted elsewhere, this inter-sector equality: (1) will show up in the form of proportionally (to the level of per capita income) less glittering cities with fewer of the luxury-goods emporiums that strike the tourist eye as signs of economic vitality; and (2) is visible only to those who look carefully and comparatively at rural living standards, away from tourist areas.

Aggregate Measures of Inequality

Income distribution statistics are available on a necessarily intermittent basis and are subject to great problems in data appraisal and summarization. It is none the less true that the available statistics for Bulgaria are relatively free of a number of potentially complicating factors and seem to provide a reasonably consistent view of Bulgaria as a country with an unusually compressed income distribution. Black-market or second economy earnings which loom very large in some other Eastern European economies and many market economies as well, are quite a small part of modern Bulgarian life and have little statistical effect. Part-time employment, which is another common source of statistical complications, is very limited in Bulgaria, because of the nearly universal, full-time labor-force participation of both adults in the household. One factor that cannot be dismissed so readily is the self-produced and consumed product of the personal plot. This category of goods production, which is of growing importance in Bulgaria, is fully counted nowhere in the world. One of the odd reasons for Western perceptions that the 'private agricultural sector' of socialist economies is highly productive (true) and efficient (not true, see pp. 106–8, above) is that these economies *collect* this information, albeit inevitably imperfectly. No one has a way of knowing what proportion of total US or UK tomato consumption is self-produced. This self-production and consumption is unlikely to be a source of overestimates of the degree of inter-sectoral equality in Bulgaria.

Interviews with managers and economists seem to confirm another aspect of the Bulgarian distributional pattern—a relatively high wage for manual workers compared to administrative-managerial employees (at all but the highest levels). Measures to reverse this profile by providing sharply higher 'incentives' for managerial staff are part of the 1986 reforms mentioned above in Chapter 4 (pp. 115–19). The series of increases in the minimum wage have partially served to offset modest inflation over the years, but have been rapid enough to raise the floor of the distribution significantly relative to both median and mean income. The higher minimum wage combined with rises in the relative wage levels in the entire state agricultural sector are likely to have decreased equality at the lower end of distribution by some additional amount beyond the figures presented below.

The best comparable income distribution figures that I have been able to find for Bulgaria were assembled by Wiles (family income) and Kiuranov (wages are shown in Table 5.1). The larger the value of the ratios at higher income levels (e.g., P5 and P10), the more concentrated is the income at the top; the smaller the values of the low income ratios (e.g., P90 and P95), the less the income going to the lower end of the distribution. The figures presented for Bulgaria are quite 'equal' by international standards.

Table 5.1 Income and wage equality in Bulgaria

Percentile†	Yearly income in 1965*		Monthly wages in 1968	
	Leva	Ratio‡	Leva	Ratio
P5	1,146	1.84	195	1.86
P10	1,000	1.61	169	1.61
P25	807	1.29	135	1.29
P50	624	1.00	105	1.00
P75	487	0.78	83	0.79
P90	362	0.58	68	0.65
P95	298	0.48	62	0.59

* Per capita family income.

† P5 is the 5th percentile from the top of the population as ranked by income. The average income of this group is 1,146 leva.

‡ The P5 'ratio' is the average income of P5 divided by the median income (1,146/624 − 1.84).

Sources: Wiles, 1975, p. 254 and Kiuranov, 1975, p. 278.

I agree with Wiles (1975, p. 253) and Michal (1975, pp. 259–62) that the commonly utilized Gini coefficient is not very useful for describing socialist income distributions (although it also shows Bulgaria to be at the most equal edge of the range of countries for which it has been calculated) and show instead the so-called decile ratio for several economies in Table 5.2.

Careful analysis of these two sets of figures provides subtle but definite support for the survey results of Apel & Strumpel. Although any individual might find themselves in quite different places in the two distributions in

Table 5.2 Decile ratios* (P90/P10) for selected countries and years

	Bulgaria	Hungary			Soviet Union		Sweden		United States	
	1963–65	1964	1967	1972	1966	1976	1971	1972	1968	1972
Family income	—	—	—	5.0	—	3.4	—	7.2	—	15.4
Family income per family member	2.7	3.0	3.0	—	3.5	—	3.5	—	6.7	—

* The decile ratio is the share of after tax income received by the top 10 percent of the population divided by the share received by the bottom 10 percent. The larger the ratio the greater the inequality of the distribution.

Sources: Wiles (1977), p. 443; Wiles (1974), pp. 20, 24, 48 and 118; Zimbalest & Sherman (1984), p. 461.

Table 5.2 (a high-salary single parent with many children, for example, or a low-salary person in a household with many working members), the overall degree of inequality scarcely changes. At first this is surprising, since as Michal (1975, p. 272) has pointed out, 'The more equalized the primary incomes, the stronger is the disequalizing effect of the varying ratio of earners to dependants within households on the distribution of household incomes.' The small difference between the distributions in Bulgaria is explained by the near universality of two earner households and apparent absence of correlation between the number of earners in a household and their average earnings. There is a double connection here to fertility, first with respect to demographic policy (discussed below, pp. 163–5), since such a high level of female labor-force participation, with predominantly a career orientation, almost automatically dictates a very low birth rate. The low fertility pattern of the Bulgarian population established in the pre-industrialization period (see pp. 20–8) reinforces this tendency. Second, the low overall birth rate with a clear prevalence of one- and two-child families means that the range of variation introduced into income-distribution figures by non-working household members is not very large.

Distribution and the 'Social Wage': Effects of Free and Subsidized Products on Inequality

Statistics on the distribution of money wages or incomes do not capture any of the distributional aspects of subsidized or socially provided goods and services. Prices of socially desirable or merit goods such as concert tickets, children's clothing and foodstuffs, books and school supplies are all very strongly subsidized from general revenues, altering the real buying power of the leva earnings of families that are more than proportionally inclined to buy those products (generally lower-income families and/or families with children). In some ultimate sense the costs are not avoided but shifted to other products, but that is only another way of restating the redistributional effects of the subsidy. The second category of goods is broad and difficult to quantify—goods provided on grounds of citizenship or membership in some age, professional or medical category, but with no money payment as a precondition to use. As Michal notes, distribution statistics 'fail to reflect the distribution of incomes in-kind, including rather important social services such as free medical service, free education, and special in-kind rewards for political, artistic, or sports achievement' (1975, p. 263).

The best we can do is note this problem and speculate on its effects.

Careful comparisons of budgetary allocations to various categories of state subsidies have been made by Pryor (1968), but this does not solve the underlying measurement problem. Efforts in popular and other sources to capture the real relative buying power of someone in Suffolk, Stuttgart, Seattle or Sofia by calculating how many minutes of work are required to pay for a particular item or service are misguided at best and in almost all cases systematically misleading. They imply that the citizens of very differently organized social and economic systems all buy, with cash out of their personal salaries, the same range of goods and services. The goods provided on an in-kind basis definitionally do not come out of the cash income of the individual. Comparing two societies where housing, medical care, education and provision of funds to support life after retirement are all social wage items in one and cash costs to the individual in the other makes utter nonsense of the question 'how many minutes work buys an egg, automobile, or sweater?' Such comparisons are never valid unless the societies compared are effectively identical in their distributional structure or 'geography'. Their unqualified use is evidence of either ignorance or intent to deceive.

Rapid Urbanization and Industrialization Bring Benefits and Problems

Bulgaria has undergone one of the most rapid and thoroughgoing processes of industry-driven urbanization in European experience. Urban growth has resulted principally from rural migration, which has led to a rapid decline in the rural population and sharp changes in all of its demographic parameters. To some degree, the 1959 regional administrative reform should be understood as a countermeasure to stem the flow of people out of the countryside, and the settlement acts and rural investment preferences of 1971, 1973 and after explicitly announce that intention. Both sets of measures are discussed in the next section.

The demographic effects of rapid migration to the cities can be seen most directly in the rising rural death rate and a rural birth rate decline so sharp as to reverse the historical differential and produce higher urban than rural crude birth rates. Both are simply results of the rapid aging of the rural population and are misleading as indicators of behavior per person at a specific age. Because there are very many old people in the rural population, even if their probability of dying at any given age does not rise, the death rate calculated for the entire rural population will rise as the proportion of the population in the highest risk categories increases. A rise in rural crude death rates (deaths per 1,000 of total rural population) suggests declining health-care standards in the countryside to the unwary, whereas Bulgaria has been the leading country in Southeastern Europe in raising the standards of health care for the rural population (Turgeon, 1983, p. 38). The so-called 'life expectancy at birth' figure (e_0), which is free of age-structural distortions, yields quite a different picture. Special programs have been established, including preferences for medical school applicants who agree to practice in rural areas, to raise health care standards in the countryside.

Similarly, the initially surprising drop in the rural birth rate below the urban birth rate in Bulgaria reverses one of the most common world-wide fertility differentials, but can easily be shown to be nothing more than the result of the predominance of young people in the urban population. Despite *higher* rural fertility rates at each given age, the urban birth rate per 1,000 population is higher because of the different age distribution within that population. (See McIntyre, 1972, pp. 187–96; 1980, pp. 158–68 and also above pp. 20–4, for a detailed discussion of the effects of these structural factors on apparent fertility differentials in Eastern Europe.)

The decline in the number of rural births, combined with the migration of large numbers of young rural residents has resulted in a rapid decline in the rural population. Table 5.3 traces population location and sectoral attach-ment from 1887 to 1985 and reveals the speed and extent of the transforma-tion. At first this was a policy goal (indeed a direct strategic element in the Soviet industrialization model that had been adopted) and was reinforced by a policy of maintaining rural wage levels well below urban rates. Eventually the rural exodus went so far as to cause alarm over farm-labor shortages and excessively rapid (and socially destructive) urban growth, leading to efforts to increase the attractiveness of rural life and create higher income professional and technical jobs in rural areas. The formation of the AICs should be viewed as in part a measure to industrialize and professionalize the skill requirements of the rural work-force and thereby change the demand side of the rural labor market. As noted above (pp. 141–3), rural incomes have now risen to the urban levels (and perhaps higher), but the population drain continues, largely because of the 'place preference' of rural youth.

A detailed study of 10,000 rural youth conducted in 1967 and published in 1973 showed that only one-third clearly intended to remain in the countryside. Despite the age of this study it is useful in revealing a level of attraction to urban life that appears to have endured (Taaffe, 1977, pp. 161–2; Semov, 1973, pp. 116–19). According to Taaffe (1977, p. 163),

a large share of the young rural population of Bulgaria perceives the place utility of cities to be considerably greater than that of villages because of a variety of

Table 5.3 Urbanization and industrialization, 1887–1985

Year	Population (1,000)			Economically active population (%)		
	Total	Urban	% urban	Agriculture and forestry	Industry	Other
1887	3,154	593	18.8	–	–	–
1900	3,744	742	19.8	–	–	–
1920	4,847	966	19.9	82.4	7.9	9.7
1934	6,078	1,303	21.4	79.8	7.7	12.5
1948	7,162	1,888	26.4	82.1	7.9	10.0
1956	7,614	2,556	33.6	70.5	12.9	16.6
1960	7,906	3,005	38.0	55.5	21.9	22.6
1965	8,228	3,823	46.5	45.3	26.3	28.4
1970	8,490	4,442	52.3	35.7	30.4	33.9
1975	8,728	5,061	58.0	28.2	33.5	38.3
1980	8,862	5,507	62.1	24.2	35.2	40.6
1985	8,943	5,795	64.8	20.9	37.2	41.9

Sources: *Statisticheski Godishnik 1985*, pp. 27, 31, 104; *1975*, p. 84; *Statisticheski Spravochnik 1986*, pp. 36–7, 179, 182–3; Mitchell, 1975, p. 162.

economic, social, and cultural differences; and, as long as these attitudes persist, planning efforts to reduce the outflow of young villagers will be difficult to implement.

A significant set of regional development and settlement policies were introduced in the early 1970s and involved efforts to direct new investment away from the provincial capitals and into the central villages in the more remote countryside. The quality of life in the countryside has been very greatly affected by the broad range of direct and indirect programs undertaken since 1959, but the outflow has remained at a level sufficient to make the agricultural labor shortage a continuing object of policy concern (Carter & Zagar, 1977, pp. 219–23; Taaffe, 1977, pp. 168–70, 176–7). Net migration from countryside to the cities has steadily constituted an unusually high proportion (more than half) of the total annual migratory movement in Bulgaria (Taaffe, 1977, pp. 158–60).

1959 Territorial Reorganization and the Quality of Rural Life

An important factor in raising the quality of life in rural areas and small towns and in slowing the rate of migration to the large cities has come as a possibly unintended result of the major territorial reorganization implemented in 1959 and slightly modified in 1964. District and regional boundaries have been changed many times in the century of Bulgarian independence; however, the 1959 reform was fundamentally different. It occurred as part of a coordinated package of measures designed to decentralize economic management and make the local government units the locus of first line economic coordination and management. The result was the creation of an entire new level of employment, with supporting cultural and social services in the newly designated provincial capitals. A decade later the reorganization of the agricultural sector into the large AIC units had a similar effect on those villages and very small towns that became AIC administrative centers.

According to Poulsen (1976), the province level of administration dating from 1934 was eliminated in the 1947 Constitution and all ninety-five rural and seven urban districts (*okolii*) were administered directly from the center. In 1949 a province level was re-established in the form of fifteen *okruzi*. The roughly 2,000 rural communes (*obshtini*) had an unbroken administrative existence during this period. As early as 1956 a serious study of the possible advantages of a redesigned regional structure was undertaken. After the adoption of the regional economic councils (*sovnarkhozy*) reform in 1957 in the Soviet Union, Bulgarian plans turned in a similar decentralization direction. When the territorial reform of 1959 emerged it was described as being principally a measure to rationalize economic administration. The forces set in motion by the creation of a new set of thirty provincial capitals with wide authority in economic and social administration was part of a coordinated plan which moved up to 2,000 ministerial employees out of Sofia, eliminated the district level of administration and consolidated the 1,930 communes into 867 to make them match single farm units. When the Bulgarian economic reforms were reversed and the ministries reconstituted (following the removal of Khrushchev from power and the abandonment of the *sovnarkhozy* in the Soviet Union), the thirty-unit provincial network remained in place and retained many of its functions. Poulsen (1976, p. 199) observes that

The provinces proved to be a suitable framework for the provision of services, the running of local industry, and the direction of agricultural production. However, the provinces proved not to be satisfactory vehicles for planning and managing industry, and they were replaced by a nonterritorial decentralization in the form of the 'economic association.'

The transition after 1964, from first-line coordination by the regional economic councils to ministries dealing with the large new economic associations (DSO), set the framework for the next two decades of development in the industrial sector. In agriculture, however, the AIC development after 1970 embodied the considerable degree of local autonomy that had been created in the 1959 reforms, but in a slightly different form. It is interesting to note that some characteristic features of the contemporary AIC system, such as an emphasis on regional autonomy in the production of primary food stuffs, had already emerged as goals under the 1959 reforms. By the mid-1970s the so-called central villages of the AICs were 'often indistinguishable from small towns as far as general development and amenities are concerned' (Taaffe, 1977, p. 169).

Reorganization to Nine Large Provinces in 1987

In many respects the 1959 reorganization was successful, creating such strong economic expansion in the new provincial capitals that the central villages program had to be established to prevent excessive depopulation of all the surrounding countryside. By the early 1980s Bulgarian geographers were arguing for a further realignment of boundaries to conform more completely with natural economic regions and political analysts were arguing that if the municipal governments were to receive additional powers of self-government they would have to be insulated from province level control. The new system of nine provinces, proposed and approved in August 1987 to take effect on 1 January 1988, has both aspects of centralization and decentralization when seen from the point of view of the local level. Obviously fewer provinces make the system more centralized if no other changes occur, and this aspect has been noted by some as evidence of failure of the 1959 reform (*RFER*, Bulgarian Situation Report/8, 18 September 1987, pp. 3-14). On the other hand, the measures to increase local level autonomy would, if in fact implemented, reduce the role of province level administration in local economic and social management. It should also be noted that the demoted province capitals are now strongly established economic centers unlikely to wither as the result of this change. In four of the eight relevant cases (the Sofia-city 'province' remains unchanged) the newly selected province capitals are surprising choices over major cities within the new regions (Razgrad over Ruse, Lovech over both Pleven and Veliko Turnovo, Haskovo over Stara Zagora, and the expansion of the Sofia region, which surrounds the separate Sofia-city, to include the cities of Pernik, Kystendil and Blagoevgrad). This may in all but the last case be a new effort to stimulate development in relatively weak areas. Cities like Ruse and Pleven will obviously prosper in any case. The new province boundaries systematically combine relatively weak and relatively strong economic districts. This reorganization also has the effect of reducing the weight of the population groups that were the objects of the 1985–6 name-changing campaign (discussed above, pp. 72–5) within any given district.

In addition to the various positive incentives to encourage people to stay in rural areas, in 1966 Bulgaria introduced restrictions on migration to the several most densely populated cities (Carter & Zagar, 1977, p. 216; Taaffe, 1977, p. 169). These restrictions are similar to those covering the largest Soviet cities. Since the largest cities all have labor shortages, the requirement that a person desiring to move to one of these cities show proof of employment is a small impediment. One result is that roughly one-eighth of the population of Sofia live there with only temporary permits which are periodically renewed (Taaffe, 1977, p. 170). A similar phenomenon has developed in the Soviet Union where such workers are known as *shabashniki* (Murphy, 1985, pp. 48–57).

Regional, Cultural and Artistic Diversity

In several respects Bulgaria presents a more varied and diverse society than would be expected on the basis of its foreign reputation, similarities to Soviet society, and small physical size. The regional decentralization of 1959 clearly had important and subtle effects on social development all across the country. The different approaches and styles of redevelopment programs has been mentioned above. The use of development advisory services on a contractual basis (also cited above) is evidence of the extent of real ability of local government to influence the details of construction and development efforts.

Mention has also been made of the relatively progressive policy toward new and experimental forms of expression in the fine arts and, to a lesser extent, literature. Especially during the period of leadership of Ludmilla Zhivkova, but continuing to the present, there is a fairly wide variety of artistic work seen in state-sponsored galleries and expositions, which often deals with the darker and more pessimistic sides of human existence. The degree of emphasis on positive (inspirational and hortatory) styles and themes is low, except for monumental art. The evocative power of the monumental sculpture at the newly restored Veliko Turnovo have been widely praised by Western critics. These are aspects of a relatively open and accommodating cultural policy for most of the last two decades.

Housing and the Quality of Life

Housing is a perennial problem area in modern Bulgarian urban life. After falling 57,000 units short of the planned total of 400,000 new apartments to be constructed during the 1980–5 plan period, the target for the 9th Five Year Plan (1986–90) was cut back to 360,000. Of this total 100,000 are scheduled to be built in Sofia, which may be compared with a waiting list of 80,000 at the beginning of the period. While the number of units completed has regularly lagged behind plans, the size of units built has risen significantly and as a result the housing space per person has jumped from 13.3 sq.m. in 1975 to 16.6 sq.m. in 1985. Although Bulgarian housing problems are severe in both quantitative and qualitative dimensions, the situation suggested to be typical of all Eastern European countries in one recent study, where 'unrelated families often share kitchen and bathroom facilities; [and] large numbers of people live for years in hotels or dormitories' (*RFER*, vol. 11, no. 25, part I, 20 June 1986, p. 3), are unheard of. The modest gap between total households and total housing units in urban areas is fully explained by two generations of the same family sharing an apartment.

Contrary to the assumptions of even frequent visitors, Bulgaria (like Hungary and Poland) has a population which mostly lives in privately owned apartments or houses.

The private ownership over the residences is the prevailing form in Bulgaria. Every citizen is entitled to a private residence in order to provide for personal and family dwelling necessities. It is not allowed to use the personal residence for collecting unearned revenues.

The private sector building construction in the country is not restricted and is even stimulated, when it is made to satisfy personal residential necessities. [Ministry of Construction and Architecture, 1982, pp. 30, 56]

As of 1975, 88.5 percent of the existing housing stock was privately owned and nineteen of twenty units were owner occupied (ibid., p. 31). The state originally set 1990 as the date for achieving the dual goals of each family having its own residence and each family member their own bedroom, but in light of the underfulfillment of the housing target for each of the last two

Five Year Plans further delay is likely. Private construction of housing for both year-round and summer (dacha) use is large scale and (especially in rural areas) dominated by three story houses of large size and good quality. State produced cooperative apartments (for example, of 70 sq.m. floor space, excluding hallways, toilet and bath) sell for 10,000 to 20,000 leva, as compared to an average household income of 6,000 leva per year in 1980. Loans are available for up to 12,000 leva, payable over thirty years at 2 percent interest (ibid., pp. 32-9).

The design and construction standards for most modern Bulgarian apartment developments are quite awful, but efforts to mix styles and heights of building have increased and measures to raise construction quality, in part by involving the new apartment owners in the finishing work, have been taken. The situation is by far the worst in Sofia, with much higher design standards evident in the new areas of Varna, Plovdiv, Tolbukhin, Ruse and other cities. The new Prime Minister Georgi Atanasov made an extraordinarily harsh attack on the performance of capital area housing construction groups.

The time has come to tell the whole truth about the architectural policies followed in Sofia—there have been unforgivable decisions that will have future consequences for the new housing estates. The appalling decisions have no equivalent anywhere in the country. [*RFER*, vol. 11, no. 25, part 1, 20 June 1986, p. 7]

Construction and design standards have improved and apartment size has definitely increased, but the barren and sometimes squalid atmosphere of the new housing blocks is one of the least attractive features of contemporary Bulgarian life. The problem of care for public areas has been emphasized elsewhere. A tendency to plant masses of new trees after totally clearing the site does lead (despite poor care) to relatively rapid and comprehensive reforestation.

Some innovative regional development and restoration efforts appear to derive directly from the 1959 reforms, partly explaining the surprisingly sophisticated and well-constructed character of the redevelopment work done in a number of remote towns such as Sandanski and Vidin. Some towns have even created independent labor market and educational policies, offering from their own resources educational and housing assistance to young people who will agree to return and reside in the town after their training. These policies were sufficiently effective in several of these towns to have produced an inverted age-structure, with a heavy preponderance of young adults.

Bulgaria has a comprehensive *Unified Plan for the Long-Term Development of Settlements* which serves more as a statement of intentions than a detailed guide to specific project design. Some elements of this policy have been put into effect and have had some influence in directing and civilizing the development process. Some success in slowing the growth of the urban population after 1975 is claimed for these measures, especially those aiming at raising the convenience and amenity level of life in the small towns and villages. The relatively good record of Bulgaria in health-care provision in rural areas is part of this central village strategy. The decisions to avoid building parking facilities in central city areas, develop electric bus systems for all towns of 80,000 or more, comprehensively electrify the Sofia transportation system (including a new wide tram and a metro system), and encourage concentration of private house construction on waste agricultural land or in already established villages, have all been put into effect to some considerable degree. It is useful to discuss the last example in some detail for the light it throws on Bulgarian property relationships.

Both land and buildings can be personal property in the fullest sense of the words. Apartments are generally built by the local People's Council for rental and (mostly) sale to individual owners. A priority list is established which takes account of age, number of children, and waiting time. Owners of buildings razed to make way for the project are compensated at an appraised and non-trivial rate and put at the top of the list for the new building on the same site. Efforts have been made since 1978 to provide preferential access to apartment for newly married couples as an encouragement to fertility, but press criticism suggests that the People's Councils have often ignored this priority. As of 1983 socialist enterprises have been invited to construct housing for their employees with their own resources, but the extent of this activity (which is substantial in a number of other countries) is unknown.

Land for private construction may be purchased from existing private owners or from local People's Council at a rate which varies directly with settlement size (1 to 10 leva per sq.m. for residential construction, 0.8 to 2 leva per sq.m. for recreation and summer-house construction, plus a tax of from 5 to 29 leva per sq.m. of floorspace of the former and 2 to 3 leva for the latter type building). The seller must pay the state a prohibitively high fee of from 100,000 to 400,000 leva per hectare (2.471 acres) if agriculturally useful land is appropriated for housing use (Ministry of Construction and Architecture, 1982, pp. 13–15, 25–6). Building is encouraged on sloping surfaces of low agricultural value. This policy is undoubtedly violated, but it has none the less had some effect on development patterns.

Each party conference is marked by some special new construction projects, almost always involving upgrading of the main shopping-walking streets in the center of the capital. For the XIII Congress in 1986 a new set of ring boulevards, rapid subway progress and a comprehensive reworking of the Vitosha Boulevard shopping area (which links the Ludmilla Zhivkova cultural center with the central department store (TsUM)), were completed. The results included the creation of a new walking street with tram lines running up the center, ornamented with street fixtures (lamps, benches, sign boards) and new shops at a markedly higher technical and artistic level than has been seen before in Bulgaria, outside luxury hotel developments. Mention of these hotels brings to mind another interesting social policy feature in Bulgaria. Luxury hotels, which are constructed by foreign contractors with a primary goal of attracting convertible currency customers, are open to Bulgarians paying in leva at prices roughly a third those charged foreigners. While these are still very high leva prices, the fact of the availability of these services is attractive. Expectations may rise more rapidly yet, but it is obvious to any experienced visitor to Bulgaria that popular access has been created to a whole new set of products, services and experiences— some approaching advanced northern European standards and others markedly improved over previously available alternatives.

Energy and Energy Policy

The traumatic winter of 1984–5 seems to have produced serious Bulgarian attention to energy conservation, whatever the relative importance of the contributory factors. Power cut-backs in the form of total blackouts for several hours in alternating subregions and strict policing of rules against utilization of electric space heaters during peak demand hours, were used. Some of the difficulty in dealing with the winter undoubtedly were the result of bad management, but the intense and sustained cold was unprecedented and came at a time when hydropower was not available to deal with peak loads. Substantial damage was done to combustion equipment in power plant as a result of extensive use of low-quality coal. Problems were compounded by the development during 1985 of the most severe and sustained drought in decades which brought the hydropower contribution (a maximum of 20 percent of capacity and roughly 10 percent of actual power generation under normal conditions) to essentially zero. The water level of the Danube at Ruse reached the lowest level ever measured on 20 October 1985 (*FBIS*, vol. 11, no. 215, 6 November 1985, p. C9).

The equipment damage during the previous winter combined with the loss of hydropower led to a very early and intensive program of preparation for the winter of 1985-6. During the summer and early fall, systematic power shut-downs were carried out with the announced purpose of allowing full repair and reconditioning of damaged units (*FBIS*, vol. 11, no. 172, 4 September 1985, pp. C4-8). Possible alternative or supplementary explanations include the desire to save fuel for the coming winter, the need to repair damage done by terrorist bombings (a totally speculative suggestion from *RFER*, Bulgarian Situation Report/10, 2 September 1985, p. 12), and the wish to make unmistakably clear to the populace that this time there would be more than just talk of energy-saving.

If the new energy realities were still not fully clear, the drastic and dramatic price changes of 15 September 1985 settled the matter. Along with the other price changes (discussed above in Chapter 4, pp. 132-3), electric power charges were raised 41 percent for household and 58 percent for enterprises, drinking water (which for households is in part use of thermal energy) rose by 67 percent for households and 364 percent for enterprises, gasoline and diesel fuel rose by 35 percent, while the price of centrally supplied thermal services (which are very thermally efficient even after transmission losses) remained unchanged (*FBIS*, vol. 11, no. 179, 16 September 1985, pp. C1-2). Foreign press reports have sometimes made these measures appear even more dramatic than they are, but they do seem to reflect an unmistakable rise in serious attention to energy issues by both party and government officials. Despite the commissioning of the new 1,000 MW reactor at Kozloduy, plans for energy rationing were announced in advance of the winter of 1987-8, indicating that the energy imbalances remain an unresolved problem (*RFER*, SR/11, 20 November 1987, pp. 3-5).

Some Western analysts question whether changes in input prices, as represented by the energy and water price rises mentioned above, have significant effects on actual enterprise behavior as long as the overall structure of central planning remains intact. They point to the implications of what Kornai (1959, 1981, 1987) called the soft budget constraint and in effect suggest that it is infinitely soft. As long as the enterprise meets its physical output targets it will be protected against failure to honor any less important targets by transfers from the central budget. This relationship is illustrated by the complaint of the BCP daily *Rabotnichesko Delo* that

Economic principles and mechanisms have still not been introduced because everything wasted is at the expense of the state and the population. Many of the sanctions are symbolic and are being paid for by the budget of the organization. [*FBIS*, vol. 11, no. 172, 4 September 1985, p. C9]

It is, however, obvious that money magnitudes do have some independent effect on the behavior of managers in the Bulgarian (and other) system, even before the reforms that have raised the significance of net earnings or profit measures in determining managerial rewards. Price rises of this large a magnitude are bound to have some independent effect on enterprise behavior.

Three areas where Bulgarian environmental and energy performance have been good are in the planning and construction of the urban transportation system, in development of a relatively sophisticated *structure* of electricity pricing (despite very low levels for these prices prior to the fall of 1985), and in the utilization of cogeneration and central district heating.

Public Transportation and Social Policy

The public transportation systems of Sofia and the other large Bulgarian cities are an interesting mixture of advanced and backward elements. Despite the growing role of privately owned automobiles (and the construction of a large and generally well engineered highway network in part to accommodate them), the public bus and tram system have been upgraded and reorganized, and in Sofia are about to be augmented by a subway. Surface transportation is divided among self-powered buses, electric buses and trams (light rail vehicles), and the system reflects in that order a rapidly decreasing technical level. The bus system is predominantly made up of the world-class Hungarian Icarus Z80 articulated, diesel powered unit of the current model and in reasonable repair. They are fast, high-capacity, efficient vehicles which make a strong impression singly or in armada force. The fleet of hundreds of diesel buses has unpleasant effects on air quality, though not when compared to the number of private cars required to replace them. The electric bus network, potentially the optimal form of urban rail-less surface transit, is made up of quite old but serviceable Skoda units, augmented by a small force of used articulated buses from Vienna. Beginning in 1985, the first of up to 900 Icarus-Ganz electric articulated buses have been put into service, and a new Chavdar-Skoda single electric bus appeared, presumably to replace the older units and carry this part of the system to the technical level of the diesel bus component.

The tram system is extensive and very efficient, but depends on clumsy, noisy and poorly finished articulated units manufactured in Sofia. The network is in the process of simplification and road-bed-track improvement (precast road-bed units, rubber rail-bed and welded continuous rails), but will retain a Third World atmosphere until the rolling stock is replaced.

The subway system is being constructed in a deliberate but apparently carefully planned fashion. Entrances have already been built into new construction projects (and also in areas where construction of new residential estates has not yet begun) along its future route. It will be a relatively extensive system, but will have only two crossing lines with no interconnections away from the center. Soviet subway cars, which are of good mechanical quality and finish and are used in the impressive systems of Prague and Budapest as well as Soviet cities, will be used in Sofia.

It may be a decade before the central core of the city is served, but already in 1986 some sections of the system running out of the city to the south were finished. Archeological discoveries have slowed some of the work in the center of the city, but completion of at least some sections of the line running to the new housing district of Lylin is expected by 1990, with hopes of completing the entire sector by 1992 (Stanev, 1986). The track, road-bed work, and rolling stock for the metro are far above the level of the existing (narrow gauge) tram system, which itself is to be replaced by a new standard railroad gauge system, using a new generation of Bulgarian produced trams. The first section of this new 'broad tram' system was constructed at high speed in 1986 and entered service in the eastern sector of the city in 1987, thus explaining the mystery of near abandonment of maintenance work on some sectors of the old tram system.

Peak-load Pricing of Electricity

Peak-load pricing is extensively applied in Bulgaria for both residential and business users of electricity. Bulgaria produces an electric meter which computes electricity usage separately for peak (normal daytime and early evening) and off-peak (22:00–6:00) periods, which are then charged sharply different rates per kilowat-hour (0.04 vs. 0.02 leva per kWh). As of 1 December 1985 there is a penalty rate of 0.04 for consumption beyond a certain number of kWh per month (this is what is called a 'life-line' rate structure elsewhere), with a 10 percent reduction per kWh under that use level (*Rabotnichesko Delo*, 27 November 1985, p. 2). This is a form of marginal cost pricing which is very popular with Western microeconomists, but is thus far not widely adopted in the West. French application of peak-load pricing (only for large industrial customers) has received much favorable attention.

The short-run marginal costs (the operating expenses of the least efficient existing generators which are used to cover the peak) and long-run marginal costs (which take account of the need to build new capacity to be able to cover a growth of the height of the peak through time) of electricity use are actually different at different times of day, so peak-load pricing is a large step in the direction of a rational energy-pricing system. Bulgaria moved in this direction quite early and systematically so by now more than half of the urban population is billed on this dual-rate basis. A domestic heating technology has been produced to match this rate (and true social cost) structure, in the form of electric 'accumulator heaters' which charge during the off-peak hours and heat by distribution of the stored heat during the peak hours. This is a rational reaction to a relatively pronounced peak in the use profile and is perhaps the only thermodynamically defensible use of electric heating.

It should be stressed that the above-mentioned advanced developments in the *relative* pricing of electricity coexisted with an extraordinarily low *level* of these rates until September of 1985. The correct relative price signals may have been little noticed because both peak and off-peak charges were so low. This price level point is consistent with the other evidence that Bulgaria did not react strongly to the changed world energy situation until very late.

Cogeneration and Central District Heating

Cogeneration and central district heating are separate effective methods of energy conservation which can be combined to very favorable effect. Cogeneration is the utilization of the waste heat from one process for some other purpose. Central district heating involves the provision of thermal energy for space heating and hot water to a large and presumably densely populated area from a central boiler or other source. The particular technology adopted in Bulgaria involves the use of low pressure steam ('rejected' after use in its high pressure form to turn an electric turbine) to supply thermal energy to a central district heating system.

For a discussion of the related economic and technical aspects of these issues, and arguments that centrally planned Soviet economies are especially inclined to avail themselves of these energy economies, see McIntyre & Thornton (1978a, pp. 177–8; 189–90; 1978b), and in greater detail for the Soviet Union, Campbell (1980, pp. 79–84). This combination has been pursued with particular consistency by the Soviet Union since the early 1920s and has been adopted by most Eastern European countries since World War II. Bulgaria has adopted both methods and used them separately and in combination. Most low quality coal, except for what is burned at remote 'mouth of the mine' power stations, is burned in urban cogeneration facilities that feed the waste heat into central district heating systems. This is a relatively satisfactory way to burn low quality fuel, especially if the real alternative is decentralized combustion of the same fuel. Since the systems are most easily installed in advance of or at the same time as construction of development areas, they were initially confined to new construction, but in recent years have been methodically extended into the areas of low rise, middle-aged apartment buildings that make up the core of Sofia and several other large cities.

Women and the State

Bulgaria has achieved a rate of progress in integrating women into social, political and especially economic life that is very good but far from perfect. Contradictions or at least unresolved tensions exist between the official programs to achieve more complete participation by women in public sphere activities and the countervailing measures to raise the birth rate by a complex set of demographic policies. The Politburo decision of 6 March 1973 (adopted as a decision of the State Council on 26 July 1974) on 'Enhancing the Role of Women in the Building of a Developed Socialist Society' clearly reveals these tensions. After noting the lavish care for the well-being of women provided by the state and claiming great success in integrating women into economic life, it notes that the birth rate is too low and calls for a set of measures including earlier marriage, larger families, more comprehensive participation of women in high status economic and political positions (according to *Statisticheski Spravochnik 1986*, p. 48, in 1985, 76.5 percent of economists, but only 14.2 percent of enterprise managers and deputy managers were women), social provision of cooking and cleaning services, reallocation of tasks within the household, longer and more generous leave, birth bonus and family allowance payments, and special assistance for unmarried or student mothers. This list of laudable but sometimes mutually contradictory measures are presented as all being simultaneously achievable.

Efforts to raise fertility immediately call into question the sincerity of any government's commitment to sexual equality. Even in a hypothetical world where housework and household responsibility are equally shared, and where commercial and childcare support services are highly developed, fertility still imposes greater losses in time, career advancement and personal autonomy on the mother (McIntyre, 1985, pp. 270–85). Bulgaria has not reached the childcare and service development levels of the GDR, for example, but it has obviously gone far in creating the cultural conditions where women take their own worklife and career path as being a central

Table 5.4 Women workers in selected occupations, 1970–85

	Women as a percentage of all workers				Number in 1985	
	1970	1975	1980	1985	Total	Women
Total	43.3	46.5	47.1	48.1	4,105,888	1,976,045
Managers of production and other enterprises and their deputies	14.9	19.4	22.2	24.7	39,103	9,646
Division manager and their deputies	15.8	23.6	28.0	33.3	47,870	15,926
Manager of production units	11.3	14.9	14.1	15.3	42,128	6,440
Heads of shifts, masters, brigade leaders and others	9.7	11.3	10.0	11.6	13,708	1,592
Main specialists	11.6	23.6	22.1	28.8	18,901	5,451
Specialist engineers and architects	28.6	38.1	35.3	35.2	16,914	5,952
Chemists, physicists, mathematicians, geographers and historians	67.5	75.0	71.5	75.5	5,378	4,061
Crop and forestry specialist	44.2	45.1	43.2	45.8	5,552	2,543
Animal and veterinary specialists	29.5	35.1	38.8	38.7	5,366	2,074
Specialist economists and planners	62.7	75.8	71.3	76.5	29,917	22,874
Accountants, auditors and others	71.6	79.7	79.5	85.1	89,794	76,427
All others (calculated as a residual)	–	–	–	48.0	3,791,257	1,823,059

Source: Calculated from *Statisticheski Spravochnik 1986*, pp. 46–8.

aspect of their life. Once this happens, whether in the East or West, the number of children found to be appropriate moves quickly to the level of two or less on the average.

Bulgaria has done better on the employment side of the socialist commitment to full citizenship for women than might be expected from its development level. According to one study cited by Leonard (1983, p. 691),

If modern nations are ranked according to the proportion of women—or men—who would have to change their occupation or industrial classification for there to be gender equality in jobs, then as of 1976, there is less sexual discrimination in Bulgaria than in any other country in the world.

This may be too strong a claim, but it is suggestive of the high degree of female integration into the permanent labor force, and hence the difficult task of population policy in convincing women to choose to have additional births.

Bulgaria adopted a relatively unrestricted abortion-on-demand system in 1956, shortly after the restoration of the unconditional 1920 abortion law as part of the de-Stalinization drive in the Soviet Union. Beginning with very low aggregate fertility levels and experiencing further declines in the years after 1956, Bulgaria has adopted two moderate restrictions of abortion availability (David & McIntyre, 1981, pp. 291–4), but has not acted to discourage use of contraception and has largely relied on positive incentives in the form of family allowance, birth bonus, paid post-maternity leave, and special loan and housing programs to attempt to make somewhat larger families desirable to Bulgarian couples (McIntyre, 1975, pp. 366–80 and David & McIntyre, 1981, pp. 294–6). As has already been pointed out in the case of Hungary (Coelen & McIntyre, 1978, pp. 1077–1102), these payment programs must be steadily increased (to offset the effects of rising real wages and some inflation on their real power) if they are to be effective. Table 5.6 shows that Bulgaria has raised payment levels only rarely (most family allowance and birth bonus payments remained unchanged in leva amounts from 1974 to 1985), so the lack of success of Bulgarian pronatalist policy is not surprising. In the midst of considerable discussion of the 'demographic crisis,' some new pronatalist measures were introduced in mid-1985.

While the family allowance and other direct financial support programs are not as powerful as in Hungary or the GDR, the various paid, partially paid and unpaid (with re-employment guaranteed) leave arrangements in Bulgaria are both generous by world standards and typical of Eastern European countries in most respects (McIntyre, 1975, 1985, Stefanov &

Table 5.5 Women workers by industrial branch, 1970–85

	Women as a percentage of all workers			
	1970	1975	1980	1985
Total	43.3	46.5	47.1	48.1
Material production sphere				
Industry	44.7	47.8	47.6	48.1
Construction	13.9	17.1	17.8	18.6
Agriculture	49.8	46.9	45.3	45.2
Forestry	54.2	47.8	44.1	42.6
Transportation	15.1	17.0	17.3	19.6
Communications	52.0	56.3	59.1	61.7
Distribution, material-technical supply and procurement	53.6	59.2	62.7	64.1
Other branches of material production	36.8	42.5	49.9	50.8
Non-productive (service and administrative) sphere				
Housing and communal economy	45.3	51.3	48.3	48.9
Science and science services	47.4	52.3	50.3	53.1
Education	68.9	72.0	74.3	75.4
Culture and the arts	47.0	53.2	54.4	55.5
Public health, social insurance, physical culture, sports and tourism	72.3	72.6	74.3	73.6
Finance, credit and insurance	65.3	73.2	77.8	79.9
Administration	39.3	42.7	49.4	54.1
Other non-productive branches	32.3	40.8	44.0	54.3

Source: Statisticheski Spravochnik 1986, pp. 44–5.

Naoumov, 1974; Berent, 1970). Bulgaria has been a leader in extending the childcare leave provisions to fathers and employed grandparents, although the extent to which these new leaves are taken by men is not known. The various leave arrangements are complex, with specially advantageous arrangements for women who are unmarried, students, or whose spouses are in the military. Until 1985 a women giving birth to a second child had forty-

Table 5.6 Marginal monthly family allowance and birth
payments: 1960–86 (leva)

	Birth order					
	1	2	3	4	5	6
Family allowances						
1960–1967	—	13	13	13	10	5
1968*–1973	5	15	35	5	5	5
1974–1985	15	25	45	15	15	15
1986 and after	15	30†	55	15	15	15
Birth payment						
1960–1967						
1968–1972	20	200	500	20	20	20
1973–1974	100	250	500	20	20	20
1975 and after	100	250	500	100	100	100

 * Prior to January 1, 1969, there was a maximum yearly income criteria
for receipt of family allowances.
  † At the time of the second birth the payment for the first birth is also
raised to 30, so the marginal payment for a second birth appears to be
30 + 15.
  Sources: McIntyre, 1975, p. 369; David & McIntyre, 1980, p. 295; Bell,
1985, p. 268; Vassilev, 1986.

five days of prematernity leave, five months of fully paid maternity leave,
seven additional months at the established minimum wage, and the right to
further unpaid leave. There are strong re-employment guarantees as well as
arrangements to provide full credit toward retirement for time spent on
maternity related leave. As of 1 July 1985, the fully paid leave was extended to
two years for first, second and third births (ten months for higher-order
births), with the pre-maternity, partially paid and unpaid leave remaining the
same (Vassilev, 1986). This is an extraordinarily strong program (especially
for first births), even by Eastern European standards. Additional measures
include provision of low interest loans to assist in setting up a household,
with provision for cancellation of part of the principal when children are
born, attempts to reserve a quarter of annual housing construction for newly
married and three-child families, higher taxes for childless couples and a new
family code which makes divorce somewhat more difficult (Bell, 1985,
p. 268).

Violence Against Women and Modern Bulgarian Culture

An often ignored aspect of the quality of life in modern society is the degree of danger, and hence restricted freedom, felt by women because of rape or harassment. Bulgarian cities are safe for solitary pedestrians and violence directed at women is at a level so low as not to inhibit free circulation at all hours. Residential neighborhoods are very poorly lighted and there is literally no police presence in these areas, so the explanation must be sought elsewhere. This pattern seems to hold in most of the European socialist countries with very different styles of maintaining public security. There is a total absence of pornographic materials and no heavy emphasis on sexuality in motion pictures, advertisements or television in Bulgaria, although there is some considerable emphasis on the beauty of the female form in both serious and popular art. Such explanations are too easy and can be undercut by carefully selected two country comparisons, but there remains the systematic difference in sexual vulnerability to be explained. This is an important but generally overlooked positive quality-of-life feature of Eastern European societies.

The relatively good Bulgarian performance in the treatment of women is more impressive because it has occurred in a society powerfully shaped by nearly 500 years of Moslem cultural and governmental dominance, with a resulting lack of a tradition of educating women for social and economic activity outside the household. The process of integrating women into the broader spheres of social life began in the nineteenth century but sharply intensified after 1944. Although there have been individual women in high leadership positions, in particular Tsola Dragoycheva and Ludmilla Zhivkova, female participation in high political and economic leadership positions remains quite small. As elsewhere in Eastern Europe the level of participation by women in political life is higher in regional, local and district government and party bodies. Leadership at these levels is generally younger, so some change at higher levels may occur over time.

6 Summing Up: Is There a Bulgarian Economic–Political Model?

Bulgarian development after World War II has interesting and valuable comparative economic, political and social aspects, none of which can be understood apart from the role and policy of the Bulgarian Communist Party (BCP). The period of the leadership of First Secretary Todor Zhivkov covers more than two decades, but Bulgarian political life has not been intensely focused on his personality. He is a relatively humble man with a self-effacing sense of humor and, despite occasional suggestions to the contrary (*New York Times* (TWIR), 21 July 1985, p. 5), there is no personality cult in any historically meaningful sense of the word. Compared to earlier periods in a number of countries and present circumstances in Romania (Shafir, 1985; Tismaneanu, 1985), the Zhivkov persona is seen in very low profile and intensity.

The name of the First Party Secretary makes a *pro forma* appearance under sections of party and government policy decisions on billboards and displays, and his formal role in meeting and greeting foreign visitors is steadily reported, but there has been no effort to make him into a larger-than-life figure or claim significance on the world scale for his thoughts and actions. As suggested in Chapters 1 and 3, he appears to be the representative of government-by-committee rather than a supremely powerful leader in his own right. The BCP is a proud, tightly disciplined organization, but little is known about its internal realities as distinct from its visible structure. Zhivkov has superintended a government that has consistently promoted and brought to positions of power and high visibility relatively young technicians and administrative specialists. The most recent evidence of this personnel pattern is the joint promotion of Chudomir Alexandrov, Ognyan Doynov, Georgi Atanasov and Stoyan Markov to leading economic policy and management positions in early 1986. The Bulgarian government has also been willing to experiment with a considerable range of organizational changes in both governmental and economic structure. The regional reorganizations (1959 and 1987), the Small-Scale Agriculture (1971), and the Small- and Medium-Sized Enterprise (1981) initiatives are examples of this tendency.

While Bulgaria has steadfastly maintained the central and defining institutions of Soviet-type central planning, it has also been a leader in experimentation with structural economic reform. The Western tendency to exaggerate the depth and implications of such 'reforms,' which has been stressed at various points in this book, should not be allowed to obscure the sustained experimentation with structural reforms that has gone on in Bulgaria and that may well have much more direct implications for other advanced Soviet-type economies than the widely praised and noted Hungarian reform developments.

In agriculture Bulgaria carried out the collectivization process in a relatively subtle fashion that did not leave permanent marks on the rural population. The process of consolidation began almost immediately thereafter and led in 1970 to the creation of the agro-industrial complexes (AIC). Bulgaria adopted and never abandoned the machine tractor station (MTS), which eventually came to be matched in size by the agricultural production units themselves as they were amalgamated as part of the AIC development. The vertically integrated AIC was developed in Bulgaria and carried to an advanced form and very large size. Agriculture was not treated as a buffer sector, but instead a sufficient flow of investment resources was provided in the early years of the collectivization process to provide sustained improvements in income and living standards for those who remained in the agricultural work force.

This 'relatively happy fate of the peasantry' was accomplished in the presence of all of the classical Soviet-type features, with very large operating units. The Bulgarian development experience in some respects lies quite close to what Nove & Newth (1967) and Wilbur (1969) have described for the Central Asian republics of the Soviet Union. When account is taken of material living standards, health care, education and cultural services, no other country in Southeast Europe has done as well by its rural population in the post-war period. The income of farm families has risen rapidly in both absolute and relative terms, and by the mid-1970s they enjoyed living standards equal to those of urban dwellers (before consideration of the in-kind benefits of personal plot cultivation). The integration of the personal-plot sector into the state agricultural system was carried out in a fashion very much as in Hungary (Swain, 1986; 1987) and has been highly successful, contributing to a rapidly rising standard of food consumption for both rural and urban populations. The AICs have gone so far as to place newspaper advertisements to attempt to recruit city dwellers to take up cultivation of personal plots, much of the output of which is marketed through and by the AICs.

In the industrial sector talk of economic reform has been incessant for two decades, but the amount of change in the actual working environment of the

typical large enterprise has been quite small. After comprehensive consolidation of industrial units (into what is in effect the Bulgarian version of the
industrial association), the prerogatives of the managers of these larger units
have been considerably increased and detailed control by central planners has
in fact been reduced. Structural innovation has come in the form of the Small
and Medium-Sized Enterprise program which has established financially
semi-autonomous units within existing large organizations and in some new
forms of banking and financial control (McIntyre, 1988a, b; Daviddi, 1987).

These new types of enterprises have brought a rapid expansion in the
quality and availability of domestically produced consumer goods, including
clothing and food. While providing some of the benefits of smaller-scale and
more responsive production often associated with markets and private
entrepreneurial activity, these changes have occurred under the tutelage of
the Bulgarian Industrial Association and largely within the structural shell of
existing large enterprises. The BIA is in some ways like a 'Ministry of New
Products and Processes' (McIntyre, 1987b), and itself represents an institutional innovation of potentially substantial significance. The character of the
undoubtedly complex set of informal operating relationships between the
BIA and the existing central planning and economic administrative organs is
obviously worthy of detailed scholarly attention.

While Bulgaria is not in the first ranks of industrial innovation, good
progress has also been made in several high-technology areas like robotics
and automated materials handling, in part through joint ventures with
Western European and Japanese companies. Bulgaria has assumed a leading
role in the CMEA computer production plan. Bulgaria appears to be one of
the countries that will draw the greatest benefits from co-production
arrangements with the Soviet Union. Bulgaria is producer of the electrical
systems from the new model 'Samara' passenger car and has played a
conspicuous role in the Soviet space program. In addition, Bulgaria produces
Apple computers under licence and an IBM PC-AX clone, which are
available domestically at retail.

In the service sector Bulgaria long maintained a ban on private enterprises
with hired labor, but continued to permit self-employed repair and service
workers and artists. Some expansion in purely private service and small-scale
production has appeared after the implementation of the Law on Individual
Enterprise in the Soviet Union in May 1987. Holding second jobs is not as
prevalent in Bulgaria as elsewhere in Eastern Europe but considerable service,
repair and construction work is done during evenings and weekends by
persons fully employed in the state sector. It should be noted also that with
the exception of retired persons and children, workers on 'personal plots'

must be fully employed in an AIC or other state enterprise. The state service sector has been expanding and certain areas such as beauty care or custom sewing and tailoring are quite highly developed.

The net effect of these changes is to produce a Soviet-type economic structure which has provided steady qualitative and quantitative improvement in consumer living standards and carried Bulgaria from Third World levels to a position at the edge of the developed European category. Sometimes the extent of the Bulgarian achievement is obscured by the relatively even income distribution, which is itself an important achievement. The absence of an extremely high income fringe, as in Greece and other capitalist countries, leads to the absence of certain visual clues to relative abundance. Because of the very high proportion of multiple-earner households (resulting from the nearly universal full-time labor force participation of women), the distribution of income by household is remarkably even, despite what appears to be substantial inequality when incomes are viewed by single earners. The degree of income differentiation is small when comparisons are made between urban and rural, or blue- and white-collar families instead of individuals. The rural population has been especially well treated, enjoying full integration into the social security and welfare system, unusual attention to provision of good health care, as well as quite high cash incomes.

Comparative Evaluation of Bulgarian Economic and Social Performance

There is a natural tendency to compare Bulgarian social and economic performance with Romania, Greece and perhaps Yugoslavia in order to apply the resulting conclusions to the development problems and dilemmas of poor Third World countries. Romania and Bulgaria have sometimes been grouped together as 'socialist LDC's' (Reynolds, 1977), Greece is treated as a capitalist LDC, and Yugoslavia as a non-Soviet model socialist LDC. The problems with these natural comparisons are unfortunately substantial. Only Bulgaria and Romania have had to develop predominantly on the basis of their own resources while working with the social imperatives of full employment. Both Greece and Yugoslavia have had the 'advantage' of large-scale migration, reducing domestic overmanning while providing very substantial hard-currency remittances from workers in Western and Northern Europe. This pattern has been very strong in Greece for much of the century, whereas the large-scale Yugoslav *Gastarbeiter* (guest worker) outflow dates from the economic reforms of the early 1960s. In both cases the development effect of the hard-currency earnings has been modest, going mostly into housing and consumer durable goods rather than financing investment in industrial capacity. And in both cases sustained inability to employ the resident workforce (only partly remedied by putatively temporary immigration) has led to an artificially favorable measured 'efficiency' for those workers employed within the country.

Romania borrowed heavily from Western banks during the 1970s and during the 1980s has turned to intense austerity and increasingly eccentric internal policies to attempt to reduce this exposure. Bulgarian foreign-trade performance and debt management has in general been quite good. Efforts to expand exports with favorable hard-currency effects have been only partially successfull and overall export expansion has been concentrated in trade with other CMEA members and a relatively small number of Third World nations in the Middle East and Africa. A relatively large portion of the export growth that has produced a favorable export balance and a decrease in the level of net indebtedness for most of the last ten years has come from the latter group of countries. Since it is impossible to determine the role of payments in convertible currencies as against concealed subsidies or other forms of 'soft' accounting, some observers have suggested that the apparent good performance of the Bulgarian debt account is illusory. The question cannot be settled with the currently available information, but it should be stressed that at least a significant share of this trade is with oil-producing countries whose sources of hard currency have been substantial during most of the period under consideration.

Controversy with the Soviet Union and possibly other CMEA countries over the quality of Bulgarian industrial and consumer goods have been noted above. The problems of dealing with an increasingly demanding CMEA market may explain the rise in agreements for joint supervision of production in many of the new bilateral technical cooperation, development and production agreements. The significant open (and perhaps much more direct private criticism) of Bulgaria by CMEA trade partners over the 1983–6 period seems to have played an important contributory role in the developing sense among Bulgarian economists and political leaders that fundamental changes in work culture and more than superficial attention to quality are required if export-based growth is to continue. Since the Bulgarian economy combines the unusual features of being tightly centrally planned and deeply involved in foreign trade, deteriorating conditions in the latter area would imply sharply decreased overall economic prospects.

Bulgaria began the 1970s with a relatively high level of indebtedness to

Western banks, but worked strenuously throughout the decade to reduce this exposure, avoiding the kind of vulnerability to Western financial institutions that has developed in Romania and Poland. The figures in Table 6.1 show that total indebtedness in Western currencies fell from 3.6 billion current US dollars in 1980 to 2.1 billion in the middle of 1984, and then rose again during 1985 and 1986. The net debt which takes account of Bulgarian convertible currency assets abroad followed a similar path but at a lower level. The full financial effects of borrowing to offset the effects of the terrible 1985 harvest are not as yet visible in reliable statistics, which appear with some considerable delay. While overall economic performance clearly faltered during 1983–5, the rise in consumer living standards was scarcely affected. The heavy industrial sector of the economy played the role of buffer, reversing the supposedly intrinsic crisis response of the centrally planned model and perhaps showing that old dogs do occasionally learn new tricks. On the other hand this may not be such a new development, since almost all of the research on 'business cycles' in centrally planned economies has centered on investment and industrial production variations, with much smaller variations found in the other categories of output.

Table 6.1 Bulgarian estimated gross and net convertible currency debt (current US$ billion)

	1980	1981	1982	1983	1984	1985	1986 (June)
Gross debt	3.6	3.2	2.9	2.4	2.1	3.6	4.3
Net debt	—	2.4	1.9	1.2	0.7	1.5	2.9

Sources: OECD/BIS, 1986, pp. 5, 9, 13; UN Economic Commission for Europe, 1987, p. 309.

Morale, Systems Performance and Social Cohesion

There appears to be a widely shared feeling among Bulgarians that the country has made large and steady strides in economic, social and cultural realms over the last several decades. This social optimism is based on tangible progress that at least implicitly is attributed to generally good and highly flexible leadership. Whether the economic difficulties of 1983–5 have fundamentally changed this view cannot yet be discerned. The growth experience of the balance of the 1986–90 Five Year Plan thus bears watching for more than simply economic reasons. It is of course impossible to judge even longer-term changes in this relationship between public opinion and social cohesion in the absence of opinion polling or electoral processes that pose 'systems' questions. Still, the tendency to view the country as well run and intelligently managed is strong and contributes to or perhaps defines the considerable level of popular approval and respect for the leadership of the Zhivkov period.

There may be an important ideological element in the predominantly optimistic social consciousness of contemporary Bulgarian society and in its self-satisfied tone that (for reasons of language, geography and immediately adjoining 'alternatives') has not been subject to qualification or subversion by outside forces to the extent observed in many other Eastern European countries. Apel & Strumpel speculate on the question of the extent to which individual perceptions of progress and desirable change are the result of successful official efforts to create system-supporting values and a particular way of experiencing social reality.

The claims of equality, opportunity and prosperity continuously voiced by the state and its institutions, together with a relatively egalitarian wage and salary distribution and a convergence of sex roles, reduce the likelihood that an individual will perceive the sort of relative deprivation that colors situational assessments. [Apel & Strumpel, 1976, p. 179]

There appear to be very similar personal goals across the two Balkan social systems they have studied, so that

The consistent and pervasive differences in reported economic and social experience between Bulgaria and Greece . . . no doubt reflect a hard core of different conditions and roles for the individual in society. [ibid., p. 179]

They observe that this popular state of mind, which may be a 'learned optimistic response,' none the less represents a high level of satisfaction with the performance of the state which has considerable implications for the functioning of the Bulgarian economy and society, since

Regardless of the extent to which it is rooted in either experience or ideology . . . the attitude does exist, and certainly will facilitate governmental success. [ibid., p. 172]

It is this positive state of mind and active approval of the achievements during the 1960s and 1970s that appear to lie behind the apparently placid but also relatively steadily progressive development of the Bulgarian economic and social system at a time when signs of crisis have appeared elsewhere in Eastern Europe. This is in some ways a triumph in political management, and it is fascinating to speculate on how or if this complex of popular attitudes has changed in response to the relative extreme economic adversity of the mid-1980s. Some Western observers have been waiting, figuratively at least, since 1944 for 'another Balkan explosion.' The 1965 Vratsa conspiracy fed this expectation, and now twenty years later the Turkish minority question raises anew unanswerable questions about inherent system stability. But with forty years of generally shared progress, no significant *émigré* culture, no attractive adjoining alternative system to study, and no plausible claim to restoration of power by pre-1944 ruling groups, it seems that the BCP will be the forum for settling any foreseeable social-political conflicts.

Bulgaria as a Development Model

There is on balance some basis for considering Bulgarian economic experience as a growth model or exemplar for developing countries. Nove & Newth (1967) and Wilbur (1969) have evaluated the development experience of the Central Asian region of the Soviet Union from this same perspective. Bulgarian development since World War II holds a series of unconventional lessons and does clearly show both that the classical Soviet central planning institutions can be made to work better than study of the original would suggest and that it is possible to sustain the favorable growth aspects of that model beyond the initial climb out of extreme backwardness and well into the middle-income levels. The success of Bulgarian Small Enterprise and (and to a lesser extent) technology policy has been noted, both occurring in an environment heavily influenced by and oriented toward foreign trade. Generally good agricultural performance has also been considered above and would appear to merit study as a development case. Kirkland (1985) has drawn similar conclusions about the potential transferability of common features in the Hungarian agricultural system.

The fact that the growth process in Bulgaria has been carried out with a highly egalitarian income distribution undercuts the motivational presumptions of both classical capitalist and Stalinist theories about the need for sharp performance-based income differentials if good work effort is to be elicited. Pressure for sharper differentiation of performance rewards is an element in the post-1982 reform discussions and was stressed at the XIII Party Congress in April 1986, which may do something to erode the current relatively even distribution. Some of the reform proposals simply involve reallocation within the existing range of observed incomes, while others do imply extension of that range.

The pace of change in the physically obvious signs of higher living standards has been greater in Bulgaria (noting very different initial levels) than in countries such as Hungary, whose development has been regularly and approvingly noted in the West. The failure to appreciate fully Bulgarian developments undoubtedly has manifold roots, including the geo-political filter applied with opposite effect to countries perceived to be close to versus moving away from Soviet forms of organization. Under this interpretation favorable Western attention can be secured by either foreign (e.g. Romania) or domestic (e.g. Hungary) policy deviation from the Soviet mode. Romania long enjoyed unduly favorable Western reviews on the basis of its relatively autonomous foreign policy which at times has seemed to seek to offend the Soviet Union. Bulgaria has generally been among the most enthusiastic advocates of Soviet-sponsored views on the whole range of foreign policy, Warsaw Pact and CMEA integration questions. Despite continuing problems and intermittent small crises there has been generally quite good economic performance, but while there have been important organizational changes in Bulgaria, they have not thus far been in the direction of significantly greater use of market forces and so they have been largely ignored. Changes in Hungary have included decentralization, limited privatization and increased use (and even more talk about use) of the market as the key coordinating force, explaining the generally uncritical Western response and the exaggerated sense of the extent and significance of the NEM measures there.

When comparison is explicitly or implicitly made between Bulgaria and countries such as Hungary or Czechoslovakia, it is important to note that very large differences in living standards existed prior to the socialist period. Rapid Bulgarian progress has occurred over the last several decades and has closed much, but far from all, of this historical and cultural gap. This experience has been different in almost all important respects from that of countries like Hungary, the GDR, and Czechoslovakia, which already in 1900 were (or were part of) relatively highly developed industrial states strongly integrated in the general European economic system. The Bulgarian experience is much more closely aligned with the problems and conditions faced by contemporary developing countries (Wilbur, 1969). By providing such a complex mixture of classical Soviet-type and original institutions, and pursuing policies leading to a significantly different urban–rural balance even within familiar institutions, it shows the range of variation that may exist within the often shapeless blanket of 'real, existing' Eastern European socialism. Bulgaria provides a valuable study in comparative communism. Its experience does not provide easy solutions (although it has some relevance) for the sustained economic–political problems of Poland, Czechoslovakia, or the Soviet Union, but calls into question the case of those who see Poland and Romania as metaphors for the necessary future of all Soviet-type economic-political systems.

Finally, in considering the likely future developments in Bulgaria itself it is necessary to take note of the unusually stressful economic conditions during the 1984–5 period, and consider what this may portend for the future. It is easy to find evidence above to suggest that this experience mobilized a new seriousness in pursuit of economic and political reforms. It is equally easy to find evidence of a quick return to the old ways, once economic conditions rebounded in 1986 and 1987. The elements of revitalization and determined resistance to change contest with each other, with no clear victor for the future. As noted, improved economic performance in 1986 and 1987 set the 1986–90 plan period off on a generally optimistic note, but long-term economic and political trends in Bulgaria will at the very least be interesting and worthy of attention by all those concerned with comparative politics, sociology and economics.

Bibliography

Alexiev, Alex 1985. Demystifying Bulgaria. *Problems of Communism*, vol. 34, no. 5, pp. 89–94.

Allen, Mark 1977. The Bulgarian economy in the 1970's. In *East European Economies Post-Helsinki*. Joint Economic Committee, US Congress, pp. 647–97.

Alton & Associates 1982. Official and alternative price indices in Eastern Europe, selected years, 1960–1981. Occasional Paper No. 73, Research Project on National Income in East Central Europe. New York, L.W. International Financial Research, Inc.

—— 1985a. Economic growth in Eastern Europe, 1970 and 1975–1984. Occasional Paper No. 85.

—— 1985b. Agricultural output, expenses and depreciation, gross product, and net product in Eastern Europe, 1965, 1970 and 1975–1984. Occasional Paper No. 86.

—— 1985c. Money income of the population and standard of living in Eastern Europe, 1970–1984. Occasional Paper No. 88.

—— 1985d. Eastern European GNP by origin and domestic final uses of gross product, 1965–1984. Occasional Paper No. 89.

Amnesty International 1986. Bulgaria: imprisonment of ethnic Turks. New York, Amnesty International, USA.

—— 1987. Bulgaria: Continued Human Rights Abuses Against Ethnic Turks. New York, Amnesty International, USA.

Apel, Hans 1975. An inter-system comparison of postwar economic growth and its welfare effects: Bulgaria and Greece. Privately circulated, May 1975.

Apel, Hans & Strumpel, Burkhard 1976. Economic well-being as a criterion for system performance: a survey in Bulgaria and Greece. In *Economic Well-Being in a System of Social Indicators*. Ann Arbor, Survey Research Center, University of Michigan Press, pp. 163–86.

Askanas, Benedykt & Laski, Kazimierz 1985. Consumer prices and private consumption in Poland and Austria. *Journal of Comparative Economics*, vol. 9, no. 2, pp. 164–77.

Aspaturian, Vernon V. 1984. Eastern Europe in world perspective. In Rakowska-Harmstone, Teresa (ed.), *Communism in Eastern Europe*, 2nd edn. Bloomington, Indiana University Press, pp. 8–49.

Baest, Torsten 1985. Bulgaria's war at home: the People's Republic and its Turkish minority (1944–1985). *Across Frontiers*, vol. 2, no. 2, pp. 18–26.

Banks, Arthur S., ed., 1986. *Political Handbook of the World: 1986*. Binghamton, New York, CSA Publications.

Bell, John D. 1977. *Peasants in Power: Alexander Stamboliski and the Bulgarian Agrarian National Union, 1899–1923*. Princeton, NJ, Princeton University Press.

Bell, John D. 1982. Bulgaria: the silent partner, in Drachkovitch, Milorad M. (ed.), *East Central Europe: Yesterday, Today, Tomorrow*. Stanford, Hoover Institution Press, pp. 219–42.

—— 1984, 1985 and 1986, and 1987. Bulgaria. In Staar, Richard F., (ed.), *Yearbook on International Communist Affairs, 1984, 1985, 1986, and 1987*. Stanford, Hoover Institute Press, pp. 302–11, pp. 263–74, pp. 266–74, and pp. 275–83.

Berend, Ivan T. & Ranki, Gyorgy 1974. *Economic Development in East-Central Europe in the Nineteenth and Twentieth Centuries*. New York, Columbia University Press.

Berent, Jerzy 1970. Causes of fertility decline in Eastern Europe and the Soviet Union. *Population Studies*, vol. 24, no. 1–2, pp. 35–58 and 247–92.

Berliner, Joseph S. 1983. Managing the USSR economy: alternative models. *Problems of Communism*, vol. 32, no. 1, pp. 40–56.

Binder, David 1985. Bulgaria harvesting incentives. *New York Times*, 29 June, p. 2.

Blum, Patrick 1986. Bulgaria puts reforms to test. *Financial Times*, 11 April 1986, p. 22.

Boichev, Venzeslav 1985. Interviews, 29 November 1985 and 16 December 1985.

Boll, Michael M. 1984. *Cold War in the Balkans: American Foreign Policy and the Emergence of Communist Bulgaria, 1943-1947*. Lexington, University Press of Kentucky.

Bornstein, Morris 1985. Improving the Soviet economic mechanism. *Soviet Studies*, vol. 37, no. 1, pp. 1–30.

Bozhkov, Lyuben 1981. The Bulgarian Agrarian Party, in Bokov, Georgi (ed.), *Modern Bulgaria: History, Policy, Economy, Culture*. Sofia, Sofia Press, pp. 217–26.

Broadhead, Frank, Howard Friel & Edward S. Herman 1988. Darkness in Rome: the Bulgarian Connection Revisited. *Covert Action Information Bulletin*, no. 23, pp. 3–38.

Brown, James F. 1970. *Bulgaria under Communist Rule*. New York, Praeger.

Brucan, Silviu 1983. *The Post-Brezhnev Era*. New York, Praeger.

Buck, Trevor 1982. *Comparative Industrial Systems*. New York, St Martin's.

Bulgaria 1947. *The First Bulgarian Two Year Economic Plan*. Sofia, Ministry of Information and Arts.

Byrnes, James F. 1947. *Speaking Frankly*. New York, Harper.

Campbell, Robert W. 1961. Marx, Kantorovich and Novoshilov: stoimost versus reality. *Slavic Review*, vol. 20, no. 3, pp. 402–18.

—— 1980. *Soviet Energy Technologies*. Bloomington, Indiana University Press.

Carter, Frank W. 1987. Bulgaria. In Dawson, Andrew H. (ed.), *Planning in Eastern Europe*. New York, St Martin's, pp. 67–101.

—— & Zagar, Marjan 1977. Postwar internal migration in Southeastern Europe. In Kosinski, Leszek A. (ed.), *Demographic Developments in Eastern Europe*. New York, Praeger, pp. 208–23.

Central Intelligence Agency 1987. *The World Factbook: 1987*. Washington, DC, United States Government Printing Office, pp. 34–5.

Chary, Frederick B. 1972. *The Bulgarian Jews and the Final Solution, 1940-1944*. Pittsburgh, University of Pittsburgh Press.

— 1987. Stamboliski and Zhivkov: comparison of political styles. Paper presented at the AAASS Meetings, Boston, 7 November.

Choleva, Sofia 1986. Interview, 11 July 1986. (Production Manager, IPOMA, Technological and Production Center for Polymer Articles.)

Coale, Ansley J. 1967. Factors associated with the development of low fertility: an historic summary. In *Proceedings of the World Population Conference, Belgrade, 1965*. New York, United Nations, p. 207.

— 1969. The decline of fertility in Europe from the French Revolution to World War II. In S. H. Behrman, L. Corsa & R. Freedman (eds), *Fertility and Family Planning*. Ann Arbor, University of Michigan Press, pp. 3–24.

— 1972. Letter, 12 June 1972.

— 1973. The demographic transition. In *Proceedings of the International Population Conference, Liège, 1973, Vol. I*. Liège, International Union for the Scientific Study of Population, pp. 62–3, 67.

Cochrane, Nancy 1984. The private sector in East European agriculture. In *Eastern Europe: Outlook and Situation Report*, US Department of Agriculture, Economic Research Services, RS–84–7, June 1984, pp. 16–19.

Cockburn, Alexander 1984a. *The Nation*, 4–11 August, p. 71.

— 1984b. *The Nation*, 29 September, p. 261.

— 1985. *The Nation*, 17–24 August, pp. 102–3.

Coelen, Stephen P. & McIntyre, Robert J. 1978. Econometric analysis of pronatalist and abortion policies. *Journal of Political Economy*, vol. 86, no. 6, pp. 1077–102.

Cohen, Stephen F. 1984. Sovieticus. *The Nation*, 17 November, p. 503.

— 1985. *Rethinking the Soviet Experience: Politics and History Since 1917*. New York, Oxford University Press.

Cook, Edward 1986. Prospects for Bulgarian agriculture in the 1980's. In *Eastern European Economies: Slow Growth in the 1980's, vol. 3, Country Studies on Eastern Europe and Yugoslavia*, Joint Economic Committee, US Congress, 99th Congress, 1st Session, 28 March, pp. 59–83.

Cornelsen, Doris 1987. Economic development in the German Democratic Republic. In Joseph, Philip (ed.), *The Economies of Eastern Europe and Their Foreign Economic Relations*, NATO Economics Directorate, Brussels, pp. 41–57.

David, Henry P. & McIntyre, Robert J. 1981. *Fertility Behavior: Central and Eastern European Experience*. New York, Springer.

Daviddi, Renzo 1987a. Bulgaria: domestic economic performance and foreign economic relations in the 1980's. In Joseph, Philip (ed.), *The Economies of Eastern Europe and Their Foreign Economic Relations*. NATO Economics Directorate, Brussels, pp. 77–100.

— 1987b. Monetary Reforms in Bulgaria. A paper presented at the Workshop on Financial Reform in Socialist Economies, European University Institute, Florence.

DeBartolo, Gilbert & Holzman, Franklyn D. 1985. The effects of aggregation on the difference between Laspeyres and Paasche indices. *Journal of Comparative Economics*, vol. 9, no. 1, pp. 71–9.

Dellin, L. A. D. (ed.) 1957. *Bulgaria*. New York, Praeger.

— 1979. Bulgaria. In Starr, Richard F. (ed.), *Yearbook of International Communist Affairs, 1979*. Stanford, Hoover Institution Press, pp. 9–18.

Dempsey, Judy 1987. Bulgaria's road to economic reform. *Financial Times*, 9 September, p. 2.

Deutsch, Robert 1986. *The Food Revolution in the Soviet Union and Eastern Europe*. Boulder, Westview.

Diehl, Jackson 1985. Bulgaria beset by economic woes; Moscow pushes reforms in economically ailing Bulgaria. *Washington Post*, 8 November, pp. A33 & 42.

— 1986. Turks lose out in Bulgarian 'Revival'. *International Herald Tribune*, 10 April, pp. 1–2.

Dienes, Leslie & Economou, Nikos 1981. CMEA energy demand in the 1980's: a sectoral analysis. In NATO Economics Directorate, *CMEA: Energy, 1980–1990*. Oriental Research Partners, Newtonville, Massachusetts, pp. 39–58.

Dobrin, Bogoslav 1973. *Bulgarian Economic Development Since World War II*. New York, Praeger.

Ellman, Michael 1984. Agricultural productivity under socialism. In Ellman, Michael, *Collectivisation, Convergence and Capitalism: Political Economy in a Divided World*. London, Academic Press, pp. 198–214.

Enkiev, Dimiter 1986. Interview, 10 July 1986. (General Manager, IKO, Information and Consulting Complex.)

Erickson, John 1982. The Warsaw Pact: past, present, and future. In Drachkovitch, Milorad M. (ed.), *East Central Europe: Yesterday, Today, Tomorrow*. Stanford, Hoover Institution Press, pp. 143–73.

— 1983. *The Road to Berlin*. Boulder, Westview.

Feiwel, George R. 1977. *Growth and Reforms in Centrally Planned Economies: The Lessons of the Bulgarian Experience*. New York, Praeger.

Field, Mark G. 1956. The relegalization of abortion in Soviet Russia. *The New England Journal of Medicine*, vol. 255, no. 9, pp. 421–2.

Furtak, Robert K. 1986. *The Political Systems of the Socialist States*. New York, St Martin's.

Foreign Broadcast Information Service (*FBIS*), various issues.

Gerschenkron, Alexander 1962a. Economic backwardness in historical perspective, and The approach to European industrialization: a postscript. In Alexander Gerschenkron, *Economic Backwardness in Historical Perspective: A Book of Essays*. Cambridge, Mass., Harvard University Press, pp. 5–29 and 353–66.

— 1962b. Some aspects of industrialization in Bulgaria, 1878–1939, and Appendix II. In Alexander Gerschenkron, *Economic Backwardness in Historical Perspective: A Book of Essays*. Cambridge, Mass., Harvard University Press, pp. 198–234 and 422–35.

Gianaris, Nicholas V. 1982. *The Economies of the Balkan Countries*. New York, Praeger.

Granick, David 1984. Central physical planning, incentives and job rights. In Zimbalest, Andrew (ed.), *Comparative Economic Systems: An Assessment of Knowledge, Theory and Method*. Boston, Mass., Kluwer-Nijhoff.

— 1987. *Job Rights in the Soviet Union: Their Consequences*. New York, Cambridge University Press.

Gregory, Paul R. & Stuart, Robert C. 1985. *Comparative Economic Systems* (2nd edn). Boston, Mass., Houghton Mifflin.

— 1986. *Soviet Economic Structure and Performance* (3rd edn). New York, Harper & Row.

Hajda, Joseph 1980. The impact of current policies on modernizing agriculture in Eastern Europe. In Francisco, Ronald A., Laird, Betty A., and Laird, Roy D. (eds), *Agricultural Policies in the USSR and Eastern Europe*. Boulder, Westview, pp. 295–310.

Hajnal, John 1964. European marriage patterns in perspective. In Glass, David V., and D. E. C. Eversley (eds), *Population in History*. London, Arnold, pp. 101–43.

Halpern, Joel & Anderson, David 1970. The Zadruga, a century of change. *Anthropologica*, vol. 12, no. 1, pp. 83–97.

— & Halpern, Barbara 1972. *A Serbian Village in Historical Perspective*. New York, Harper & Row.

Hanson, Philip 1971. East–West comparisons and comparative economic systems. *Soviet Studies*, vol. 22, no. 3, pp. 327–43.

Harding, Neil 1981. What does it mean to call a regime Marxist? In Szajkowski, Bogdan (ed.), *Marxist Governments: A World Survey, Vol. 1*. New York, St Martin's, pp. 20–33.

Hare, Paul 1987. Hungary: internal economic development. In Joseph, Philip (ed.), *The Economies of Eastern Europe and Their Foreign Economic Relationships*. NATO Economics Directorate, Brussels, pp. 213–29.

Hartford, Kathleen 1985. Hungarian agriculture: a model for the socialist world? *World Development*, vol. 13, no. 1, pp. 123–50.

Havlik, Peter 1985. A comparison of purchasing power parity and consumption levels in Austria and Czechoslovakia. *Journal of Comparative Economics*, vol. 9, no. 2, pp. 178–90.

Helmreich, Ernst C. 1938. *The Diplomacy of the Balkan Wars, 1912–1913*. Cambridge, Mass., Harvard University Press.

Herman, Edward S. & Broadhead, Frank 1986. *The Rise and Fall of the Bulgarian Connection*. New York, Sheridan Square Publications.

Heslin, Mary 1987. The East European connection. In Baranson, Jack (ed.), *Soviet Automation*. Mt. Airy, Maryland, Lomond Publications, pp. 97–115.

Hewett, Edward 1980. Alternative econometric approaches to studying the links between economic systems and economic outcomes. *Journal of Comparative Economics*, vol. 4, no. 3, pp. 274–94.

Hill, Ronald J. 1985. *Soviet Union: Politics, Economics and Society*. London, Frances Pinter.

Hobday, Charles 1986. *Communist and Marxist Parties of the World*. Harlow, Essex, Longman, pp. 151–3.

Holmes, Leslie 1981. People's Republic of Bulgaria. In Szajkowski, Bogdan (ed.), *Marxist Governments: A World Survey, Vol. 1*. New York, St Martin's, pp. 116–44.

Hood, William 1984, Unlikely conspiracy. *Problems of Communism*, vol. 33, no. 2, pp. 67–70.

—— 1985. Reply: the KGB and the Pope. *Problems of Communism*, vol. 34, no. 1, pp. 91–2.

Hough, Jerry F. 1976. Political participation in the Soviet Union. *Soviet Studies*, vol. 28, no. 1, pp. 3–20.

—— & Fainsod, Merle 1979. *How the Soviet Union is Governed*. Cambridge, Mass., Harvard University Press.

Hristozov, Hristoz V. 1984. *The Role of the Personal Supplementary Holdings of the Population for the Self-Sufficiency of the Urban Systems*. Sofia, NAPS.

Ivanova, Vera 1985. Agroindustrial complexes and personal holdings—does that mean Bulgarian mixed policy? Vienna, Vienna Institute for Comparative Economic Studies.

Jackson, Marvin R. 1981. Bulgaria's economy in the 1970s: adjusting productivity to structure. In *East European Economic Assessment, Part 1, Country Studies*, Joint Economic Committee, US Congress, 27 February, pp. 571–618.

—— 1982a. National product and income in southeastern Europe before the Second World War. *ACES Bulletin*, vol. 14, no. 3, pp. 73–103.

—— 1982b. Agricultural output in southeastern Europe, 1910–1938. *ACES Bulletin*, vol. 14, no. 4, pp. 49–87.

—— 1986. Recent economic performance and policy in Bulgaria. In *Eastern European Economies: Slow Growth in the 1980's, vol. 3, Country Studies on Eastern Europe and Yugoslavia*, Joint Economic Committee, US Congress, 28 March, pp. 23–58.

Jackson, Marvin R. & Lampe, John R. 1982a. War and economic development, 1912–1950. In Lampe, John R. & Jackson, Marvin R., *Balkan Economic History, 1550–1950: From Imperial Borderlands to Developing Nations*. Bloomington, Indiana University Press, pp. 329–599.

—— 1982b. The evidence of industrial growth in southeastern Europe before the Second World War. *East European Quarterly*, vol. 16, no. 4, pp. 1–42.

Jelavich, Barbara 1983a. *History of the Balkans, Vol. 1: Eighteenth and Nineteenth Centuries*. Cambridge, Cambridge University Press.

Jelavich, Charles & Jelavich, Barbara 1977. *The Establishment of the Balkan National States*. Seattle, University of Washington Press.

—— 1983b. *History of the Balkans, Vol. 2: Twentieth Century*. Cambridge, Cambridge University Press.

Jerome, Robert T. 1985. Estimates of sources of growth in Bulgaria, Greece, and Yugoslavia, 1950–1980. *Comparative Economic Studies*, vol. 27, no. 3, pp. 31–82.

Kamm, Henry 1987a. A lifetime spent waiting for things to get better. *New York Times*, 2 October, p. A4.

—— 1987b. Back seat for *glasnost* amid Bulgarian change. *New York Times*, 3 October, p. 3.

—— 1987c. Bulgarian–Turkish tensions on minority rise. *New York Times*, 4 October, p. 9.

—— 1987d. Far-reaching economic changes stir Bulgaria. *New York Times*, 7 October, p. A10.

—— 1987e. In Babel on Danube, all tongues but one are still. *New York Times*, 14 October, p. A4.

—— 1988a. Bulgaria parley is foretaste of scaling down of change. *New York Times*, 29 January, p. A2.

—— 1988b. Bulgarian rejects political opening. *New York Times*, 30 January, p. 4.

Kaser, Michael 1981. The industrial enterprise in Bulgaria. In Jeffries, Ian (ed.), *The Industrial Enterprise in Eastern Europe*. New York, Praeger, pp. 84–94.

—— & Radice, E. A. eds. (1985). *The Economic History of Eastern Europe, 1919–1975*, vol. 1, vol. 2 and vol. 3. Oxford, Oxford University Press.

Kirk, Dudley 1946. *Europe's Population in the Interwar Years*. Princeton, League of Nations, pp. 48–50 and 55–9.

Kitchen, Martin 1986. *British Policy Towards the Soviet Union During the Second World War*. New York, St Martin's.

Kiuranov, Chavdar 1975. Aspects of the distribution of personal earnings and earnings stratification in Bulgaria. In Fallenbuchl, Zbigniew M. (ed.), *Economic Development in the Soviet Union and Eastern Europe, Vol. 1*. New York, Praeger, pp. 276–86.

Kornai, Janos 1959. *Overcentralization in Economic Administration*. London, Oxford University Press.

—— 1983. *Growth, Shortage and Efficiency: A Macrodynamic Model of the Socialist Economy*. Berkeley, University of California Press.

—— 1986. The Hungarian reform process: visions, hopes, and reality. *Journal of Economic Literature*, vol. 24, December, pp. 1687–737.

—— 1986b. *Contradictions and Dilemmas: Studies on the Socialist Economy and Society*. Cambridge, MIT Press.

Kosinski, Leszek A., ed. 1977. *Demographic Developments in Eastern Europe*. New York, Praeger.

Kostanick, Huey L., ed. 1977. *Population and Migration Trends in Eastern Europe*. Denver, Westview.

Kostov, Natalya & Kostov, Vladimir 1983. *Sotsializmat v Bulgariya*. Paris, Peev and Popov.

Kraus, Richard & Vanneman, Reeve D. 1985. Bureaucrats versus the state in capitalist and socialist regimes. *Comparative Studies in Society and History*, vol. 27, no. 1, pp. 111–22.

Krause, John T. 1960. On the possibility of increasing fertility in the under-developed nations. *Comparative Studies in Society and History*, vol. 2, no. 4, pp. 485–7.

Kuczynski, Robert R. 1931. *The Balance of Births and Deaths, Vol. II.* [*Eastern and Southern Europe*]. Washington, DC, The Brookings Institution.

—— 1936. *The Measurement of Population Growth*. New York, Oxford University Press.

Kuttner, Robert 1983. Trials of two welfare states: Sweden and Denmark. *The Atlantic*, November, pp. 14–22.

Lalkov, Milcho 1981. Bulgaria—a newly sovereign state. In Bokov, Georgi (ed.), *Modern Bulgaria: History, Policy, Economy, Culture*. Sofia, Sofia Press, pp. 67–102.

Lampe, John R. 1975a. Varieties of unsuccessful industrialization. *Journal of Economic History*, vol. 35, no. 1, pp. 56–85.

—— 1975b. Finance and pre-1914 industrial stirrings in Bulgaria and Serbia. *Southeastern Europe*, vol. 2, no. 1, pp. 23–52.

—— 1982. New markets in the old empires, from the sixteenth to the nineteenth centuries, and Modernization in the new nation-states, 1860–1914. In Lampe, John R. & Jackson, Marvin R., *Balkan Economic History, 1550–1950: From Imperial Borderlands to Developing Nations*. Bloomington, Indiana University Press, pp. 21–158 and 159–322.

—— 1986. *The Bulgarian Economy in the Twentieth Century*. London, Croom Helm.

Lane, David 1987. *Soviet Labour and the Ethic of Communism: Full Employment and the Labour Process in the USSR*. Boulder, Westview.

Lazarcik, Gregor & Znayenko, Wassyl 1979. Bulgaria and East Germany: domestic final uses of gross product, structure and growth, selected years, 1965–1978. Occasional Paper 58 of the Research Project on National Income in East Central Europe. New York, L.W. International Financial Research, Inc.

League of Nations 1938. *Chronology of Political and Economic Events in the Danube Basin, 1918–1936*. Paris.

—— 1940. *Bulgaria* (European Conference on Rural Life Monograph No. 28). Geneva, League of Nations, pp. 10–15.

Leonard, John 1983. Let's not be so beastly to the Bulgarians. *The Nation*, 31 January, pp. 689–91.

Livi-Bacci, Massimo 1971. *A Century of Portuguese Fertility*. Princeton, NJ, Princeton University Press, pp. 11–13, 66–9.

McCloskey, Donald N. 1975. The persistence of the English common fields. In Parker, William N. & Jones, Eric L. (eds), *European Peasants and Their Markets: Essays in Agrarian Economic History*. Princeton, NJ, Princeton University Press, pp. 91–3.

McIntyre, Robert J. 1972. The effects of liberalized abortion laws in Eastern Europe. In Clinton, Richard L. & Godwin, R. Kenneth (eds), *Research in the Politics of Population*. London, D. C. Heath & Co., pp. 181–216.

—— 1975. Pronatalist programmes in Eastern Europe. *Soviet Studies*, vol. 27, no. 3, pp. 366–80.

—— 1980. The Bulgarian anomaly: demographic transition and current fertility. *Southeastern Europe*, vol. 7, no. 2, pp. 147–70.

—— 1982. On demographic policy debates in the USSR. *Population and Development Review*, vol. 8, no. 2, pp. 363–4.

—— 1985. Demographic policy and sexual equality: value conflict and policy appraisal in Hungary and Romania. In Meyer, Alfred G. & Wolchik, Sharon (eds), *Women, State and Party in Eastern Europe*. Durham, Duke University Press, 1985, pp. 270–85.

—— 1986a. The New Economic Mechanism in Bulgaria: Fact or Fiction? Russian Research Center, 29 October 1986.

—— 1986b. Reform on the periphery of the central planning system: new forms of service and small scale production in Bulgaria and the GDR. New Orleans, Allied Social Science Association Meeting, 30 December 1986.

—— 1987a. False measurements of productivity in socialist agriculture. Manuscript.

—— 1987b. The ministry of new products and processes in a collectivist state. Manuscript.

—— 1988a. The small enterprise and agriculture initiative in Bulgaria: institutional invention without reform. *Soviet Studies*, vol. 40, forthcoming.

—— 1988b. Small-scale industrial and service developments in Bulgaria and the GDR. Paper presented at the NATO Colloquium, Brussels, 23 March.

—— 1988c. Economic change in Eastern Europe: other paths to socialist construction. *Science and Society*, vol. 52, forthcoming.

—— & Thornton, James R. 1978a. On the environmental efficiency of economic systems. *Soviet Studies*, vol. 30, no. 2, pp. 173–92.

—— & —— 1978b. Urban design and energy utilization: a comparative analysis of Soviet practice. *Journal of Comparative Economics*, vol. 2, no. 4, pp. 334–54.

Makov, Nikola 1985. Coal is back. *Sofia News*, 20 November, p. 5.

Marer, Paul 1987. Hungary's foreign economic relations in the mid-1980s: a retrospective and predictive assessment. In Joseph, Philip (ed.), *The Economies of Eastern Europe and Their Foreign Economic Relationships*. NATO Economics Directorate, Brussels, pp. 231–54.

Markov, Georgi 1983. *The Truth That Killed*. London, Weidenfeld & Nicolson.

Mehlan, Karl-Heinz 1965. The socialist countries of Europe. In Berelson, Bernard (ed.), *Family Planning and Population Programs: A Review of World Developments*. Chicago and London, University of Chicago Press, pp. 207–26.

Michal, Jan M. 1975. An alternative approach to measuring income inequality in Eastern Europe. In *Economic Development in the Soviet Union and Eastern Europe, vol. 1, Reforms, Technology and Income Distribution*. New York, Praeger, pp. 256–75.

Miller, Marshall L. 1975. *Bulgaria During the Second World War*. Stanford, Stanford University Press.

Ministry of Construction and Architecture 1982. On the settlement situation and related trends and policies. National Monograph submitted to the Economic Commission for Europe. Sofia, 56 pp.

Mishev, Stoyan 1985. Interviews, 1 November and 27 November 1985. (Vice President, BIA)

Mishev, Stoyan 1986. Interview, 4 July 1986.

Mitchell, Brian R. 1975. *European Historical Statistics, 1750–1970*. London, Macmillan.

Moore, Patrick 1984. Bulgaria. In Rakowska-Harmstone, Teresa (ed.), *Communism in Eastern Europe*, 2nd edn. Bloomington, Indiana University Press, pp. 186–212.

Moore, Wilbert E. 1945. *Economic Demography of Eastern and Southern Europe*. New York, Columbia University Press.

Murphy, Patrick 1985. Soviet *Shabashniki*: material incentives at work. *Problems of Communism*, vol. 34, no. 6, pp. 48–57.

Narkiewicz, Olga A. 1986. *Soviet Leaders: From Cult of Personality to Collective Rule*. New York, St Martin's.

Natan, Zhak 1957. *Ikonomicheska istoriia na Bulgariia*. Sofia.

Neuberger, Egon 1959. The Yugoslav Investment Auctions. *Quarterly Journal of Economics*, vol. 73, no. 1, pp. 88–115.

Nove, Alec 1983. *The Economics of Feasible Socialism*. London, Allen & Unwin.

— 1987a. 'Radical reform', problems and prospects. *Soviet Studies*, vol. 39, no. 3, p. 452–67.

— 1987b. Trotsky, markets, and East European reforms. *Comparative Economic Studies*, vol. 29, no. 3, pp. 30–9.

— & Newth, J. A. 1967. *The Soviet Middle East: A Model for Development*. London, Allen & Unwin.

OECD 1982. *Prospects for Agricultural Production and Trade in Eastern Europe, Vol. 2, Bulgaria, Czechoslovakia, Romania*. Paris, OECD, pp. 135–216.

— 1986. Statistics on external indebtedness: bank and trade-related non-bank external claims on individual borrowing countries and territories. Organization for Economic Co-operation and Development and the Bank for International Settlements, Paris and Basle.

Ognyanov, Lyubomir 1981. Along the road to socialism. In Bokov, Georgi (ed.), *Modern Bulgaria: History, Policy, Economy, Culture*. Sofia, Sofia Press, pp. 103–27.

Ofer, Gur 1977. Economizing on urbanization in socialist countries: historical necessity or socialist strategy. In Brown, Alan A. & Neuberger, Egon (eds), *International Migration: A Comparative Perspective*. New York, Academic Press, pp. 270–90.

Oren, Nissan 1971. *Bulgarian Communism: The Road to Power, 1934–1944*. New York, Columbia University Press.

— 1973. *Revolution Administered: Agrarianism and Communism in Bulgaria*. Baltimore, The Johns Hopkins University Press.

Parenti, Michael 1987. *Inventing Reality: Politics and the Mass Media*. New York, St Martin's.

Peroncel-Hugoz, Jean-Paul 1985. Political and cultural life in Sofia. *Le Monde*, 15–16 December, 1985, p. 4, as translated and reprinted in *JPAS-EER*, 27 February 1986, pp. 111–14.

Petrov, Krustiu 1984. *The Personal Holding in the People's Republic of Bulgaria*. Sofia, NAPS.

Pick, Hella 1975. Bulgaria: development model. *New York Times* (*B&F*), 9 November, p. 8.

Popkova, L. 1987. Where are the pastries lightest? *CDSP*, vol. 39, no. 35, pp. 9–10.

Potts, Malcolm 1967. Legal abortion in Eastern Europe. *The Eugenics Review*, vol. 59, pp. 232–49.

Poulsen, Thomas M. 1976. Administrative and economic regionalization of Bulgaria: the territorial reform of 1959. In Butler, Thomas (ed.), *Bulgaria: Past and Present*. Columbus, American Association for the Advancement of Slavic Studies, pp. 187–201.

Pryor, Frederic L. 1968. *Public Expenditures in Communist and Capitalist Nations*. London, Allen & Unwin.

— 1977. Some costs and benefits of markets: an empirical study. *Quarterly Journal of Economics*, vol. 91, no. 1, pp. 81–102.

— 1985. *A Guidebook to the Comparative Study of Economic Systems*. Englewood Cliffs, NJ, Prentice-Hall.

Puchev, Plamen 1986. Interview, 9 July 1986.

Pundeff, Marin 1986. Dimitrov at Leipzig: was there a deal? *Slavic Review*, vol. 45, no. 3, pp. 545–9.

Radio Free Europe Research (*RFER*), various issues.

Reynolds, Lloyd G. 1977. Growth acceleration under socialism. In *Image and Reality in Economic Development*. New Haven, Conn., Yale University Press, pp. 397–428.

Rothschild, Joseph 1959. *The Communist Party of Bulgaria: Origins and Development, 1883-1936*. New York, Columbia University Press.

— 1974. *East Central Europe between the Two World Wars*. Seattle, University of Washington Press.

Sanders, Irwin T. 1949. *Balkan Village*. Lexington, University of Kentucky Press.

Shabad, Theodore 1981. Electrical energy: supply and demand in the CMEA economies in the 1980's including nuclear energy prospects. In NATO Economics Directorate, *CMEA: Energy, 1980-1990*. Newtonville, Mass., Oriental Research Partners, pp. 117–28.

Shafir, Michael 1985. *Romania: Politics, Economics and Society*. London, Frances Pinter.

Sherman, Howard J. 1969. *The Soviet Economy*. Boston, Mass., Little, Brown & Co.

Sklar, June L. 1974. The role of marriage behavior in the demographic transition: the case of Eastern Europe around 1900. *Population Studies*, vol. 28, no. 2, pp. 231–47.

Spassov, Boris 1981. Socialist democracy in action. In Bokov, Georgi (ed.), *Modern Bulgaria: History, Policy, Economy, Culture*. Sofia, Sofia Press, pp. 187–216.

Spulber, Nicolas 1957. *The Economics of Communist Eastern Europe*. New York, Wiley.

Staar, Richard F. 1975. Bulgaria. In Richard F. Staaar (ed.), *Yearbook on International Communist Affairs, 1975*. Stanford, Hoover Institution Press, pp. 13–18.

Stanev, Nikol 1986. Interview, 18 July 1986 (Deputy Mayor of Sofia).

Statesman's Yearbook, 1985-1986 1985. Bulgaria. New York, St Martin's, pp. 241–8.

Statistecheski Godishnik (various years), Sofia, Central Statistical Office.

Statistecheski Spravochnik (various years), Sofia Central Statistical Office.

Stefanov, Ivan & Naoumov, Nicola 1974. Bulgaria. In Berelson, Bernard (ed.), *Population Policy in Developed Countries*. New York, McGraw-Hill.

Stern, Jonathan P. 1981. Natural gas: resources, production possibilities and demand in the 1980's. In NATO Economies Directorate, *CMEA: Energy, 1980-1990*. Newtonville, Mass. Oriental Research Partners, pp. 99-115.

Sugar, Peter F. 1977. *Southeastern Europe under Ottoman Rule, 1354-1804*. Seattle, University of Washington Press.

Swain, Nigel 1986. *Collective Farms Which Work?* Cambridge, Cambridge University Press.

— 1987. Hungarian agriculture in the early 1980s: retrenchment followed by reform. *Soviet Studies*, vol. 39, no. 1, pp. 24-39.

Sweezy, Alan 1973a. Recent light on the relationship between socioeconomic development and fertility decline. Caltech Population Program Occasional Paper No. 1. Pasadena, Caltech Population Program, pp. 2-6 & 18-19.

— 1973b. Letter, 13 February 1973.

— 1973c. Letter, 24 July 1973.

Szajkowski, Bogdan 1982. *The Establishment of Marxist Regimes*. London, Butterworth.

Taaffe, Robert N. 1974. Urbanization in Bulgaria: 1946-1970. *Études Balkaniques*, vol. 3, nos. 2-3, pp. 50-63.

— 1976. The urbanization of Communist Bulgaria. In Butler, Thomas (ed.), *Bulgaria: Past and Present*. Columbus, American Association for the Advancement of Slavic Studies, pp. 171-86.

— 1977. The impact of rural–urban migration on the development of Communist Bulgaria. In Kostanick, Huey L. (ed.), *Population and Migration Trends in Eastern Europe*. Boulder, Westview, pp. 157-79.

Tampke, Jürgen 1983. *The People's Republic of Eastern Europe*. New York, St Martin's.

Terry, Sarah M. 1985. The implications of economic stringency and political succession for stability in Eastern Europe in the eighties. In *Eastern European Economies: Slow Growth in the 1980's, vol. 1, Economic Performance and Policy*, Joint Economic Committee, U.S. Congress, 28 October, pp. 502-40.

Tonkov, Georgi. Interview, 14 July 1986.

Totev, Anastas I. 1935. Indeksni chista za obema na rastiteluoto zemedelsko proizvodstvo v Bulgaria. *Trudove na statisticheskiia institut za stopanski prouchvaniia pri SDU*, 2-3, p. 95, Sofia. Cited in Jackson (1982b).

Tsonev, Vladimir 1985. The housing problem and the birth rate. *Naselenie (Population, in Bulgarian)*, vol. 3, no. 4, pp. 3-15.

Turgeon, Lynn 1983. A quarter century of non-Soviet East European agriculture. *ACES Bulletin*, vol. 15, no. 3, pp. 27-41.

United Nations, *Demographic Yearbook*. New York, various years.

— 1985. Adjustment and investment policies in the centrally planned economies of Eastern Europe. In *World Economic Survey 1985: Trends and Policies in the World Economy*. New York, United Nations, pp. 89-101.

— 1986. Adjustment, investment and structural change in centrally planned economies. In *World Economic Survey 1986: Current Trends and Policies in the World Economy*. New York, United Nations, pp. 121–34 and 169–72.

—— 1987. *Economic Survey of Europe in 1986-1987*. New York, United Nations, pp. 115–206, 229–36 and 306–12.

van de Walle, Étienne 1972. Letter, 30 November 1972.

van den Berg, Ger P. 1985. Joint Party and government decrees in the USSR and other socialist countries. *Review of Socialist Law*, vol. 11, no. 1, pp. 47–73.

Vassilev, Dimiter 1986. Interview, 22 July 1986.

Vassilev, Vassil A. 1979. *Bulgaria—Thirteen Centuries of Existence*. Sofia, Sofia Press (in English).

Vogel, Heinrich 1975. Bulgaria. In Hoheman, Hans-Hermann, Kaser, Michael & Thalheim, Karl C. (eds), *The New Economic Systems of Eastern Europe*. Berkeley, University of California Press.

Vulkanov, V. 1979. *Normativnite aktove na ministerskiia suvet*. Sofia.

Wädekin, Karl-Eugen 1980. Conclusion. In Francisco, Ronald A., Laird, Betty A., & Laird, Roy D. (eds), *Agricultural Policies in the USSR and Eastern Europe*. Boulder, Westview, pp. 311–27.

—— 1982. *Agrarian Policies in Communist Europe: A Critical Introduction* (Studies in Eastern European and Soviet Russian Agrarian Policy, Vol. 1). London, Allanheld, Osmun.

Waller, Michael & Szajkowski, Bogdan 1981. The Communist movement: from monolith to polymorph. In Bogdan Szajkowski (ed.), *Marxist Governments: A World Survey, Vol. 1*. New York, St Martin's, pp. 1–19.

Warriner, Doreen 1939. *Economics of Peasant Farming*. London, Oxford University Press, pp. 9–10, and 160.

—— 1965. Introduction. In Doreen Warriner (ed.), *Contrasts in Emerging Societies*. Bloomington, Indiana University Press, pp. 7–10 and 15–16.

Wiedemann, Paul 1980a. The origins and development of agro-industrial development in Bulgaria. In Francisco, Ronald A., Laird, Betty A., & Laird, Roy D. (eds), *Agricultural Policies in the USSR and Eastern Europe*. Boulder, Westview, pp. 97–135.

—— 1980b. Economic reform in Bulgaria. *Forshungsberichte 62*, Vienna, Weiner Institute für Internationale Wirtschaftsvergleiche.

—— 1983. Transforming traditional socialist agricultural organization. A Case Study of Bulgaria. *ACES Bulletin*, vol. 14, no. 4, pp. 125–35.

Wilbur, Charles K. 1969. *The Soviet Model and Underdeveloped Countries*. Chapel Hill, University of North Carolina Press.

Wiles, Peter J. D. 1974. *Distribution of Income East and West*. Amsterdam, North Holland.

—— 1975. Introduction. In *Economic Development in the Soviet Union and Eastern Europe, Vol. 1*. New York, Praeger, pp. 253–5.

—— 1977. *Economic Institutions Compared*. Oxford, Basil Blackwell.

—— 1982. East Central Europe as an active element in the Soviet empire. In

Drachkovitch, Milorad M. (ed.), *East Central Europe: Yesterday, Today, Tomorrow*. Stanford, Hoover Institution Press, pp. 81–105.

Wolf, Thomas A. 1985. Estimating 'Foregone Gains' in Soviet–East European Foreign Trade: A Methodological Note. *Comparative Economic Studies*, vol. 27, no. 3, pp. 83–97.

Wyzan, Michael L. 1988. The Bulgarian experience with centrally-planned agriculture: lessons for Soviet reformers? In Gray, Kenneth R. (ed.), *Contemporary Soviet Agriculture: Comparative Perspectives*. Ames, Iowa State University Press.

Zaslavsky, Victor 1982. *The Neo-Stalinist State: Class, Ethnicity and Consensus in Soviet Society*. Armonk, NY, M. E. Sharpe.

Zdraveopazrane 1985. Ministry of National Health, Sofia.

Zimbalist, Andrew & Sherman, Howard J. 1984. *Comparing Economic Systems: A Political-Economic Approach*. Orlando, Academic Press.

Zwass, Adam 1984. *The Economies of Eastern Europe In a Time of Change*. Armonk, NY, M. E. Sharpe.

Index